P9-CRU-526

LANGUAGE AND LITERACY SERIES

Dorothy S. Strickland and Celia Genishi, SERIES EDITORS

(Continued)

Engaged Reading

PROCESSES, PRACTICES, AND POLICY IMPLICATIONS

EDITED BY

John T. Guthrie and Donna E. Alvermann

FOREWORD BY **Kathryn H. Au**

Teachers College, Columbia University
New York and London

Published by Teachers College Press, 1234 Amsterdam Avenue, New York, NY 10027

The work reported herein is a National Reading Research Center project of the University of Maryland and the University of Georgia. It is supported under the Educational Research and Development Centers Program (PR/AWARD NO. 117A20007) as administered by the Office of Educational Research and Improvement, U.S. Department of Education.

Library of Congress Cataloging-in-Publication Data

Engaged reading : processes, practices, and policy implications /
  edited by John T. Guthrie and Donna E. Alvermann ; foreword by
  Kathryn H. Au.
     p.   cm. — (Language and literacy series)
  Includes bibliographical references and index.
  ISBN 0-8077-3816-6 (pbk.: alk paper)
  1. Reading—United States. 2. Motivation in education—United
States. 3. Students—United States—Attitudes. I. Guthrie, John
T. II. Alvermann, Donna E. III. Series: Language and literacy
series (New York, N.Y.)
LB 1573.E65   1999
428.4—dc21   98-40022

ISBN 0-8077-3816-6 (paper)

Printed on acid-free paper
Manufactured in the United States of America

06 05 04 03 02 01 00 99   8 7 6 5 4 3 2 1

To Stacey and Jack

Contents

Foreword

DURING A VISIT TO A SMALL, RURAL school on the island of Hawaii, I noticed a group of fifth graders sitting on the steps outside their classroom and reading. The bell rang, signaling that it was time to go to lunch, and the teacher came out to collect the students. Mahina remained glued to her book, pleading as the teacher approached, "One more page, just one more page."

Something magical happens when students become engaged in reading. Time for sustained silent reading starts with the scrape of a chair, mumbling, the rustling of paper. A moment later, a hush falls. The teacher and students are lost in their books. When the teacher says, "Time," several students groan, "Aw, already?"

This volume provides an authoritative overview of the engagement perspective on reading. The editors, John Guthrie and Donna Alvermann, are two of the most distinguished figures in the field of reading. There are few books on my shelves to which I refer again and again, but this will be one of them. These thoughtful syntheses of current research on reading highlight studies conducted at the National Reading Research Center (NRRC) and place this work in the context of the field as whole. The chapters address issues at the elementary through secondary levels, factors in the home and community, research methods, and policy implications. The general reader and specialist alike will appreciate the logical organization and clear writing needed to convey such a wealth of information so succinctly.

When we address engagement in reading, we recognize the importance of students' motivations for becoming literate and learning to read. As Guthrie and Anderson state in Chapter 2, the engagement perspective requires us to consider not just *how* people read, but *why* they would choose to read. Certainly, the pleasure of being lost in a book, as Mahina experienced it, is one of the reasons people choose to read. We may read to keep up with current events, to figure out how to program a new VCR, or to find solace, but we always read with some purpose in mind. Reading is motivated by these purposes.

To some, a volume emphasizing the centrality of engagement to students' development as readers may seem out of step with these times, when reading researchers and educators once again find themselves embroiled in a heated public debate about phonics and basic skills. Let there be no mistake—this book summarizes research of direct relevance to this debate. All who share the goal of teaching students to read well, of starting students on the road to becoming lifelong readers and informed citizens, should take the time to understand the research presented here.

After 25 years spent working on the question of how schools can help students of diverse backgrounds to become excellent readers, I have reached the conclusion that we cannot—we must not—return to simplistic notions of reading. For our students to thrive as readers, we must embrace the kind of rich and complex understanding reflected in the engagement perspective. I began my career as an educator in the 1970s, and as a beginning teacher I painstakingly followed the sequence of skill lessons presented in the teacher's guide to our school's basal reading series. It did not take me long to discover that these lessons made little sense to my kindergarten and first-grade students, many of whom lived in public housing projects and had little or no experience with books before coming to school. My students had to be captured by the magic of books before they took the slightest interest in learning letter names and letter sounds. Once they had experienced the joys of reading, they could see the sense in learning skills, and skill instruction proceeded much more smoothly and quickly.

I am a great believer in the explicit instruction of skills. But I no longer believe that skills and strategies can be the starting point for instruction. It is students' interests that must serve as the starting point. As indicated in surveys conducted by the NRRC, classroom teachers, who have detailed knowledge of students' needs in learning to read, do not rank phonics and basic skills as their greatest concern. Instead, their greatest concern is "creating interest in reading." Whether educators work with students of diverse backgrounds or mainstream students, in schools in the inner city or in affluent suburbs, they worry that many of their students do not care about reading and do not choose to read. Here are a few of the comments I have heard recently:

> Principal at a suburban elementary school: "I'll tell you the main problem we have with reading. It's motivation. I'm not worried about skills. When our students want to read, they learn the skills."

> Sixth-grade teacher in an elementary school in a low-income community: "The problem I have is that my students don't care about reading. They'd rather be playing video games or watching TV. Anything but reading."

> Librarian at a prestigious preparatory school: "I see the elementary students borrowing books all the time, but once they get to seventh grade, I never see

them again. Well, they may come in once in a while to look up information for a report, but they don't borrow books to read for pleasure."

Students can be quite frank about their lack of interest in reading. In an interview study, I encountered a considerable number of fifth graders who indicated that they never read a book outside of school except for homework. One of the problems, I found, was that many students did not have strategies for deciding what to read next. They did not have ideas about books they might enjoy because they did not participate in communities of readers, either at school or at home. One boy, asked how he chose books when his class went to the school library, answered, "I just grab any book!"

It is students like this boy who have convinced me that we must make ownership of literacy the overarching goal of reading instruction. Students who have ownership value literacy so much that they make it a part of their lives whether they are at home or at school. They see reading in terms of the purposes it can fulfill in their lives, rather than in terms of random acts, such as "grabbing any book."

This same interview study revealed to me the power of the teacher in leading students to connect with books. At one school, when asked the name of their favorite author, student after student replied, "Roald Dahl." These students had been inspired by a third-grade teacher who loved Roald Dahl. She began by reading aloud to them. Then they read books by Roald Dahl on their own and discussed them in literature circles. Two years later, the students still harked back to this experience. A boy at this school described the importance of sustained silent reading in his becoming an avid reader. This same third-grade teacher had made him read everyday. Week after week, he went through the motions of reading, but only because everyone in the class was required to do so. Then, one day, he happened to read a book he loved. From that moment on, he was hooked on reading.

Some may shy away from terms such as *engagement* and *ownership*, thinking that they lack the toughness or rigor of terms such as phonics, basic skills, or cognitive strategies. I want to reassure those who feel any hesitation on this score. The authors in this volume recognize fully the importance of bringing students to high levels of proficiency in skills and strategies, and to high levels of knowledge in the academic content areas. Many of those whose work is cited here, as contributors to the development of the engagement perspective on reading, have distinguished themselves previously through years of work on students' learning of strategies for comprehending text and for recognizing words. The engagement perspective builds upon and encompasses this earlier work on strategies within a broader framework that acknowledges students' interests and motivations and their experiences in the home and community.

Engagement is at the very heart of what it means to be a reader. The other evening, while visiting my sister's house, I found my niece with her nose buried in a new Nancy Drew book. She explained to me that it was hard to put down one of these books because of the way the chapters end: "Like the last sentence might be, 'The elevator started to plunge to the ground.' So you can't stop there, you have to keep reading." It grew late, and my sister went to tell my niece that it was time to get ready for bed. Floating down the hall came the words I love to hear: "One more page, just one more page."

Kathryn H. Au
University of Hawaii

Acknowledgments

THE EDITORS WOULD LIKE to acknowledge the contributions of all members of the National Reading Research Center. This includes participants at the Universities of Georgia and Maryland, as well as affiliated universities and schools in many states. We recognize and appreciate the chapter authors who integrated the findings of NRRC research for this volume. We are especially indebted to Eileen Kramer and Barbara Neitzey for their typing and editorial expertise devoted to this book. We are obliged to the editors of Teachers College Press for their confidence and continuing support. We are, finally, grateful to Anne Sweet, who served as the monitor of the NRRC from the Office of Educational Research and Improvement and who approved an initial draft of this volume as part of the final reporting to the U.S. Department of Education.

CHAPTER 1

Understanding Engagement: Historical and Political Contexts

Peter B. Mosenthal

THE YEAR WAS 1975. I had been teaching for 2 years in a Columbus, Ohio, elementary school. I also was in the homestretch to completing my doctoral degree at Ohio State University. At a February meeting that year, the principal announced that our school was going to hire a consultant to improve students' flagging reading achievement. Many of these students were third- and fourth-grade boys who demonstrated absolutely no interest in reading. These boys had been subjected to every remedial intervention possible, from their first grade on, but, as the principal noted, "These students continued to show no motivation to read anything, anywhere, anytime." (The principal commonly would refer to these students as the "no-way readers.") The principal hung a sign in his office that read, "Everything begins with motivation or it doesn't begin at all," and then initiated a program to implement this belief.

Early in the morning on March 2, the entire elementary school was brought to the gym to be introduced to the new reading consultant. It was none other than Ohio State's Archie Griffin. Archie had just been awarded his second Heisman Trophy in recognition of his uncanny running ability. As a reading consultant, it was Archie's job to promote reading by personally adding a brief note of encouragement to every fifth book report that a student submitted based on a book the student had selected and read. A thermometer was set up in the entrance to the school, which registered the number of books that the entire school had read by the end of each week, starting on March 9. By the time June arrived, the mercury had exceeded the top of the thermometer. As for those "no-way" readers who wouldn't read anything, anywhere, anytime, anyplace—they were remarkable!

They read more sports stories than one possibly could have imagined; in Fader and McNeil's (1966) terms, they had become "hooked on books."

Two years later the principal noticed a significant drop on the standardized tests. As a friend of mine later reported, the program had declined into a disappointment. Maybe the program failed because not all the athletes were Heisman Trophy recipients. Or it might have been, as the teachers complained, that there was no longer any novelty in the approach; they grumbled about all the extra work that was involved. Teachers were concerned that their students weren't reading quality literature, and several noted that students did little actual reading in their social studies and science texts. The following year, the students' standardized reading achievement scores hit an all-time low. In June 1978, the principal took down his motivation sign and replaced it with one that read, "Too many agendas spoil the broth."

ENGAGEMENT THEORY IN EDUCATION

How well had the principal and the students grasped the essence of engagement and motivation? Motivation is one of those terms that we find just about everywhere—on the walls of administrative offices; in speeches to sales representatives; in locker rooms at half time; in the homes of toddlers earmarked for potty training; in journals of psychology, sociology, education, and marketing. In all its ubiquitous settings, motivation ultimately deals with a fundamental set of actions: setting and achieving goals (Ames, 1992; Dweck & Leggett, 1988; Maehr & Pintrich, 1991; Meece, Blumenfeld, & Hoyle, 1988; Urdan & Maehr, 1995) or identifying and solving problems (Bransford & Vye, 1989; Dewey, 1910, 1929, 1938; Prawat, 1993). The reasoning goes something like this. First, an individual establishes a goal. This represents the desire to achieve a valued outcome. Or an individual identifies a problem. Problems are undesired things; they prevent goal attainment. Clear the problem and this sets the way for goal attainment. Second, as long as the goal or problem identified remains a concern to an individual (for whatever reason), she will engage in goal attainment or problem solving. Third, during this period of engagement, an individual ideally learns how to develop and refine strategies for attaining goals or solving problems. As strategies become more efficient and effective, proficiency in goal attainment and problem solving typically increases. This, in turn, enables an individual to achieve more complex goals and solve more difficult problems.

This view of engagement has many interpretations (Prawat, 1993). Perhaps the best known of these is Dewey's (1910, 1929, 1938) notion of "reflective inquiry," which explains engagement in terms of three stages: (1) problems are identified; (2) problems are studied through active engagement; and (3) conclusions are reached as problems are solved. For Dewey, the first stage was critical for

engagement of any type to occur. As Dewey (1910) argued, "The origin of thinking is some perplexity, confusion, or doubt. Thinking is not a case of spontaneous
combustion" (p. 12). And stated somewhat differently, "All reflective inquiry starts
from a problematic situation" (Dewey, 1929, p. 189). The importance of Dewey's
argument here is that, before one becomes engaged in learning, one must engage
in reflective inquiry by seeking out problems. This step of problematizing results
in the identification or creation of ideas. These ideas, in turn, result in a radical
reorientation in one's thinking. Ideas about familiar objects, including subject
matters in school, are viewed as "challenges to thought. . . . They are *to be* known,
rather than objects of knowledge. . . . They are things *to be* understood" (Dewey,
1929, p. 103, emphasis in original). "The subject-matter which had been taken as
satisfying the demands of knowledge, as the material with which to frame solutions [becomes] something which sets *problems*" (Dewey, 1929, p. 99, emphasis
in original).

Dewey (1929) further argues the point that, when one problematizes an object or action as an idea, one begins to understand it, to gain more control over it,
and begins to verify it. If objects are not problematized, knowledge remains merely
facts, which, according to Dewey (1933/1986), do not promote engagement:

> Mere facts or data are dead, as far as mind is concerned, unless they are used to sug-
> gest and test some idea, some way out of difficulty. Ideas, on the other hand, are
> *mere* ideas, ideal speculations, fantasies, dreams, unless they are used to guide new
> observations of, and reflections upon, actual situations, past, present, or future.
> Finally, they must be brought to some sort of check by actual given material or else
> remain ideas. (p. 199, emphasis in original)

Once objects have been problematized as ideas, engagement is said to transpire.
In this stage, learners attempt to solve their problem by calling up and searching
out related information, formulating hypotheses, interacting with the problem, and
observing the results. As such, engagement at this stage involves the process of
weighing ideas against data, and anticipations against obtained outcomes, for the
purpose of judging the worth and values of ideas: "Data (facts) and ideas (suggestions, possible solution)," Dewey (1892/1969) argues, "form the two indis-
pensable and correlative factors of all reflective activity." In this process, Dewey
adds, ideas are verified by being "carried over into the particular conditions or
facts"; the latter, in turn, are "connected together or given meaning, instead of
remaining so many blank, separate particulars" (p. 233). In the process of verify-
ing ideas, activity is central; this is why Dewey (1929) emphasizes that "the
experimental procedure is one that installs doing as the heart of knowing" (p. 36).
Another aspect of engagement at this stage "involves willingness to endure a condition of mental unrest and disturbance" (Dewey, 1910, p. 13). For the learner, it
is always a temptation to establish certainty too quickly by jumping to conclusions. But this short-circuits the engagement process. Reflective inquiry, which

Dewey (1929) equated with scientific forms of investigation, emphasizes that "a disciplined mind takes delight in the problematic. . . . The scientific attitude may almost be defined as that which is capable of enjoying the doubtful" (p. 228).

After engagement has been undertaken for a considerable time, learners reach some sort of conclusion, which Dewey (1929) refers to as an "outcome": "The outcome of the directed activity is the construction of a new empirical situation in which objects are differently related to one another, and such that the *consequences* of directed operations form the objects that have the property of being *known*" (pp. 86–87, emphasis in original). According to Dewey, the benefits of engagement lie not in the new solutions to the problems but rather in the new relations that are discovered and the problem being understood at a deeper level. This, in turn, enables the learner to problematize (and hence understand) an object at a more complex level when "the object is revisited."

More important, after sustained engagement in reading, achievement is increased. As Stanovich and others have reported, high levels of "print exposure" are solid predictors of reading achievement. According to Stanovich (1986), reading extensively has spiraling benefits, which he describes as follows:

> The effect of reading volume on vocabulary growth, combined with the large skill differences in reading volume, could mean that a "rich-get-richer" or cumulative advantage phenomenon is almost inextricably embedded within the developmental course of reading progress. The very children who are reading well and who have good vocabularies will read more, learn more word meanings, and hence read even better. Children with inadequate vocabularies—who read slowly and without enjoyment—read less, and as a result have slower development of vocabulary knowledge, which inhibits further growth in reading ability. Walberg (Walberg, Strykowski, Rovai, & Hung, 1984; Walberg & Tsai, 1983) . . . has dubbed those educational sequences where early achievement spawns faster rates of subsequent achievement "Matthew effects," after the Gospel according to Matthew: "For unto everyone that hath shall be given, and he shall have abundance: but from him that hath not shall be taken away even that which he hath" (XXV:29). (p. 381)

Not only is engagement productive for achievement, but it is an integral part of reading proficiency. This notion has a long history. Some 40 years ago, Gray and Rogers (1956) found in an extensive interview study that

> Maturity in reading as one aspect of total development is distinguished by attainment of those interests, attitudes, and skills which enable young people (and adults) to participate eagerly, independently, and effectively in all the reading activities essential to a full, rich, and productive life. (p. 56)

A fusion of motivation and cognition, of skill and will, of interest and thought is integral to reading engagement. Unfortunately, this fusion was little understood by the principal in the school with the Archie Griffin program. The simple view that motivation, as temporary excitement, will fuel achievement is insufficient. This book explores a more enriched set of processes, including cognition and social interaction, as well as affect within the dynamics of reading engagement.

THE NATURE OF AGENDAS FOR SCHOOLING

While I agree with the sentiment of the principal's first sign, "Everything begins with motivation or it doesn't begin at all," I agree even more with the sentiment of the second that "too many agendas spoil the broth." Motivation, engagement, strategies, and level of outcome achievement are not just things that have to do with an individual's goals or problems; in addition, they have to do with the agendas of many individuals—especially in school contexts. To understand this, let's first consider what makes up an agenda.

Agendas Defined

Although the dictionary would have us believe that an *agenda* is little more than "a list of things to be done or matters to be acted upon," agendas are actually more complex, consisting of eight important dimensions (Mosenthal, 1993, 1995). First, agendas, like motivation itself, involve identifying goals or problems as a basic starting point for behavior. As I noted earlier, goals are not neutral outcomes; they represent *desired outcomes*. As such, goals are outcomes that *should be* obtained according to some set of beliefs, values, perspectives, or practices. When a desired goal is blocked, a problem is said to exist. Thus, problems are undesired outcomes, or outcomes that *shouldn't be*. Problems represent an impasse in our ability to change "what was," "what has been," or "what is" into "what should be."

In the Archie Griffin episode, the principal began his odyssey of improving reading in his school by identifying a fundamental goal, that is, to raise his school's standardized reaching achievement scores. Since the no-way readers contributed significantly to the school's lower scores, a major emphasis of the principal's goal was to improve these readers' individual scores; as their scores went, so went the school's.

Second, agendas cannot be set by just anyone; rather, only certain individuals or groups have the legitimacy, ability, and power to set agendas. Moreover, certain individuals or groups—and not others—are held accountable for setting agendas. In my school district, principals were the ones held most accountable for test scores in each school. For the most part, the school board, as well as the parents, equated the quality of education with the level of standardized test scores. Therefore, principals in my district maintained and exercised their powers to promote higher test scores as the primary agenda for their school buildings (see my accounting of this in Mosenthal, 1989).

Third, agendas are set to benefit some but not others. In addition, of those who benefit, agendas may benefit some more than others. In the opening episode, the principal was fortunate the first time that everyone felt they were benefiting by participating in the program. The second time around, few teachers saw benefit in the program; girls objected that the program was more beneficial to boys, given that the athlete was a male football player.

Fourth, agendas are set to have an impact on different levels of social organization, for example, an individual, a class, a school, a district, a state, or even a nation. In the Archie Griffin example, the principal's main concern was that his innovative program would have an effect primarily at the school level; to the extent that individuals and individual classrooms benefited, that was a bonus.

Fifth, the extent to which agendas can be carried out is often limited by available resources, such as money, time, and (wo)manpower. The principal in the above account was fortunate enough to have an Ohio State booster support the new program; without this support, the program would not have been possible.

Sixth, to achieve goals or solve problems, agenda setters prescribe a set of ideal actions to be taken. In this regard, prescribed actions, like goals that should be and problems that shouldn't be, also reflect values, that is, they are actions that *should be taken*. Prescribed actions, like prescribed goals, often represent what agenda setters perceive as "better" or "best" choices. In the example above, the principal, in collaboration with a teacher committee, carefully detailed each of the steps for implementing the new motivational reading program.

Seventh, once actions have been prescribed, agendas then include actions taken. In brief, these are the actual actions that agenda implementers follow in order to achieve the desired goal or solve the undesired problem. In implementing the program, care was taken to provide many different kinds of books in class. Students were given library cards to check books out at the local library. Teachers discussed criteria for book selection. Teachers also taught students how to read a book so students would have the necessary information to complete a book report. Finally, teachers spent considerable time in helping students understand how to write the book report itself (which many students also illustrated).

Finally, agendas often include some form of evaluation. On the one hand, evaluation is used to determine the extent to which actions actually taken relate to actions prescribed. It is often the case that new constraints arise when prescribed actions are, in fact, implemented. This may create inconsistency between what ideally has been prescribed and what actually transpires; evaluation is used to measure the degree of this inconsistency. On the other hand, evaluation may be used to determine the extent to which the outcomes of the actions taken result in successful goal achievement or problem solution.

In the Archie Griffin motivational reading program, evaluation was carried out by recording the number of books read and book reports submitted on a variety of thermometers. In addition, evaluation of the program was based on students' standardized reading achievement scores the following year.

Prevailing Agendas of Education and Literacy Instruction

To date, a variety of agendas of education and literacy have been identified (Larabee, 1997; Mosenthal, 1983a, 1984a, 1987, 1993; Walmsley, 1981). These agendas espouse different and often contradictory goals of education and literacy. In addition, these agendas espouse different means for engaging in literacy learning. Finally, these agendas often suggest different interpretations of what it means to be proficient in literacy. For illustration purposes, consider: (1) the good citizen agenda, (2) the equality agenda, and (3) the economic agenda. These are discussed below.

The Good Citizen Agenda. The oldest agenda is *let's-inculcate-good-citizenship*, which serves to promote democratic equality. Broudy (1986) summarizes the sentiment of this agenda by noting, "The underlying faith of a democratic society is that the common good will be achieved if the citizens legislate rationally and remain loyal to the ideals of the commonwealth" (p. 247). This agenda dates back to the time in the 1800s when the new American republic had many more personal agendas operating than public agendas. To counteract the growth of self-interest and to preserve the integrity of the republic, schools were given the responsibility of instilling personal dedication to the preservation of democracy.

According to this agenda, the goal of schools should be to prepare good citizens by promoting established political, cultural, and moral ideals (Bloom, 1987; Cremin, 1980; Gutmann, 1987; Hirsch, 1987; Strike, 1991). A related goal is to promote belief in a common heritage and faith in the democratic system of government. Although these goals date back to the founding of the United States (Meyer, Tyack, Nagel, & Gordon, 1979), they still surface today in most of the federal government's political tracts. For example, the national report *A Nation at Risk* (National Commission on Excellence in Education, 1983) argued that "a high level of shared education is essential to a free, democratic society and to the fostering of a common culture" (p. 7). Moreover, the National Education Goals Panel (1995) stressed the need for increased "competency over challenging subject matter . . . to ensure that all students learn to use their minds well, so they may be prepared for responsible citizenship" (p. 11). We also find this goal argued in such works as Gutmann's *Democratic Education* (1987), which argues the need to educate all citizens to a high "democratic threshold." This threshold requires that, with few exceptions, all students must be educated up to the threshold of knowledge and skills required of democratic character. Unless this threshold is attained, not everyone will have an effective voice, and as a consequence true democracy will not be achieved.

Such goals, in part, are to be achieved by teaching a common language in the elementary grades, which includes correct handwriting, spelling, grammar, pronunciation, capitalization, and rhetorical style (Mosenthal, 1983a, 1984a). The assumption here is that, if students in the elementary grades acquire the same strategies for inputting and outputting information through reading, writing, listening, and speaking, they will be more effective at reproducing information at the secondary grades. In turn, this will help solidify their belief and understanding of the "democratic way" (Kaestle, 1983). Students taught under this agenda learn that prior knowledge is not to be integrated with "current text knowledge" (or knowledge gleaned from a classroom's textbook) in the event that the former may disturb the fidelity of the latter (Mosenthal, 1983b, 1984b; Mosenthal, Conley, Colella, & Davidson-Mosenthal, 1985; Spiro, 1977).

The strategies taught to students so that they can engage in this agenda tend to be highly hierarchical and skills-based (Walmsely, 1981). Instructionally sequenced materials in the elementary grades, such as basals, often give way to texts that present history that identifies White European males and the American Founders as famous people to model. The goal that is appealed to in setting and implementing this agenda is that students should want to learn in order to be "good citizens" like George Washington, Thomas Jefferson, and Abraham Lincoln (Thornton, 1994).

The Equality Agenda. A second agenda might be called *let's equalize society*. This agenda attempts to minimize the broad social, cultural, and economic class differences found in society due to increased immigration and continued concentration of great wealth in the hands of a few. To accomplish this goal, education's purpose becomes one of providing equal education (Howe, 1994; Porter, 1995; Valli, Cooper, & Frankes, 1997). At the turn of the twentieth century, this agenda was implemented through the establishment of universal enrollment, uniform curriculum, and a shared educational experience for all students (Katz, 1987; Katznelson & Weir, 1985). More recently, this agenda has been used to help redress inequalities resulting from social and political practices of the nineteenth century. Larabee (1997) describes these efforts as follows:

> The recurring demand for equal treatment has removed the Protestant bible, public prayer, and other divisive religious practices from the public schools. It has motivated a powerful movement to provide equal educational experiences for all people regardless of race, ethnicity, and sex—resulting in the formal desegregation of schools and in attempts to remove race and gender stereotypes from textbooks, incorporate the experiences of non-Whites and females in the curriculum . . . and reduce the discriminatory practices in the classroom. (pp. 45–46)

This goal of equal treatment has been defined further in the Goals 2000: Educate America Act (1994) in terms of an opportunity-to-learn (OTL) standard that

> means the criteria for, and the basis of, assessing the sufficiency or quality of the resources, practices, and conditions necessary at each level of the education system (schools, local educational agencies, and states) to provide all students with an oppor-

tunity to learn the material in voluntary national content standards or the State content standards. (Conference Report, 1994, p. H1626)

Associated with the equal treatment that Larabee describes above and alluded to in the OTL standard is the goal of "equal access." This goal has come to mean that every individual should have an equal opportunity to acquire an education at any level. More generally, this means that education should provide all individuals with the opportunity to gain entry to what is viewed as desirable. Harvey and Klein (1989) described this as "the need to provide appropriate routes of access that allow everyone to avail themselves of existing educational treatments and benefits" (p. 57).

Also a part of equal treatment is "participation equity." This applies to structures and processes that define the everyday life in schools (often referred to as the "hidden curriculum") (Valli et al., 1997). Underlying participation equity is the need of schools ". . . to eliminate tracking, biased testing, and other arrangements that so often deny such access on grounds of race, gender and socioeconomic class" (Beane & Apple, 1995, p. 11).

Education and literacy instruction that have built upon the equity agenda have replaced tracking and ability grouping with heterogeneous grouping and cooperative learning. Moreover, they have attempted to promote inclusive education, reintegrating special education students in the regular classroom, so that handicapping conditions do not consign students to an inferior education. Moreover, they have promoted programs of compensatory education and affirmative action to make certain that educational equality is a realizable outcome. And both have helped to support the recent demand by reformers that all students be held to the same high level of educational performance standards (Larabee, 1997). Education and literacy instruction have attempted particularly to promote the equity agenda by teaching multiculturalism (Au, 1995; Banks, 1993) and cultural relevancy (Ladson-Billings, 1995).

The Economic Agenda. A third agenda might be called *let's beat the bell curve*. This agenda is based on the observation that there are differences among individuals in cognitive proficiencies and that jobs in the work force are highly stratified, with workers at the top of the stratification experiencing significantly higher socioeconomic status than those at the bottom (Bowles & Gintis, 1976; Herrnstein & Murray, 1994). This agenda is based also on the idea that work is a useful metaphor describing what one does at the job as well as in school (hence, when work is not completed at school, it becomes "homework").

As Boorstin (1973) has argued, this agenda began its ascendence when schools adopted Frederick Taylor's notions of efficiency from the workplace (as outlined in Taylor's book, *The Principles of Scientific Management*, published in 1911) and began using statistics, based on the bell curve, to classify the mental and academic aptitude of students and adult workers.

The beat-the-bell-curve agenda includes two goals in particular. The first goal assumes that education and literacy instruction must prepare students to function effectively in the real world to the best of their ability, especially in the work force (Johnston & Packer, 1987; National Center on Education and the Economy, 1990). In this regard, education is viewed as having an economic benefit not only for individuals who are well educated but also for a well-educated society.

Closer to home, the National Education Goals Panel (1995) has expressed the importance of a highly educated work force in asserting, "By the year 2000, all students will leave grades 4, 8, and 12 having demonstrated competency over challenging subject matter . . . so they may be prepared not only for 'responsible citizenship' and 'further learning' but also for 'productive employment' in our Nation's modern economy" (p. 11).

Note that this goal of beat-the-bell-curve agenda (i.e., having individuals perform above their expected aptitude level with the help of education and literacy instruction) does not attempt to promote educational equality. In short, educational equality is viewed in this agenda as largely irrelevant to the expansion of GNP and, more important, is viewed as counterproductive in a capitalist economy where the pursuit of competitive advantage is the driving force behind economic behavior. Hence, to meet the pressure to be economically productive in the most cost-efficient manner possible, education operating from this agenda has adopted a highly stratified structure.

A second goal associated with the beat-the-bell-curve agenda views the educational advancement of students not in terms of collective economic needs but rather in terms of the needs of individual educational consumers. From the individual consumer perspective, it doesn't matter who fills jobs at any given level of stratification—as long as all jobs are filled with well-educated and well-trained people.

THE PUBLIC SIDE OF ENGAGEMENT THEORY

The three agendas described above have played a prominent role in shaping education in the United States in all aspects of research, practice, and policy. Unfortunately, many educators have tended to ignore the contradictions inherent in these agendas. Rather than developing strategies to engage these agendas simultaneously, they have tended to view each agenda as a separate and independent problem. This has created a no-win situation, for whatever agenda is being advanced at a given time, another also is being undermined (Mosenthal, 1989).

Rather than ignoring the contradictions of educational agendas (as well as those that preoccupy our daily lives), Dewey and those holding an engagement perspective would remind us that such contradictions should be acknowledged; contradictions should be part of the cornerstone of the educational curriculum.

By making life's contradictions the reflective challenge of educational communities, strategies can be proposed, implemented, refined, and evaluated to continually identify the most propitious way of maximizing the interactive benefits of the different agendas as they affect those communities (Mosenthal, in press).

Coping with these apparent contradictions requires new forms of curriculum. As Mohr (1988) has pointed out:

> Official authorized public curriculum and unofficial, more personal curricula exist in every classroom. Teachers and students contribute to both. They each have perceptions of the official curriculum, they each have their own unofficial curriculum, and they each are making use of all at any one time in the classroom. . . . Teachers work with all curricula at once, learning the students' official and unofficial curricula and managing their own, while looking for and seizing opportunities to cause as many students as possible to absorb the official authorized curriculum. . . . When all curricula intersect at once, the classroom curriculum becomes functional. At the intersection, student learning of the teacher's official authorized curriculum can take place. (pp. 64, 66)

This intersection brings the official curriculum alive by connecting with students' interests and intentions. The path to such an effective classroom curriculum involves the craft of fully engaging students in learning the required curriculum through the curriculum of interest. As Case (1990) has argued, "Successful teaching engages the students with the subject, and their engagement affects the teacher and the subject, as well as the students themselves" (p. 28).

It is such thinking, in the Deweyan tradition, as of late that invites all educators to reconsider engagement theory as a way of linking the contradictions of personal and public, official and unofficial agendas for the purpose of enhancing learning in general and reading in particular (Almasi, McKeown, & Beck, 1996; Baker, Afflerbach, & Reinking, 1996; Guthrie & Alao, 1997; Guthrie et al., 1996; Wigfield & Guthrie, 1997). The spirit of this call goes back to Dewey in his invocation of reflective thinking that involves the use of ideas in goal setting and problem identification, the use of engagement to attain goals and solve problems, the use of patience to persevere, and the use of outcomes to begin reflective inquiry anew. And the spirit of this call goes back to Gray and Rogers's (1956) earlier-cited observation that, through engagement with learning and reading, students are better able to realize "a full, rich, and productive life" (p. 56).

CHALLENGES: ENGAGEMENT IN ACTION

It is against this broad relief of lifelong learning that the contributors to this volume discuss engagement. This discussion addresses three themes that challenge the way many educators currently think about learning and reading. First, it moves us beyond the simple view of window-dressing the public curriculum with motivational aids, to understanding the more complex view of how the public curriculum is to be constructed in concert with students' personal curricula.

In brief, in the simple view, motivation is limited to the appeal of bells and whistles, or "amusements," as Dewey called them. These are often simple add-ons to the official curriculum, which come in the form of games and trite rewards. In contrast, in the chapters that follow, the authors present a deeper, more realistically complex picture of motivation that is grounded in the cognitive and affective systems of learners and readers. Motivation that inspires lifelong learning and reading, the authors argue, is rooted in the need to problematize and self-actualize. This, in turn, can be accomplished only by providing students with the opportunity to explore their personal curricula in the context of the public curriculum. Such opportunity involves integrating motivation with strategically conceptualized systems that promote learning, reading, expressing, and conflict resolution. Moreover, such opportunity involves allowing students to both create choice and select choice in what they learn and how they learn it.

A second important theme of this book goes back to Case's (1990) observation above that successful teaching engages the students with the subject, and the subject with the student. In other words, as the contributors to this book remind us, engagement has a short life apart from substance; extended learning and reading engagement rely on extended subject matter, as well as interest and intention. A number of chapters discuss the importance of integrating learning and reading across the full expanse of public and personal curricula. How this can be accomplished is effectively illustrated.

Finally, a third important theme of this book addresses the problem raised in this chapter—the problem of competing educational agendas. While acknowledging that such agendas exist, the authors also make the point that none of these agendas—pursued either individually or interactively—can be realized without engagement. Simply put, reading engagement is a requirement for promoting any educational agenda. It is as Dewey noted: Action begins with a problem and the intent to solve this problem; action is enhanced through the implementation of effective strategies; actions result in outcomes that result in the identification of new problems, the generation of new ideas, and a renewed intent to address these problems. Remove these elements of engagement and the likelihood of any student participating in any educational agenda is greatly diminished. Despite the obviousness of this argument, the question remains as to whether engagement is politically viable in our schools today. The final chapter explores this question.

Taken as a whole, this book attempts to re-establish a conversation between Dewey, Gray, and Rogers, of the past, and reading researchers, teachers, and administrators of the present. It attempts to move us beyond what Dewey (1988/1929) called the "spectator theory of knowledge," to one that embraces an engagement theory of learning and reading:

The mind is within the world as a part of the latter's own on-going process. It is marked off as mind by the fact that wherever it is found, changes take place . . . from knowing as an outside beholding to knowing as an active engaged participant in the drama of problems, contradictions, and meaningful ideas. (p. 232)

REFERENCES

Almasi, J. F., McKeown, M. G., & Beck, I. L. (1996). The nature of engaged reading in classroom discussions of literature. *Journal of Literacy Research, 28,* 107–146.

Ames, C. (1992). Classrooms: Goals, structures, and student motivation. *Journal of Educational Psychology, 84,* 261–271.

Au, K. (1995). Multicultural perspectives on literacy research. *Journal of Reading Behavior, 27,* 85–100.

Baker, L., Afflerbach, P., & Reinking, D. (Eds.). (1996). *Developing engaged readers in school and home communities.* Mahwah, NJ: Erlbaum.

Banks, J. A. (1993). Multicultural education: Historical development, dimensions, and practice. In L. Darling-Hammond (Ed.), *Review of research in education* (Vol. 19, pp. 3–49). Washington, DC: American Educational Research Association.

Beane, J., & Apple, M. (1995). The case for democratic schools. In M. Apple & J. Beane (Eds.), *Democratic schools* (pp. 1–25). Alexandria, VA: Association for Supervision and Curriculum Development.

Bloom, A. (1987). *The closing of the American mind.* New York: Simon & Schuster.

Boorstin, D. (1973). *The Americans: The democratic experience.* New York: Random House.

Bowles, S., & Gintis, H. (1976). *Schooling in capitalist America: Educational reform and the contradictions of economic life.* New York: Basic Books.

Bransford, J. D., & Vye, N. J. (1989). A perspective on cognitive research and its implications for instruction. In L. B. Resnick & L. E. Klopfer (Eds.), *Towards the thinking curriculum: Current cognitive research* (pp. 173–205). Washington, DC: Association for Supervision and Curriculum Development.

Broudy, H. S. (1986). Technology and citizenship. In J. A. Culbertson & L. L. Cunningham (Eds.), *Microcomputers and education* (Eighty-fifth yearbook of the National Society for the Study of Education, Part I, pp. 234–253). Chicago: National Society for the Study of Education.

Case, J. H. (1990). Unexpected responses: Interaction in the classroom. *The Teacher's Journal, 3,* 18–28.

Conference Report on H. R. 1804, Goals 2000: Educate America Act. (1994). *Congressional Record, 140*(32), H1625–H1684.

Cremin, L. (1980). *American education: The national experience, 1783–1876.* New York: Harper & Row.

Dewey, J. (1910). *How we think.* Boston: Heath.

Dewey, J. (1929). *The quest for certainty.* New York: New York: Minton, Balch.

Dewey, J. (1938). *Logic: The theory of inquiry.* New York: Holt.

Dewey, J. (1969). Introduction to philosophy: Syllabus of course 5. In J. A. Boydston (Ed.), *John Dewey: The early works, 1889–1892* (Vol. 3, pp. 34–437). Carbondale: Southern Illinois University Press. (Original work published 1892)

Dewey, J. (1986). How we think: A restatement of the relation of reflective thinking to the educative process. In J. A. Boydston (Ed.), *John Dewey: The later works, 1925–1953* (Vol. 8, pp. 105–352). Carbondale: Southern Illinois University Press. (Original work published 1933)

Dewey, J. (1988). *The quest for certainty.* Carbondale: Southern Illinois University Press. (Original work published 1929)

Dweck, C. S., & Leggett, E. L. (1988). A social-cognitive approach to motivation and personality. *Psychological Review, 95,* 256–273.

Fader, D. N., & McNeil, E. B. (1966). *Hooked on books: Program & proof.* New York: Putnam.

Goals 2000: Educate America Act of 1994. Pub. L. No. 103–227, 1–3, 108 Stat. 125 (1994).

Gray, W. S., & Rogers, B. (1956). *Maturity in reading.* Chicago: University of Chicago Press.

Guthrie, J. T., & Alao, S. (1997). Designing contexts to increase motivations for reading. *Educational Psychologist, 32*(2), 95–105.

Guthrie, J. T., Van Meter, P., McCann, A. D., Wigfield, A., Bennett, L., Poundstone, C. C., Rice, M. E., Faibisch, F. M., Hunt, B., & Mitchell, A. (1996). Growth of literacy engagement: Changes in motivations and strategies during Concept-Oriented Reading Instruction. *Reading Research Quarterly, 31,* 306–332.

Gutmann, A. (1987). *Democratic education.* Princeton, NJ: Princeton University Press.

Harvey, G., & Klein, S. (1989). Understanding and measuring equity in education: A conceptual framework. In W. Secada (Ed.), *Equity in education* (pp. 43–67). Philadelphia: Farmer.

Herrnstein, R. J., & Murray, C. (1994). *The bell curve: Intelligence and class structure in American life.* New York: Free Press.

Hirsch, E. D. (1987). *Cultural literacy: What every American needs to know.* Boston: Houghton Mifflin.

Howe, K. R. (1994). Standards, assessment, and equality of educational opportunity. *Educational Researcher, 23*(8), 27–33.

Johnston, W. B., & Packer, A. H. (1987). *Workforce 2000: Work and workers for the twenty-first century.* Indianapolis, IN: Hudson Institute.

Kaestle, C. F. (1983). *Pillars of the republic.* New York: Hill & Wang.

Katz, M. B. (1987). *Restructuring American education.* Cambridge, MA: Harvard University Press.

Katznelson, I., & Weir, M. (1985). *Schooling for all: Class, race, and the decline of the democratic ideal.* New York: Basic Books.

Ladson-Billings, G. (1995). Toward a theory of culturally relevant pedagogy. *American Educational Research Journal, 32,* 465–491.

Larabee, D. F. (1997). Public goods, private goods: The American struggle over educational goals. *American Educational Research Journal, 34,* 39–81.

Maehr, M. L., & Pintrich, P. R. (Eds.). (1991). *Advances in motivation and achievement: Goals and self-regulatory processes* (Vol. 7). Greenwich, CT: JAI Press.

Meece, J. L., Blumenfeld, P. C., & Hoyle, R. H. (1988). Students' goal orientation and cognitive engagement in classroom activities. *Journal of Educational Psychology, 80,* 514–523.

Meyer, J. W., Tyack, D., Nagel, J., & Gordon, A. (1979). Public education as nation-building in America: Enrollments and bureaucratization in the American states, 1870–1930. *American Journal of Education, 85,* 591–613.

Mohr, M. (1988). Classroom curriculum: Expectations and configurations. In Langston Hughes School-Based Research Group, *Teacher research on student learning* (pp. 63–72). Fairfax, VA: Fairfax County Public Schools.

Mosenthal, P. B. (1983a). Defining classroom writing competence: A paradigmatic perspective. *Review of Educational Research, 53*(2), 217–251.

Mosenthal, P. B. (1983b). The influence of social situation on children's classroom comprehension of text. *Elementary School Journal, 83*(5), 537–547.

Mosenthal, P. B. (1984a). Defining reading program effectiveness: An ideological perspective. *Poetics, 13,* 195–216.

Mosenthal, P. B. (1984b). The effect of classroom ideology on children's production of narrative text. *American Educational Research Journal, 21*(3), 679–689.

Mosenthal, P. B. (1987). The goals of reading research and practice: Making sense of the many theories of reading. *Reading Teacher, 40,* 694–698.

Mosenthal, P. B. (1989). The whole-language approach: Teachers between a rock and a hard place. *Reading Teacher, 42,* 628–629.

Mosenthal, P. B. (1993). Understanding agenda setting in reading research. In A. P. Sweet & J. I. Anderson (Eds.), *Reading research into the year 2000* (pp. 115–128). Hillsdale, NJ: Erlbaum.

Mosenthal, P. B. (1995). Why there are no dialogues among the divided: The problem of solipsistic agendas in literacy research. *Reading Research Quarterly, 30,* 574–577.

Mosenthal, P. B. (in press). Reframing the problems of adolescence and adolescent literacy: A dilemma-management perspective. In D. E. Alvermann, K. A. Hinchman, D. W. Moore, S. Phelps, & D. Waff (Eds.), *Reconceptualizing the literacies in adolescents' lives.* New York: Erlbaum.

Mosenthal, P., Conley, M., Colella, A., & Davidson-Mosenthal, R. (1985). The influence of prior knowledge and teacher lesson structure on children's production of narratives. *Elementary School Journal, 85,* 621–634.

National Center on Education and the Economy. (1990). *America's choice: High skills or low wages* (Report of the Commission on the Skills of the American Workforce). Rochester, NY: Author.

National Commission on Excellence in Education. (1983). *A nation at risk.* Washington, DC: U.S. Government Printing Office.

National Education Goals Panel. (1995). *The national education goals report* (Core Report). Washington, DC: U.S. Government Printing Office.

Porter, A. (1995). The uses and misuses of opportunity-to-learn standards. *Educational Researcher, 24,* 21–27.

Prawat, R. S. (1993). The value of ideas: Problems versus possibilities in learning. *Educational Researcher, 22*(6), 5–16.

Spiro, R. J. (1977). Remembering information from text: The "state of schema" approach. In R. C. Anderson, R. J. Spiro, & W. E. Montague (Eds.), *Schooling and the acquisition of knowledge* (pp. 137–166). Hillsdale, NJ: Erlbaum.

Stanovich, K. E. (1986). Matthew effects in reading: Some consequences of individual differences in the acquisition of literacy. *Reading Research Quarterly, 21*, 360–407.

Strike, K. A. (1991). The moral role of schooling in a liberal democratic society. In G. Grant (Ed.), *Review of research in education* (Vol. 17, pp. 413–483). Washington, DC: American Educational Research Association.

Taylor, F. W. (1911). *The principles of scientific management*. New York: Harper.

Thornton, S. J. (1994). The social studies near century's end: Reconsidering patterns of curriculum and instruction. In L. Darling-Hammond (Ed.), *Review of research in education* (Vol. 20, pp. 223–254). Washington, DC: American Educational Research Association.

Urdan, T. C., & Maehr, M. L. (1995). Beyond a two-goal theory of motivation and achievement: A case for social goals. *Review of Educational Research, 65*, 213–243.

Valli, L., Cooper, D., & Frankes, L. (1997). Professional development schools and equity: A critical analysis of rhetoric and research. In M. W. Apple (Ed.), *Review of research in education* (Vol. 22, pp. 251–304). Washington, DC: American Educational Research Association.

Walberg, H. J., Strykowski, B. E., Rovai, E., & Hung, S. S. (1984). Exceptional performance. *Review of Educational Research, 54*, 87–112.

Walberg, H. J., & Tsai, S. (1983). Matthew effects in education. *American Educational Research Journal, 20*, 359–373.

Walmsley, S. A. (1981). On the purpose and content of secondary reading programs: An educational ideological perspective. *Curriculum Inquiry, 11*, 73–93.

Wigfield, A., & Guthrie, J. T. (1997). Relations of children's motivation for reading to the amount and breadth of their reading. *Journal of Educational Psychology, 89*(3), 420–432.

CHAPTER 2

Engagement in Reading:
Processes of Motivated, Strategic,
Knowledgeable, Social Readers

John T. Guthrie and Emily Anderson

F OR MOST OF THE TWENTIETH CENTURY, teaching and research in reading have emphasized language and cognitive issues. Cognitive science and educational research have revealed how strategies, skills, and background knowledge enhanced students' abilities to comprehend text and learn new ideas (Barr, Kamil, Mosenthal, & Pearson, 1991). This traditional emphasis points to the "how" of reading. Our engagement perspective incorporates the "why" of reading into this frame. Although reading researchers have acquired a theoretical and empirical literature on "how" people read words and books, we need to complement this knowledge with an understanding of "why" people choose to read.

Reading traditionally has been defined as a set of skills or competencies (Anderson, Hiebert, Scott, & Wilkinson, 1985; Huey, 1908; Ruddell, Ruddell, & Singer, 1994). In this view, expertise in reading is the automatic coordination of a fluid cognitive system. Learning to read has been defined as the acquisition of skills such as understanding stories, comprehending paragraphs, and recognizing words. We believe this achievement-oriented view of reading is accurate but incomplete. In our view, reading should be conceptualized as an engagement. Engaged readers not only have acquired reading skills, but use them for their own purposes in many contexts. They possess beliefs, desires, and interests that energize the hard work of becoming literate. From this perspective, motivations and social interactions are equal to cognitions as foundations for reading (Alvermann & Guthrie, 1993).

Understanding why people read is valuable because wide and frequent reading confers many benefits. Studies show that being a wide and frequent reader increases a student's reading achievement by 10–15 percentile points on standard tests. Students in the top third of a class in amount of reading will be more than 10 percentile points higher than students of equal ability who are lower on amount of reading (Cipielewski & Stanovich, 1992). For students of equal ability, the more avid reader will receive higher grades in all subjects than the less avid reader.

Not only does the amount of reading correlate with reading achievement, but also it is strongly related to level of knowledge. For example, practical knowledge of topics such as the federal budget size, World War II allies, world languages, and Middle East religions is determined largely by amount of reading. Frequent readers possess 200–400% higher knowledge levels than less frequent and less active readers. Even controlled for amount of TV viewing and intellectual ability, amount and breadth of reading determine knowledge levels (Stanovich & Cunningham, 1993).

Frequent reading propels people toward active citizenship. Among young adults, active readers are more likely to participate in society by joining local and civic organizations (Guthrie, Schafer, & Hutchinson, 1991). Active readers are 30% more likely to vote, to join civic organizations, to participate in a parent/teacher association, and to be members of community religious groups. Wide and frequent reading fosters societal participation by providing a common information base among members in the community.

Active reading is grounded in intrinsic motivations. It is common sense that people read for a reason. Reading is a conscious, deliberate act prompted by a plausible purpose. When an individual's reasons for reading include curiosity, the desire for aesthetic involvement, or the disposition for social interchange, that individual is likely to be an active reader. In one study, the more curious, involved students with a solid sense of self-efficacy spent 140% more time reading than less intrinsically motivated readers. Intrinsically motivated students read a 70% wider variety of books than less intrinsically motivated students (Wigfield & Guthrie, 1997). Students who want to read for personally significant reasons will invest time in reading. *Our view is that engagement in reading is a motivated mental activity with vital consequences for world knowledge and social participation.*

PROFESSIONAL PRIORITIES FOR READING ENGAGEMENT

At least three forces prompted us to adopt an engagement perspective on reading. One of them was the high priority given to this topic by reading teachers across the nation. The National Reading Research Center (NRRC) conducted a poll of 1,000 reading teachers randomly selected from the membership of the International Reading Association (IRA). The poll asked, "What are your priorities for research in reading?" Given a choice of 99 alternatives, these professional educators ranked "creating interest in reading" above all others. The most highly rated issues were "intrinsic desire for reading," "increasing amount and breadth of children's reading," and the "roles of teachers, peers, and parents in motivation" (O'Flahavan, Gambrell, Guthrie, Stahl, Baumann, & Alvermann, 1992). Confirming this priority, the National Elementary Principals Association reported that in a membership survey the top research priority was "finding ways to motivate students" (Baumann, Allen, & Shockley, 1994; National Association of Elementary School Principals, 1996).

Our perspective was shaped by a second influence, consisting of the burgeoning professional literature on motivation. Since the 1980s an increasing body of research has documented that student beliefs, goals, values, and self-perceptions dramatically affect achievement (Maehr & Pintrich, 1993; Pintrich, Brown, & Weinstein, 1994; Schunk & Meece, 1992). However, most of these studies have been general to all of school learning or they have been conducted in science and math. Despite the ample research in motivation generally, motivation for reading has been virtually neglected until very recently.

Third, the intellectual roots of our engagement perspective can be traced to Dewey and Freire. Dewey identified reading interest with unified activity. He noted that "the genuine principle of interest is the principle of the recognized identity of the fact to be learned or the action proposed with the growing self; that it lies in the direction of the agent's own growth, and is therefore, imperiously demanded, if the agent is to be himself" (Dewey, 1913, p. 7). Our view of intrinsic motivation is akin to Dewey's sense of interest. An interested reader personally identifies with the conceptual content of a text so fully that absorbing its meaning is an effortless activity. Beyond the individual pursuit of self-development, Dewey argued that reading is a social enterprise (Archambault, 1964). Extending this view, Freire observed that literacy enables people to understand, and even change, the social order. We concur with Freire that "the reader's development of a critical comprehension of the text, and the sociohistorical context to which it refers, becomes an important factor in our notion of literacy" (Freire & Macedo, 1987, p. 157).

In this brief space, we cannot compare and contrast our engagement perspective with all aspects of the whole language movement. While we emphasize reading as meaning-making, consistent with Goodman and Goodman (1994) and Holdaway (1979), we place language processes in the web of a motivational, conceptual, and social system. In this web, conceptual processes in reading are predominant. That is, reading is primarily an act of knowing. Language is a pathway in the pursuit of understanding. For educators, the foremost challenge is motivating students to learn through reading. Helping students become self-determining agents of their own development through reading is our deepest concern. While all language processes are valuable tools, the full set of motivational, conceptual, strategic, and social operations are central to the engaged reader.

ENGAGEMENT IN READING: A PROCESS MODEL

Reading engagement is the condition in which a person builds on existing conceptual knowledge by using cognitive strategies in order to fulfill motivational goals and to understand or participate in a social world. Thus, we define reading engagement as the joint functioning of motivation, conceptual knowledge, strategies, and social interactions during literacy activities. These processes operate dynamically, increasing over time. Our view of reading is submerged within the engagement construct. In this context, reading is the motivated, strategic, conceptual, social interaction with text and written language.

Engagement as a dynamic system is shown in Figure 2.1. As motivation increases, engagement increases. When students are intrinsically motivated, they learn to use cognitive strategies for reading (Path A). These reading strategies, such as recognizing words, comprehending, predicting, summarizing, and self-monitoring, when properly deployed and fully executed, lead to conceptual understanding (Path B). Social interaction patterns in the classroom can amplify or constrict students' intrinsic motivations, their use of self-regulated strategies, and their attainment of deep conceptual knowledge (Paths C, D, E). As students gain conceptual understanding, their sense of self-efficacy grows and their motivations for reading increase (Path F) (Baker, Afflerbach, & Reinking, 1996; Guthrie, Schafer, Wang, & Afflerbach, 1995).

In this map of reading, strategies occupy a central location. It is undeniable that reading strategies are difficult to learn. Recognizing words, the most basic

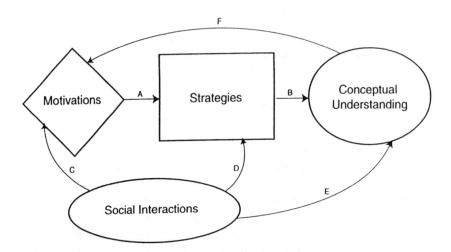

Figure 2.1. Processes of engagement in reading.

set of strategies, is an obstacle for some learners (Adams, 1990). Many students fail to comprehend stories. Besides struggling with narratives, students are often frustrated by informational texts (National Assessment of Educational Progress, 1994). A majority of elementary students are unable to learn the strategies for integrating diverse texts and composing in multiple genre. Strategies for comprehending demand effort and persistence, and learning them is not inherently enjoyable. However, students will exert the needed effort and attention if they possess powerful, personal motivations like involvement and curiosity (Pintrich & DeGroot, 1990; Pintrich & Schrauben, 1992). When a particular strategy helps a student complete an exciting story or learn about a favorite topic, the reader will learn and use that strategy. Yet, the motivations and reasons for using reading strategies are only beginning to be understood and used in classrooms.

Beyond providing a purpose for strategy learning, motivations give students a reason for using their background experience. The importance of background experience and knowledge in reading comprehension is widely accepted (Anderson & Pearson, 1984). However, the role of motivation in using background knowledge has been recognized only recently. Students who are motivated to read will recall what they know to integrate it with new information. In addition, motivated readers interact socially. Motivation increases and students' strategic expertise expands as they talk with peers, share books, and discuss their texts (Almasi, 1995). Connections among the components of reading engagement will be explained later in this chapter, but first we turn to the nature of reading motivation.

What Are the Motivations for Reading?

In our engagement perspective, motivations are "reasons for reading." A motivation for reading answers the question, "Why are you reading that text?" This is consistent with goal-oriented theories of motivation (Wigfield & Eccles, 1992). In this school of thought, motivations are internalized goals and beliefs leading to strategies for learning and choices of activities that are consistent with the goals and purposes of the learner.

One motivation for reading is *involvement*. Many adults and children alike have had the experience of "getting lost" in a book. People report that they "fall into" a text and dwell within it. We call that involvement. In addition to enjoying involvement, many people seek to find books in which they expect to "get lost." Wanting this experience, involvement becomes a purpose for reading. When getting lost or being involved in a book is something a person wants to do, involvement becomes the motivation for reading.

A second common motivation for reading is *curiosity*. This refers to an intense interest in a particular topic, such as turtles, astronauts, or gardening. Interests such as these propel people to seek books and magazine articles on the topics. In our view, specific interests often become generalized into a curiosity, a desire for learning overall about the world through reading. In several studies, these two motivations—involvement and curiosity—consistently have predicted students' frequency of reading and amount of time spent reading books (Guthrie, Van Meter, et al., 1996).

A third motivation for reading is *social*. Many adults recommend books to friends and enjoy discussing books. Children are equally social, reporting that they read to share or to keep pace with friends and peers. In these cases the social interchange is the reason for reading, and the motivation for literate activity is social.

A fourth motivation for reading is *challenge*. Some students choose to read a particular text because it appears to be more difficult or stimulating than other choices. Students who enjoy challenge are willing to persist in the face of difficult text. They may report that they like learning complex ideas or figuring out a complicated plot. Fifth, a motivational construct is *importance*. The belief that reading is valuable supports student effort and commitment. These students say, "It is important to me to be a good reader," and this motivation leads to achievement in reading. A sixth motivation is *efficacy*, which refers to the individual's belief in his or her capacity to read well. Students with reading efficacy have confidence in their abilities to read. They spend time reading independently and are optimistic about their future achievement. Reading efficacy is not as obvious a "reason for reading" as the other motivations presented here. However, the enabling power of efficacy, especially for primary children, is substantial.

Another set of motivations is more external to the learner. One extrinsic motivation is *recognition*. This refers to the desire to be known as a good reader or to be seen as competent by peers, teachers, or parents. A certificate or gold star may be awarded as an incentive to increase students' motivation of recognition. Another extrinsic motivation is *competition*. Students like to "be the best." Some want to be better than their friends or peers. A strong motivator is *grades*. Students read and work for positive evaluations from their teacher. Finally, *work avoidance* is a motivation. This operates negatively to reduce the amount of reading and effort. A student with a work-avoidance motivation tries to minimize the act of reading. Low achievers are often work-avoidants in reading.

In general, students possess both intrinsic and extrinsic motivations. However, in a population of inner-city students, Wigfield reported that the strongest motivations were grades, followed by importance, compliance, and recognition (Wigfield, Wilde, Baker, Fernandez-Fein, & Scher, 1996). Three of the four highest motivations were relatively external to the learner (extrinsic). The more internal (intrinsic) motivations of curiosity and involvement were lower in prominence. This is problematic in light of evidence that intrinsic motivations are correlated with reading achievement and amount of reading (Wigfield & Guthrie, 1997).

Motivations and Interest

Interest is a fascination with a topic or a subject matter. Readers may be interested in movie stars in Hollywood, black holes in space, or ballet. A person with an interest in one of these topics is likely to read about it, perhaps with rapt attention. High interest for a topic leads to high comprehension of text on that topic, according to a variety of research, even when background knowledge on the topic is held constant (Schiefele, 1996). Although the benefits of interests for comprehension are robust among college students, those benefits do not always appear for younger students, such as third graders. For example, Carr and Thompson (1995) found that younger students may not be able to connect their interests to comprehension-enhancing strategies. Whereas interest is specific to a topic, such as dinosaurs, motivation refers broadly to multiple topics and genres. For example, Guthrie, Van Meter, and colleagues (1996) found that young students who possess intrinsic motivations for reading, read a wide range of topics and use a variety of effective strategies for finding books, understanding them, and reducing distractions as they read.

Development of Motivations

Motivations for reading are not static. They develop and evolve as students become more self-determining (Deci, Vallerand, Pelletier, & Ryan, 1991). As the student becomes aware of herself, she becomes the agent of her own engagement in reading. Oldfather (1994) illustrated this process in an exploration of how students motivate themselves. She asked fifth- and sixth-grade students the following question, "Do you remember a time when you were supposed to do some reading in school and you really didn't feel like doing it? Did you do it? Why or why not? How did you feel when this happened?" Students fell into three categories: (1) those who motivated themselves and completed tasks; (2) those who did not motivate themselves but completed the tasks; and (3) those who did not become motivated and did not complete the tasks.

Students in the first group reported that they chose a positive attitude. One student reported that although a science project seemed boring at first, "I have to think of it as important, because if you thought it wasn't important you wouldn't do anything about it" (Oldfather, 1994, p. 9). Students reported that they try to make tasks worthwhile. One student reported, "If I come into something open minded and I think it might be worthwhile, I will probably get to like it." Some students simply plunged into an activity. One of them said, "If I can just start to do it, I get really into it and start to put more effort into it. I don't like having to sit down, but once I make myself get there I get involved" (p. 10). These students were self-determining, able to take charge of their own motivations. They set motivational goals and exerted effort to participate in activities that yielded motivational benefits. These students saw themselves as engaged in their own development.

Central to our notion of engagement is the self-determining learner: those learners whose intrinsic motivations energize their wide and frequent reading. Students who read for involvement, curiosity, challenge, importance, and self-efficacy spend more time reading books than students who read for recognition, grades, competition, and compliance with the demands of a program. Motivation, however, cannot thrive in a vacuum.

In isolation, intrinsic motivational goals cannot sustain engagement in reading. The home environment, social milieu, and cognitive strategies of students also contribute to reading. Students who are socially inclined, talk with their friends, share books, and discuss their writing are most likely to become avid readers. Thus, motivations for reading cannot be considered in isolation from their social and cultural contexts. As Serpell asserted, individuals participate in activities (e. g., literacy) embedded in cultural settings (Serpell & Boykin, 1994). These settings, in turn, are shaped by the beliefs of the participants. Because these beliefs have meaning for the individual, they become a source of intrinsic motivation. Motivational potency of the social group leads to greater enjoyment and persistence in reading activity and the development of motivational goals. Acts of reading take place not in a void, but in a stream of cultural practices into which young students are enculturated (Guthrie et al., 1991).

Can the tie between amount of reading and intrinsic motivation be confirmed with studies of classroom intervention? Guthrie and a team of collaborators addressed this question by creating a year-long curriculum to enhance intrinsic motivations, strategies, and amount of reading (Guthrie, McGough, Bennett, & Rice, 1996). Known as Concept-Oriented Reading Instruction, this curriculum integrated reading/language arts and science (Guthrie, Van Meter, Hancock, McCann, Anderson, & Alao, in press). Over the school year, increases in motivation according to in-depth interviews were tied to an increased amount of reading. For the elementary students in this study, 85% of the students who increased in intrinsic motivation from fall to spring increased in the amount and breadth of their reading. Consistent with previous research, some students decreased in motivation. Seventy percent of students who decreased in intrinsic motivation from fall to spring also declined in amount and breadth of reading. In other words, reading widely is the natural consequence of personal goals, aspirations, and motivations of learning about the world, immersing in new experiences, and interacting with peers.

Motivations Correlate with Reading Achievement

Motivational goals are connected to achievement. Students who want to understand the core concepts in a subject matter attain higher grades and higher scores on measures of knowledge than students who are less intrinsically motivated. These motivational goals, however, do not directly confer achievement. Intrinsic motivations increase achievement by leading to productive strategies. Students who are interested in a course topic will use strategies to regulate their own learning and studying. They will do an outline when it is needed, reread when they are confused, self-question to foster connections between ideas, and identify key terms that are important, all of which lead to achievement.

By many definitions, achievement in reading is linked to motivations. Reading comprehension ability on a standardized test is significantly associated with the motivations of involvement, recognition, social interchange, and competition. Standardized reading vocabulary measures also are significantly associated with involvement and social interchange (Wigfield et al., 1996). Defined by teacher grades or ratings, student achievement is associated with motivation in a similar pattern. Third and fifth graders who receive high grades possess higher self-efficacy (e. g., higher perceived self-competence) than lower achievers. Higher achievers reported that "my friends think that I am a good reader," and "when I read aloud, I feel proud that I can read so well." A solid self-concept leads to reading achievement in the elementary grades (Gambrell, Codling, & Palmer, 1996). Among high school students, similar connections exist. For example, Hynd reported that intrinsic motivational and attitudinal characteristics of high school students predicted knowledge gained in content courses such as physics (Hynd, McNish, Qian, Keith, & Lay, 1994).

How do teachers view motivations and their relation to achievement? To understand teachers' viewpoints, Sweet (Sweet & Guthrie, 1994) conducted focus groups and interviews with a range of elementary school classroom teachers and reading teachers. She asked teachers, "What is motivation?" and "What are motivated students like?" Teachers replied that some students were disposed to be "engrossed" and "immersed" in reading, whereas others were less so (*involvement* motivation). Some students were fascinated with a particular topic, whereas others were less so (*curiosity* motivation), teachers reported. Teachers said that some students were energized by being given choices (*autonomy* support), whereas some students were interested in reading books connected to an activity such as a field trip, visitor, or hands-on experience (*activity* support). Sweet examined how these motivations of involvement, curiosity, autonomy support, and activity support were related to achievement.

Teachers perceived that higher-achieving students possessed a different profile of motivations than lower achievers. High-achieving students, whom teachers reported as "A" students in reading, were more motivated by internal involvement and curiosity than they were by external support for autonomy and activity. In contrast, the students rated by teachers as "C" in reading were perceived to be more highly motivated by teacher support for autonomy and activity than they were by involvement and curiosity. In other words, the "A" students were higher on the intrinsic than the extrinsic motivations. The "C" students were the opposite, being higher on the extrinsic than the intrinsic motivations. Higher achievers had acquired personal interests that guided their reading, whereas lower achievers were more reliant on situational supports to stimulate their reading. These findings were consistent with the theory of self-determination proposed by Deci (Deci et al., 1991). Children develop intrinsic motivations by gradually internalizing the goals and values held by parents and teachers around them.

Motivations Decline Throughout School Years

How do motivations change as students progress through elementary school to middle school? Harter and her colleagues reported that intrinsic motivations for schooling declined as students progressed through school (Harter, Whitesell, & Kowalksi, 1992); preference for challenge, curiosity, and independent thinking decreased. Extrinsic motivations (e.g., preference for easy work, studying to get good grades, and dependence on the teacher) increased during the same period. This pattern of change was more pronounced for students who perceived themselves to be competent than for students who perceived themselves to be relatively less competent in school. Although all students declined in intrinsic motivation, students with the highest perceived self-competence experienced the most dramatic decreases in intrinsic motivation. These students with the highest self-competence perception also showed the most marked increases in extrinsic motivations for schooling. The educational conditions needed to sustain high intrinsic motivation seem to disappear in middle and high school (see Guthrie, Alao, & Rinehart, 1997).

These declines in intrinsic motivation also occur for reading. Comparing students across grades, Wigfield (Wigfield & Guthrie, 1997) found that students declined in reading efficacy (I'm a good reader), social motivations (I like to share books with friends), and recognition (I like to be known as a good reader). Both boys and girls declined at the same rate. Likewise, Gambrell (Gambrell et al., 1996) reported that value of reading declined in the elementary grades among a cross-section of students. Students were less likely in grade 5 than in grade 3 to believe that reading is important and useful. Across grades 1–6, a positive attitude toward reading erodes steadily, with a more dramatic drop for low achievers than for others (McKenna, Kear, & Ellsworth, 1995).

This decline in children's intrinsic motivation for reading is cause for alarm. Since reading achievement depends on motivation, and this motivation decreases in elementary school, we can expect declines in achievement. If intrinsic motivation declines, children do not have desire or energy for higher-order strategy learning, which is necessary to their reading comprehension. Educational programs and principles to increase engagement are presented in later chapters. In addition, a research-based set of principles is proposed and explained by Guthrie, Alao, and

Rinehart (1997), and curriculum possibilities for increasing motivation are presented in Guthrie and Wigfield (1997).

Most vital is the following implication. If students exit school with low intrinsic motivation to read, they will be "at risk" of being nonreaders who shun books. They will be nonparticipants in the literate community.

ENGAGED READING IS CONCEPTUAL

People read to make meaning. The nature of meaning constructed from text, however, may vary dramatically from lower-order, rote, literal meanings to higher-order, interpretive, conceptual meanings. As students read, they gain important facts and bits of information. With this information, motivated readers construct explanations and attempt to account for the particular elements they have comprehended. Readers build principled meaning to integrate the particular features of text they have understood. Basically, people read to grasp concepts that hold personal and social significance.

What Is Conceptual Learning?

Conceptual learning emphasizes the building of rich mental models. For example, Chi and others reported that higher levels of conceptual knowledge about the biology of the human heart consisted of enriched mental models (Chi, DeLeeuw, Chiu, & Lavancher, 1994). A student with a good mental model of the heart possesses a relatively large number of features and a systemic, dynamic sense of how the heart operates. As students learn about the functions of the heart, they learn more features and they learn about the interactions among the heart's functions. Consistent with this view, Mayer showed that conceptual knowledge of a bicycle can be described as a mental model. For example, understanding a bicycle consists of knowing the parts, the actions of the parts, and the principles that govern those actions, including friction, resistance, and motion. Students who learned these principles through reading could answer high-level questions and solve problems better than students who did not possess such a dynamic mental model (Mayer & Gallini, 1990).

The enrichment view of conceptual learning from text is espoused by diSessa. She stated that "understanding evolves toward compactness involving a few principles that are as general as possible" (diSessa, 1993, p. 190). She continued, "Cultivating the sense of a mechanism (how systems work) can help students to develop adequate scientific models of situations" (p. 206). In a review of research on knowledge representation, Alexander and Judy (1988) concluded that as students become more knowledgeable in a subject, their understanding is increasingly organized around fundamental principles. Both diSessa and Alexander underscored the view that conceptual learning consists of generalizations that embrace particular features, structures, and functions.

Examples of Conceptual Knowledge

In the examples below, elementary school students (grade 3) read several trade books to learn about the differences between ponds and deserts. Their learning reflected different levels of conceptual understanding (Guthrie, Van Meter, et al., 1996). The first student showed the lowest level:

> Ponds and deserts are different from each other because ponds are wet places with animals in the pond and some people throw food in for the ducks to eat.

The second student learned an intermediate level of conceptual knowledge:

> Ponds have alot of water deserts have not alot of water. Deserts have the hottest air. Ponds have cool air. Deserts have lizards ponds do not have lizards. Ponds have ducks deserts do not have ducks. Deserts have camels ponds do not have camels. Ponds have alot of grass. Deserts a little thing of grass. Ponds have alot of rain deserts have not alot. A desert can have no rain for a year. Deserts have big bad tornados, but ponds have no tornados. Ponds have fish, but deserts have no fish.

The third student gained a relatively high level of conceptual knowledge about the features of biomes and why they support different species:

> Ponds and deserts are different in all kinds of ways. First of all ponds have water birds and ducks. And they also have water snakes, duck weed, lily pads. They both have sun light. Deserts are places that have tumble weed which is a plant that lives in a desert. They also have sand, cactuses, Lizards, Cobra & Scorpions and much more. In a cold desert you can see lots of rain and it is cold. Cold deserts and hot/dry deserts are different because one is hot and the other is cold. The animals that live in the pond get water from the pond and get food from fish, flies, grass and other things. If the animals from the pond go to the desert I think they wouldn't survive. The animals that live in the desert get their water from when it rains and the plants. They get their food from other animals and plants. If the animals that live in the desert go and try to live in the pond I think some of them wouldn't survive.

This showed how knowledge increased in several respects. The third student gained command of more elements, features, and functions in this domain than the other students. She also formed principles to organize these particulars into relationships. At the highest levels of conceptual understanding, students possess interrelated, explanatory principles for phenomena and events. They have the ability to coordinate theory and evidence, and they can express the interplay between them (Alexander & Judy, 1988; Guthrie, Anderson, Alao, & Rinehart, 1997).

Vosniadou (1994) suggested that conceptual learning requires restructuring of existing information. She documented that across grades 1–6, children restructure their knowledge of the earth's shape. Most younger students believe a dual earth theory in which the earth is round but you can fall off it if you walk far enough. By age 8, one-third of the students believe the earth is a sphere; by age 10, two-thirds believe the earth is a sphere that people on all sides can occupy. Conceptual learning, in this perspective, entails the revision of one form of explanatory understanding into a different form of understanding. The particular facts and features of the concept change little, but the principle of explanation changes substantially.

How Do Students Learn Conceptual Knowledge from Reading?

Glynn (1994; Glynn & Duit, 1995) proposed a model of conceptual learning based on an extensive review of research. Students learn concepts readily when five conditions are provided:

- Existing knowledge is activated.
- New information and educational experiences are related to existing knowledge.
- Intrinsic motivation is developed.
- New knowledge is constructed.
- New knowledge is applied, evaluated, and revised.

The process of building new understanding begins with background experience.

Understanding a new text is dramatically influenced by what the student already understands about the topic. As students encounter new information, they organize and construct it into a fluid understanding. New information can be one of two forms. It may be textual, from books, articles, or textbooks; it also may be experienced through the senses of seeing, hearing, feeling, and smelling. Sensory experiences, often called "hands-on" activities in classrooms at the elementary level or "laboratory" activities at the high school level, often are used in teaching science, but they rarely are employed to enhance reading development.

Because new knowledge can be gained both directly through hands-on experiences and indirectly through reading or viewing videos, many teachers provide both avenues to students. However, both avenues are almost never combined to increase the skills of reading. Teachers rarely have tangible hands-on experiences to support reading development.

The power of combining experiential and text-based learning has been demonstrated by Hynd and her collaborators (Hynd, Alvermann, & Qian, 1993). Hynd asked half of the students in a class to observe phenomena of motion, such as the path of a penny being shoved off a table or a bullet being fired from a gun. After observing a demonstration, all students read a text explaining the Newtonian principle of forward motion. Students who viewed the demonstration and read the text developed higher conceptual understanding than students who read the text but did not view the demonstration. The combination of reading and hands-on experience enabled students to learn structural features (i.e., size, weight, and speed of objects) and the relations among structures that form the principles of motion. Sensory experiences arouse interest and lead students to pose questions. These interests and self-questioning processes that come from experiential learning help students explain what they have read and seen.

Understanding stories is a conceptual endeavor. Stories contain conventional elements of setting, characters, plot, conflict, and resolution. Stories contain a sequence of episodes that change dynamically across time. Grasping these elements of character, setting, plot, and sequence is necessary to perceiving one or more of the plausible themes in the story. Britton has shown that as students read a literary narrative, they build an internal model of what is happening (Britton & Gulgoz, 1991; Stahl, Hynd, Britton, McNish, & Bosquet, 1996). This model shifts to assimilate new information, and it can be used to predict. Readers regularly test the story against the view of the world as they have experienced it. This constructive process of understanding stories parallels the constructive process of understanding a new idea such as the formation of volcanos. Reading comprehension is a process of building meanings, whether literary or expository. In either case the meanings are conceptual, containing specific information, inferences, and broad patterns. Whether the patterns reflect an observable event such as a volcano or an imagined character, comprehending the text is an act of building a conceptual understanding.

Motivations for Conceptual Learning

Intrinsic motivation is a fundamental condition for conceptual learning. Intrinsically motivated readers possess a desire to explain and understand. This desire to explain is related to the "curiosity" motivation that predicts both reading achievement and amount of reading. Students who possess the motivational goal of explaining concepts are likely to be attentive, concentrated, and focused on text meanings. Curious students will elaborate ideas that come to mind as they read. They make inferences and integrate new information with what they already know. Intrinsically motivated readers ask, "Am I understanding this text?" and "What should I do to fix up my misunderstandings?" Schiefele (1996) found that interested, motivated readers developed high-level conceptual understanding of texts despite how much they already knew. At the same time, interested readers tended to avoid distracting particulars and did not spend time memorizing trivia. Hynd (Hynd et al., 1994) confirmed that intrinsically motivated high school physics students gained more knowledge than less motivated learners because they used strategies more effectively. Motivated students gave more attention, more thought, and more planning to their reading.

ENGAGED READING IS STRATEGIC

Strategies and Skills

To make meaning, readers use skills and strategies. Defined as a plan of action, a strategy can be applied to different situations. Strategies are crucial for all types of planning, from vacations, to tennis, to reading. Overall, strategies are cognitive processes that are controllable and conscious (Baker & Brown, 1984; Pressley et al., 1994). Strategies are different from skills, which usually are defined as "automatic sequences of complex actions." Skills are continuous performances executed quickly. Bike riding is a skill for the experienced rider, but deciding where to ride is a strategy.

Expert readers (and riders) differ from novices in their awareness of strategies. Expert readers have control over their strategies and monitor their use. Expert learners take into consideration the task at hand. They evaluate different strategies and decide which ones are most appropriate. This evaluation also may include an evaluation of the learner's effort, intelligence, and amount of prior knowledge that might be needed to accomplish the task. Strategic readers are better than nonstrategic readers not only at reading but also at monitoring, controlling, and adapting their strategic processes while reading.

Nonstrategic readers are unaware of what works for them. If a strategy is not working, the poor reader is unaware of this problem and unable to adjust the strategy use to increase understanding of various texts. Strategies rarely are learned well. Because they are difficult to acquire, children need sustaining motivations and excellent teaching.

Using Prior Knowledge

A few powerful strategies are widely recognized as fundamental to reading at all ages. These include the following: (1) using prior knowledge, (2) searching for information, (3) comprehending, and (4) learning and automating word recognition. First, *using prior knowledge* is a prerequisite to comprehending new information, and it is imperative to the advancement of conceptual knowledge. Activating their prior knowledge about a topic gives students a way to connect their new knowledge to their previous understanding, which is how comprehension and learning occur. Experiences create *a schema* in our brains, which is recalled when cued from text. For example, we have a schema about how to order dinner in a restaurant, how to travel by airplane, and how to get ready for school or work each morning. These common events in our lives are loaded with different kinds of declarative and procedural knowledge. When reading new text, students' prior knowledge allows them to reflect upon what they already know about the topic, which enhances their understanding of new information.

Searching for Information

Engaged learners are motivated to understand and explain the world they see around them. As they explore their environment, they inevitably are involved in a process of *searching for information* (Dreher, 1993; Guthrie, Weber, & Kimmerly, 1993). Pursuing their personal goals, they seek information from multiple sources, including libraries, multiple media, and informational books. Engaged readers browse, examine a variety of documents, and extract critical details during their search. Students tailor their strategies to the content goals of the classroom. For example, if students are asked to learn about facts such as the location and architecture of Rome, their strategies will be adapted (Dreher, 1995). If the instructional goals are factual, students will learn fact-finding strategies. If students are expected to learn conceptual knowledge (e.g., adaptation in science, or roles of government in history), their searching will include an extensive amount of self-monitoring and integrating.

Comprehending

As engaged learners succeed in searching, they are drawn into strategies of *comprehending* new information and texts. Summarized by Dole and others, these strategies include grasping the critical elements of a single text, questioning, summarizing, inferencing, and drawing conclusions about the theme of a narrative (Dole, Duffy, Roehler, & Pearson, 1991). Questioning is one comprehension strategy that aids in the understanding of new information in single texts. Commeyras (Commeyras & Sumner, in press) found that students were eager to pose questions. Students want to raise questions about literature and life, and teachers who encourage these questions will improve students' reading. Strategies for imagery (making pictures in one's mind) increase comprehension and interest. Engaged readers use imagery spontaneously, but less engaged learners need direction. Thinking aloud is another strategy for comprehension. By thinking aloud as they read, students can develop an awareness of whether or not comprehension is occurring (Baumann, Jones, & Seifert-Kessell, 1993; Truscott, Walker, Gambrell, & Codling, 1995).

In a multitext environment, students need different strategies. Learners need to connect information across texts, link illustrations with prose, and abstract common themes from multiple genres. For example, students will integrate texts only if instruction has been provided. Stahl (Stahl, Hynd, Glynn, & Carr, 1996) found that high school students need explicit strategy instruction to understand multiple interpretations of historical events. These strategies may entail drawing, charting, note taking, and composing either in narrative, expository, or persuasive rhetorical structures. However, even at the high school level, students do not know, without help, how to integrate multiple texts.

Learning and Automating Basic Processes

When children first learn to read, they learn strategies necessary for making sense of text at the word and sentence levels. These strategies include: (1) reading unfamiliar words (e.g., decoding), (2) using contextual cues to make meaning from text (e.g., inferencing), (3) predicting and questioning, (4) vocabulary, and (5) story comprehension. This finite set of skills is representational of primary reading skills that are most important because they predict overall competence in first-grade readers (Metsala & Ehri, 1998). Emergent readers' ability to apply these strategies to word reading evolves over time, in a developmental sequence. Each stage prepares the reader to become more proficient.

Strategy development in word reading, according to Ehri (1994), occurs in three phases: logographic, alphabetic, and orthographic. The first phase, *logographic*, refers to using the visual features of words that are nonphonemic, contextual, or graphic. Children in this stage use visual images of a word, rather than letter–sound correspondences, to read a word (e.g., a store logo). Logographic readers move to the alphabetic stage when they stop attending to global shapes and begin to read the print. The *alphabetic* stage begins when readers can read words by processing and understanding letter–sound relationships. Alphabetic readers can phonologically recode written words into pronunciations. They know the names and sounds of letters and can break words into pronounceable segments or chunks. The ability to break words down allows readers at this stage to decode unfamiliar words accurately. Alphabetic readers also are able to store the spellings of sight words and letter–sound connections in memory. Children in the *orthographic* stage have word knowledge that includes prefixes and suffixes. These readers can use letter–sound patterns that recur across words that they have learned to read. Orthographic readers can recognize spelling patterns (e.g., -ate, -ment, -ed) and can store these patterns in memory. As Adams (1990) found, the best differentiator between good and poor readers is their knowledge of spelling patterns and proficiency with spelling–sound translations.

Using contextual clues to make meaning is another strategy for beginning readers. Contextual clues are important in decoding unfamiliar words because the text preceding a word enables readers to form exceptions about what the word is. We know that young readers form expectations because they substitute words that are semantically and syntactically consistent with the text up to the point of the unfamiliar word.

Strategies that trigger students' prior knowledge allow them to attach new knowledge and meaning to their previous knowledge. For example, when students make predictions before reading a book, they create an expectation based on what they know. New information in the story then links easily into their understanding. Asking questions helps engage students in the text, brings out their background knowledge, and focuses their attention on what is about to happen in the story.

Vocabulary comprehension is necessary for beginning readers. Rapid learning of abstract and concrete words is essential to semantic processing during reading. For young readers (e.g., grades 2 and 3), concrete words are easier to understand because there is a direct sensory referent to the word that is not available for abstract words. Older children (e.g., grade 5 and up) tend to learn abstract words rapidly through contextual information and prior knowledge. Teachers can support these developmental trends.

There are two aspects of becoming a strategic reader. One aspect is becoming more automatic in using strategies; the other is becoming more deliberate and conscious. Young readers work toward becoming efficient with word-level strategies (e.g., letter–sound relationships, decoding, using contextual cues for recognizing words). Word recognition becomes automatic, as less attention is needed for this process, allowing the reader to focus on making meaning. In their development, young readers become more proficient in word recognition and comprehension strategies, such as inferencing, using analogy, predicting, and questioning simultaneously. They all become automatic. When text is challenging or unfamiliar, however, engaged readers can be conscious and deliberate. Conscious of their own strategies, engaged students talk about their own comprehension so they can better understand what works (Booth & Hall, 1994, 1995; Hiebert, 1994; Hoffman et al., 1993; Hoffman et al., 1995; McFalls, Schwanenflugel, & Stahl, 1994). McCarthey, Hoffman, and Galda have studied the teaching of these strategies and discuss instruction in Chapter 3.

Motivational Conditions for Learning the Strategies of Reading

Strategies are difficult to learn and use. Many investigators report that strategies require long-term teaching and, once learned, strategies may not be used frequently or widely. For this learning, students must be motivated. However, students are motivated by the plot of an exciting story or details of an intriguing topic, not by strategies themselves.

In reading, strategies are a means to an end. The end is content understanding and the means are the strategies. If students are personally invested in the end of learning, they will be more likely to gain the means being promoted by the teacher. The goals of learning will be adopted and pursued vigorously by students, if the students make a personal investment. This personal investment can be supported by encouraging student autonomy and freedom. Teachers can empower students to help define the goals, choose among options, and pursue their own interests. With autonomy support, students become engaged readers, showing persistence, effort, and a sense of self-efficacy in learning the strategies of reading (Allen, Michalove, Shockley, & West, 1991; Meece, Blumenfeld, & Hoyle, 1988; Skinner & Belmont, 1993).

ENGAGED READING IS SOCIAL

Within classrooms, engaged readers often interact socially in their pursuit of understanding. Given the opportunity, students form partnerships and small teams. Highly influential in determining the nature and extent of the social interaction in these teams are the goals of the individuals in the group. When the goals are shared, group collaboration is enhanced, according to extensive studies by Johnson, Johnson, and Stanne (1989). When individuals believe and feel that they belong to a group, they show positive interpersonal interactions. Beyond goals and beliefs, the quality of social interaction depends on equity. When all students in a team are equally contributing, group interchange is most likely to be affectively positive and intellectually productive.

SOCIAL INTERACTION CONTRIBUTES TO MOTIVATION

Social interaction patterns in the classroom affect student motivation. (See Path C in Figure 2.1.) When students in a small-group activity believe that they can trust other students to listen and accept their suggestions, they become personally invested in the group activity. Among students in the elementary schools of Newark, New Jersey, Morrow found that a social place for reading is motivating (Morrow, Sharkey, & Firestone, 1993). Classroom settings that invite collaboration are more likely to spark interest, effort, and attention than settings in which individuals are isolated. Given a supply of books and sensible purposes, students who interact intensively by talking with friends about books, sharing writing, and discussing homework are likely to be the most avid readers (Allen et al., 1991; Guthrie, Schafer, Wang, & Afflerbach, 1993).

Within families, a similar pattern appears. In families where caretakers and siblings share books, talk about what they read, and find literacy to be entertaining, children develop positive dispositions toward reading. In a longitudinal study in an eastern urban area, Baker and her colleagues (1996) reported that when parents believed reading was a valuable source of family fun, children grew to see reading as enjoyable and important (Pellegrini, Galda, Shockley, & Stahl, 1994; Sonnenschein, Baker, Serpell, Scher, Fernandez-Fein, & Munsterman, 1996).

Influences of Social Interaction on Reading Strategies

Social interaction patterns can enhance the development of strategies for reading. In an award-winning dissertation, conducted at the University of Maryland at College Park, Almasi (1995) showed that particular forms of social interaction during literature discussion in elementary school classrooms fostered growth of literary interpretation strategies. When teachers encouraged students to listen closely to each other, entertain multiple interpretations of text, and recognize alternative perspectives, the students gained. When students can talk to each other about their writing, they learn an acute sense of audience and authorship. In other words, strategies for reading and writing are influenced by the social structure of peer interactions within the classroom.

Most book discussions in classrooms are conducted with literary texts. Meloth and Deering (1994), however, showed that discussion of informational books is also productive. In particular, students seeking explanations in science books asked "why" questions and read thoroughly. They learned a keen awareness of reading strategies such as collecting evidence, weighing information, and drawing elaborate conclusions.

Central to effective social interactions are students' beliefs. When students believe that they can influence their learning activities, they are more likely to interact socially, for example, by seeking help. If students have a sense of control, they ask questions, request clarifications, and inquire about resources, according to Newman and Schwager (1992). These help-seeking strategies lead to subject matter achievement. In help seeking, social interaction is itself a strategy.

How Does Social Interaction Affect Conceptual Learning?

Socially responsible behaviors are associated with academic achievement. For example, Wentzel (1993) reported that students who possessed the social goals of sharing, cooperating, and complying with teacher requests had higher grades and standardized test scores. These student goals were associated with grades and tested achievement. It is not clear, however, how these social goals and behaviors lead to conceptual understanding of subject matter content.

One explanation is that social goals may lead to social interactions, which, in turn, influence learning. Brown and Campione (1990) found that conceptual understanding "is most likely to occur when students are required to explain, elaborate, or defend their position to others; the burden of explanation is often the push to make students evaluate, integrate, and elaborate knowledge in new ways"

(p. 114). This interchange can be encouraged by reciprocal teaching. A review of studies on reciprocal teaching by Rosenshine and Meister (1994) showed that students who interacted by predicting, questioning, summarizing, and clarifying learned concepts from informational texts. Compared with other groups, pairs of students who participated in reciprocal teaching gained a deep, explanatory understanding of life science concepts, such as *predation* and *extinction*. Dialogue is a social event that can foster conceptual understanding (Alvermann et al., 1996).

Students are often aware of the dynamics in group discussion. Alvermann (Alvermann et al., 1996) reported that students perceive the quality of interaction during group discussion as important to their conceptual understanding. Students who participated in groups in which members listened to each other were more likely to report that they understood stories in depth than students in less interactive groups. Thus, social interaction contributes to conceptual understanding partly through the students' self-perceptions of acceptance.

IMPLICATIONS OF THE ENGAGEMENT
PERSPECTIVE ON READING

We have seen that reading is not merely a skill. It is not limited to an achievement in the cognitive domain. Reading is better understood as an engagement of the person in a conceptual and social world. This view of reading has profound implications for education and people who have a stake in education. Taken seriously, the engagement perspective on reading changes the landscape. It alters the classroom for teachers, the home for parents, the problem-space for researchers, and the challenges for policy makers. The challenges of teaching, parenting, researching, and policy making will be mentioned here and will be developed more fully in the remainder of this book. In the chapters that follow, the authors portray their viewpoints. They take an informed stance on their topics, bringing the existing research, the findings of the NRRC, and their professional experience into the picture.

Teaching

A classroom teacher who adopts the engagement perspective builds a classroom that looks very different than a traditional classroom. In an engaging classroom, reading lessons are designed to develop long-term motivation, knowledge, social competence, and reading skill. Effective lessons are designed as frequently by students as by teachers. Long blocks of time may be given to debate and writing as well as to skill teaching. The "outcome" of a unit may be a set of student portfolios or a classroom exhibit rather than a definable statement of textbook coverage.

Engaging classrooms are often noisy. Because students are both involved and social, they talk. This talk will disturb the traditional teacher across the hall or the principal who holds a different model of effective teaching, in which students work individually on skills. In the midst of a student-centered curriculum, however, skills need not be abandoned. Outstanding teachers embed skill instruction with meaningful engagements. The principles that describe engaging, primary-level classrooms are presented by McCarthey, Hoffman, and Galda in Chapter 3.

Teaching reading in the intermediate grades (3–6) is changing rapidly. Reading is being integrated into the content of social studies and science at these grades. This context gives students the substantive content they need to learn the complex reading strategies of summarizing, integrating multiple texts, searching for information, and critically evaluating their own understanding. The principles that describe engaging classrooms at this level are presented by Hynd. She also portrays the characteristics of engaging classrooms at the middle and high school levels to the extent that they have been investigated.

Parenting

Everyone recognizes that homes influence reading. Parents who are interested in reading have children who are more motivated, more competent readers. Research on the engagement perspective of reading sheds new light on how this home influence works. For example, storybook reading has long been considered the way that family members increase reading for their children. Without subtracting from this focus, recent studies show that the beliefs of the parents and caretakers are crucially important. The conviction of family members who do the reading makes a substantial difference. Because both the beliefs and actions of parents matter, the implications for home–school programs are significant. In Chapter 5, Baker captures the trends of this new perspective.

Researching

Inquiry into reading covers a broader terrain now than 5 years ago. Investigators are asking dramatically new questions that would have been regarded as irrelevant until recently. Questions of social and motivational factors have appeared on the horizon. The answers are only dimly perceived, but the process has begun. Besides new questions, new modes of inquiry are proliferating. For example, laboratory-based experiments with hypothesis testing had been the most prevalent mode of inquiry. Although this methodology is still necessary for some crucial questions in reading, the knowledge base from this experimental literature rarely influenced the practice of schooling because it was not obviously relevant to instruction. Many investigators, and policy makers, have been frustrated by this apparent failure of dissemination.

The engagement perspective suggests that a second limitation of laboratory research is its decontextualized nature. By controlling out factors successfully, many experiments left out the messy "real-world" contexts that make a new idea useful for teachers. Placing research into context has led to qualitative research strategies (e.g., case studies and participant observation) as well as quantitative strategies (e.g., surveys, quasi-experiments, and causal modeling) that bring many factors together rather than separating them from each other.

Significant tensions exist among reading researchers who use different methods of inquiry. Currently, reading researchers do not agree on what constitutes data. Some researchers would count one child's story of yesterday's reading as data; other researchers would insist that multiple stories from multiple children should be compiled in an economical form. Differences in beliefs among researchers are clearly visible. Some investigators assume that the world has an "objective" reality that can be understood in similar ways by different people. Others suppose that our experience of reality is so "subjective" that general principles of reading are not attainable or interesting.

Amid this diversity, it is intriguing that many researchers find the engagement perspective to be generative for them. Both traditionally quantitative investigators and qualitative researchers have published studies of reading engagement. Both have portrayed what engaged reading looks like in children and how it is nurtured in classrooms. Part of the purpose of this book is to identify the threads of the current fabric of our understanding as affirmed by investigators using different research methods. Alvermann, who is known for publishing studies from more than one belief system, displays in her chapter the many modes of inquiry into reading that have informed the engagement perspective on reading.

Policy Making

One prevalent policy issue is the standards movement, which is advocated by state departments of education (Allington & Walmsley, 1995; Fuhrman, 1993). Adopting standards in English language arts from the IRA/NCTE project or writing their own, more than 50% of the states are in the process of conducting standards-based reform. The engagement perspective on reading raises questions about the current reform movement. At present, standards are predominantly collections of cognitive strategies for reading and writing. Usually, insufficient attention is given to questions of motivational goals and social competence. If the engagement perspective is adopted widely throughout the nation, including the policy community, then the discussion of standards will change so that a richer, more comprehensive system for promoting reading can be implemented.

The IRA/NCTE standards are consistent with an engagement perspective. For example, standard number 2 states that "students read a wide range of literature." This refers to the activity of being a reader, not merely the cognitive skill of reading. To read a wide range of texts requires interest and knowledge as well as skill. In addition, standard number 11 states that "students participate as knowledge-

able, reflective, reactive, critical members of a variety of literacy communities."
This implies social interaction in literacy, which is central to the notion of engagement. To implement the IRA/NCTE standards meaningfully, educators will need to
see reading as an engagement as well as a skilled performance.

At its heart, the engagement perspective points to a new aim for education.
With this new aim, reading is taught and learned as an avenue for exploring the
inner world of personal experience and the outer world of people, places, and
things. Our engagement perspective says that we need a new type of reading, and
we need this reading to become the cornerstone of schooling. Wilkinson, in Chapter 7, shows how school policies can cultivate or cripple student engagement in
reading. She raises questions that everyone concerned with the future of schooling should address.

REFERENCES

Adams, M. J. (1990). *Beginning to read: Thinking and learning about print.* Cambridge,
    MA: MIT Press.
Alexander, P. A., & Judy, J. E. (1988). The interaction of domain-specific and strategic
    knowledge in academic performance. *Review of Educational Research, 58,*
    375–404.
Allen, J., Michalove, B., Shockley, B., & West, M. (1991). I'm really worried about
    Joseph: Reducing the risks of literacy learning. *The Reading Teacher, 44,* 458–467.
Allington, R. L., & Walmsley, S. A. (Eds.). (1995). *No quick fix.* New York: Teachers
    College Press.
Almasi, J. F. (1995). The nature of fourth graders' sociocognitive conflicts in peer-led
    and teacher-led discussions of literature. *Reading Research Quarterly, 30,* 314–351.
Alvermann, D. E., & Guthrie, J. T. (1993). The National Reading Research Center. In
    A. P. Sweet & J. I. Anderson (Eds.), *Reading research into the year 2000* (pp. 129–
    150). Hillsdale, NJ: Erlbaum.
Alvermann, D. E., Young, J. P., Weaver, D., Hinchman, K. A., Moore, D. W., Phelps,
    S. F., Thrash, E. C., & Zalewski, P. (1996). Middle- and high-school students' per-
    ceptions of how they experience text-based discussions: A multicase study. *Read-
    ing Research Quarterly, 31,* 244–267.
Anderson, R. C., Hiebert, E. H., Scott, J. A., & Wilkinson, I. A. (1985). *Becoming a na-
    tion of readers: The report of the Commission of Reading.* Washington, DC: Na-
    tional Institute of Education.
Anderson, R. C., & Pearson, P. D. (1984). A schema-theoretic view of basic processes in
    reading. In P. D. Pearson, R. Barr, M. Kamil, & P. Mosenthal (Eds.), *Handbook of
    reading research* (pp. 255–291). New York: Longman.
Archambault, R. D. (Ed.). (1964). *John Dewey on education: Selected writings.* Chicago:
    University of Chicago Press.
Baker, L., Afflerbach, P., & Reinking, D. (Eds.). (1996). *Developing engaged readers in
    school and home communities.* Mahwah, NJ: Erlbaum.

Baker, L., & Brown, A. L. (1984). Metacognitive skills of reading. In P. D. Pearson, R. Barr, M. Kamil, & P. Mosenthal (Eds.), *Handbook of reading research* (pp. 353–394). New York: Longman.

Barr, R., Kamil, M. L., Mosenthal, P., & Pearson, P. D. (Eds.). (1991). *Handbook of reading research* (Vol. II). New York: Longman.

Baumann, J. F., Allen, J., & Shockley, B. (1994). *Research questions teachers ask: A report from the National Reading Research Center school research consortium* (Reading Research Report No. 30). Athens, GA: Universities of Georgia and Maryland, National Reading Research Center.

Baumann, J. F., Jones, L. A., & Seifert-Kessell, N. (1993). *Monitoring reading comprehension by thinking aloud* (Instructional Resource No. 1). Athens, GA: Universities of Georgia and Maryland, National Reading Research Center.

Booth, J. R., & Hall, W. S. (1994). *Relationship of reading comprehension to the cognitive internal state lexicon* (Reading Research Report No. 14). Athens, GA: Universities of Georgia and Maryland, National Reading Research Center.

Booth, J. R., & Hall, W. S. (1995). *A hierarchical model of the mental state verbs* (Reading Research Report No. 42). Athens, GA: Universities of Georgia and Maryland, National Reading Research Center,.

Britton, B. K., & Gulgoz, S. (1991). Using Kintsch's computational model to improve instructional text: Effects of repairing inference calls on recall and cognitive structures. *Journal of Educational Psychology, 83*, 329–345.

Brown, A. L., & Campione, J. C. (1990). Interactive learning environments and the teaching of science and mathematics. In M. Gardner, J. G. Greeno, F. Reif, A. H. Schoenfeld, A. DiSessa, & E. Stage (Eds.), *Toward a scientific practice of science education* (pp. 111–140). Hillsdale, NJ: Erlbaum.

Carr, M., & Thompson, H. (1995). *Brief metacognitive intervention and interest as predictors of memory for text* (Reading Research Report No. 35). Athens, GA: Universities of Georgia and Maryland, National Reading Research Center.

Chi, M. T. H., DeLeeuw, N., Chiu, M., & Lavancher, C. (1994). Eliciting self-explanations improves understanding. *Cognitive Science, 18*, 439–477.

Cipielewski, J., & Stanovich, K. E. (1992). Predicting growth in reading ability from children's exposure to print. *Journal of Experimental Child Psychology, 54*, 74–89.

Commeyras, M., & Sumner, G. (in press). Questions children want to discuss about literature: What teachers and students learned in a second-grade classroom. *Elementary School Journal.*

Deci, E. L., Vallerand, R. J., Pelletier, L. G., & Ryan, R. M. (1991). Motivation and education: The self-determination perspective. *Educational Psychologist, 26*, 325–346.

Dewey, J. (1913). *Interest and effort in education.* Boston: Houghton Mifflin.

diSessa, A. A. (1993). Toward an epistemology of physics. *Cognition and Instruction, 10*, 105–225.

Dole, J. A., Duffy, G. G., Roehler, L. R., & Pearson, P. D. (1991). Moving from the old to the new: Research on reading comprehension instruction. *Review of Educational Research, 61*, 239–264.

Dreher, M. J. (1993). Reading to locate information: Societal and educational perspectives. *Contemporary Educational Psychology, 18*(2), 129–139.

Dreher, M. J. (1995). *Sixth-grade researchers: Posing questions, finding information, and writing a report* (Reading Research Report No. 40). Athens, GA: Universities of Georgia and Maryland, National Reading Research Center.

Ehri, L. C. (1994). Development of the ability to read words: Update. In R. B. Ruddell, M. R. Ruddell, & H. Singer (Eds.), *Theoretical models and processes of reading* (pp. 323–358). Newark, DE: International Reading Association.

Freire, P., & Macedo, D. (1987). *Literacy: Reading the word and the world.* South Haven, MA: Bergin & Garvey.

Fuhrman, S. H. (Ed.). (1993). *Designing coherent education policy: Improving the system.* San Francisco: Jossey-Bass.

Gambrell, L. B., Codling, R. M., & Palmer, B. M. (1996). *Elementary students' motivation to read* (Reading Research Report No. 52). Athens, GA: Universities of Georgia and Maryland, National Reading Research Center. (ERIC Document Reproduction Services No. ED 395 279)

Glynn, S. M. (1994). *Teaching science with analogies: A strategy for teachers and textbook authors* (Reading Research Report No. 15). Athens, GA: Universities of Georgia and Maryland, National Reading Research Center.

Glynn, S. M., & Duit, R. (Eds.) (1995). *Learning science in the schools: Research reforming practice.* Mahwah, NJ: Erlbaum.

Goodman, Y., & Goodman, K. (1994). To err is human: Learning about language processes by analyzing miscues. In R. B. Ruddell, M. R. Ruddell, & H. Singer (Eds.), *Theoretical models and processes of reading* (pp. 104–124). Newark, DE: International Reading Association.

Guthrie, J. T., Alao, S., & Rinehart, J. M. (1997). Literacy issues in focus: Engagement in reading for young adolescents. *Journal of Adolescent & Adult Literacy, 40*(6), 438–450.

Guthrie, J. T., Anderson, E., Alao, S., & Rinehart, J. M. (1997). *Influences of concept-oriented reading instruction on intrinsic motivations for conceptual learning from text.* Manuscript submitted to U.S. Department of Education, Office of Educational Research and Improvement, University of Maryland, College Park.

Guthrie, J. T., McGough, K., Bennett, L., & Rice, M. E. (1996). Concept-oriented reading instruction: An integrated curriculum to develop motivations and strategies for reading. In L. Baker, P. Afflerbach, & D. Reinking (Eds.), *Developing engaged readers in school and home communities* (pp. 165–190). Mahwah, NJ: Erlbaum.

Guthrie, J. T., Schafer, W. D., & Hutchinson, S. R. (1991). Relations of document literacy and prose literacy to occupational and societal characteristics of young black and white adults. *Reading Research Quarterly, 26*(1), 30–48.

Guthrie, J. T., Schafer, W. D., Wang, Y. Y., & Afflerbach, P. (1993). *Influences of instruction on reading: An empirical exploration of social, cognitive, and instructional indicators* (Reading Research Report No. 3). Athens, GA: Universities of Georgia and Maryland, National Reading Research Center.

Guthrie, J. T., Schafer, W. D., Wang, Y. Y., & Afflerbach, P. (1995). Relationships of instruction on reading: An exploration of social, cognitive, and instructional connections. *Reading Research Quarterly, 30*(1), 8–25.

Guthrie, J. T., Van Meter, P., Hancock, G. R., McCann, A., Anderson, E., & Alao, S. (in press). Does concept-oriented reading instruction increase strategy use and conceptual learning from text? *Journal of Educational Psychology.*

Guthrie, J. T., Van Meter, P., McCann, A. D., Wigfield, A., Bennett, L., Poundstone, C. C., Rice, M. E., Faibisch, F. M., Hunt, B., & Mitchell, A. (1996). Growth of literacy engagement: Changes in motivations and strategies during concept-oriented reading instruction. *Reading Research Quarterly, 31*, 306–332.

Guthrie, J. T., Weber, S., Kimmerly, N. (1993). Searching documents: Cognitive processes and deficits in understanding graphs, tables, and illustrations. *Contemporary Educational Psychology, 18*, 186–221.

Guthrie, J. T., & Wigfield, A. (Eds.). (1997). *Reading engagement: Motivating readers through integrated instruction.* Newark, DE: International Reading Association.

Harter, S., Whitesell, N. R., & Kowalksi, P. (1992). Individual differences in the effects of educational transitions on young adolescents' perceptions of competence and motivational orientation. *American Educational Research Journal, 29*, 777–808.

Hiebert, E. H. (1994). Becoming literate through authentic tasks: Evidence and adaptations. In R. B. Ruddell, M. R. Ruddell, & H. Singer (Eds.), *Theoretical models and processes of reading* (pp. 391–413). Newark, DE: International Reading Association.

Hoffman, J. V., McCarthey, S. J., Abbott, J., Christian, C., Corman, L., Curry, C., Dressman, M., Elliot, B., Maherne, D., & Stahle, D. (1993). So what's new in the new basals? A focus on first grade. *Journal of Reading Behavior, 26*, 47–73.

Hoffman, J. V., McCarthey, S. J., Bayles, D., Price, D., Elliott, B., Dressman, M., & Abbott, J. (1995). *Reading instruction in first-grade classroom: Do basals control teachers?* (Reading Research Report No. 43). Athens, GA: Universities of Georgia and Maryland, National Reading Research Center.

Holdaway, D. (1979). *The foundations of literacy.* Portsmouth, NH: Heinemann.

Huey, E. B. (1908). *The psychology and pedagogy of reading.* Cambridge, MA: MIT Press.

Hynd, C. R., Alvermann, D. E., & Qian, G. (1993). *Prospective teachers' comprehension and teaching of a complex science concept* (Reading Research Report No. 4). Athens, GA: Universities of Georgia and Maryland, National Reading Research Center.

Hynd, C. R., McNish, M. M., Qian, G., Keith, M., & Lay, K. (1994). *Learning counterintuitive physics concepts: The effects of text and educational environment* (Reading Research Report No. 16). Athens, GA: Universities of Georgia and Maryland, National Reading Research Center.

Johnson, D. W., Johnson, R. T., & Stanne, M. B. (1989). Impact of goal and resource interdependence on problem-solving success. *The Journal of Social Psychology, 129*(5), 621–629.

Maehr, M. L., & Pintrich, P. R. (Eds.). (1993). *Advances in motivation and achievement* (Vol. 8). Greenwich, CT: JAI Press.

Mayer, R. E., & Gallini, J. K. (1990). When is an illustration worth ten thousand words? *Journal of Educational Psychology, 82*(4), 715–726.

McFalls, E. L., Schwanenflugel, P. J., & Stahl, S. A. (1994). *Influence of word meaning on the acquisition of a reading vocabulary in second-grade children* (Reading Research Report No. 25). Athens, GA: Universities of Georgia and Maryland, National Reading Research Center.

McKenna, M. C., Kear, D. J., & Ellsworth, R. A. (1995). Children's attitudes toward reading: A national survey. *Reading Research Quarterly, 30*, 934–956.

Meece, J. L., Blumenfeld, P. C., & Hoyle, R. H. (1988). Students' goal orientation and cognitive engagement in classroom activities. *Journal of Educational Psychology*, *80*, 514–523.

Meloth, M. S., & Deering, P. D. (1994). Task talk and task awareness under different cooperative learning conditions. *American Educational Research Journal*, *31*(1), 138–165.

Metsala, J. L., & Ehri, L. C. (Eds.). (1998). *Word recognition in beginning literacy*. Mahwah, NJ: Erlbaum.

Morrow, L. M., Sharkey, E., & Firestone, W. A. (1993). *Promoting independent reading and writing through self-directed literacy activities in a collaborative setting* (Reading Research Report No. 2). Athens, GA: Universities of Georgia and Maryland, National Reading Research Center.

National Assessment of Educational Progress. (1994). *1994 NAEP Reading: A first look*. Washington, DC: U.S. Government Printing Office.

National Association of Elementary School Principals. (1996). By the numbers: Elementary concerns. *Education Week*, p. 4.

Newman, R. S., & Schwager, M. T. (1992). Student perceptions and academic help-seeking. In D. H. Schunk & J. L. Meece (Eds.), *Student perceptions in the classroom* (pp. 123–146). Hillsdale, NJ: Erlbaum.

O'Flahavan, J. F., Gambrell, L. B., Guthrie, J., Stahl, S., Baumann, J. F., & Alvermann, D. E. (1992). Poll results guide activities of research center. *Reading Today*, p. 12.

Oldfather, P. (1994). *When students do not feel motivated for literacy learning: How a responsive classroom culture helps* (Reading Research Report No. 8). Athens, GA: Universities of Georgia and Maryland, National Reading Research Center.

Pellegrini, A. D., Galda, L., Shockley, B., & Stahl, S. A. (1994). *The nexus of social and literacy experiences at home and school: Implications for first-grade oral language and literacy* (Reading Research Report No. 21). Athens, GA: Universities of Georgia and Maryland, National Reading Research Center.

Pintrich, P. R., Brown, D. R., & Weinstein, C. E. (Eds.). (1994). *Student motivation, cognition, and learning: Essays in honor of Wilbert J. McKeachie*. Hillsdale, NJ: Erlbaum.

Pintrich, P. R., & DeGroot, E. V. (1990). Motivational and self-regulated learning components of classroom academic performance. *Journal of Educational Psychology*, *82*(1), 33–40.

Pintrich, P. R., & Schrauben, B. (1992). Students' motivational beliefs and their cognitive engagement in classroom academic tasks. In D. H. Schunk & J. L. Meese (Eds.), *Student perceptions in the classroom* (pp. 149–184). Hillsdale, NJ: Erlbaum.

Pressley, M., El-Dinary, P. B., Brown, R., Schuder, T. L., Pioli, M., Green, K., & Gaskins, I. (1994). Transactional instruction of reading comprehension strategies. *Reading and Writing Quarterly*, *10*, 5–19.

Rosenshine, B., & Meister, C. (1994). Reciprocal teaching: A review of the research. *Review of Educational Research*, *64*, 479–530.

Ruddell, R. B., Ruddell, M. R., & Singer, H. (Eds.). (1994). *Theoretical models and processes of reading*. Newark, DE: International Reading Association.

Schiefele, U. (1996). Topic interest, text representation, and quality of experience. *Contemporary Educational Psychology*, *21*, 3–18.

Schunk, D. H., & Meece, J. L. (Eds.). (1992). *Student perceptions in the classroom.* Hillsdale, NJ: Erlbaum.

Serpell, R., & Boykin, A. W. (1994). Cultural dimensions of cognition: A multiplex, dynamic system of constraints and possibilities. In R. J. Sternberg (Ed.), *Thinking and problem solving* (pp. 369–403). New York: Academic Press.

Skinner, E. A., & Belmont, M. J. (1993). Motivation in the classroom: Reciprocal effects of teacher behavior and student engagement across the school year. *Journal of Educational Psychology, 85,* 571–581.

Sonnenschein, S., Baker, L., Serpell, R., Scher, D., Fernandez-Fein, S., & Munsterman, K. A. (1996). *Strands of emergent literacy and their antecedents in the home: Urban preschoolers' early literacy development* (Reading Research Report No. 48). Athens, GA: Universities of Georgia and Maryland, National Reading Research Center.

Stahl, S. A., Hynd, C. R., Britton, B. K., McNish, M. M., & Bosquet, D. (1996). What happens when students read multiple source documents in history? *Reading Research Quarterly, 31,* 430–458.

Stahl, S. A., Hynd, C. R., Glynn, S. M., & Carr, M. (1996). Beyond reading to learn: Developing content and disciplinary knowledge through texts. In L. Baker, P. Afflerbach, & D. Reinking (Eds.), *Developing engaged readers in school and home communities* (pp. 139–163). Mahwah, NJ: Erlbaum.

Stanovich, K. E., & Cunningham, A. E. (1993). Where does knowledge come from? Specific associations between print exposure and information acquisition. *Journal of Educational Psychology, 85,* 211–230.

Sweet, A. P., & Guthrie, J. T. (1994). *Teacher perceptions of students' motivation to read* (Reading Research Report No. 29). Athens, GA: Universities of Georgia and Maryland, National Reading Research Center.

Truscott, D. M., Walker, B. J., Gambrell, L. B., & Codling, R. M. (1995). *Poor readers don't image, or do they?* (Reading Research Report No. 38). Athens, GA: Universities of Georgia and Maryland, National Reading Research Center.

Vosniadou, S. (1994). Capturing and modeling the process of conceptual change. *Learning and Instruction, 4,* 45–49.

Wentzel, K. R. (1993). Does being good make the grade? Relations between academic and social competence in early adolescence. *Journal of Educational Psychology, 85,* 357–364.

Wigfield, A., & Eccles, J. S. (1992). The development of achievement task values: A theoretical analysis. *Developmental Review, 12,* 265–310.

Wigfield, A., & Guthrie, J. T. (1997). Relations of children's motivation for reading to the amount and breadth of their reading. *Journal of Educational Psychology, 89*(3), 420–432.

Wigfield, A., Wilde, K., Baker, L., Fernandez-Fein, S., & Scher, D. (1996). *The nature of children's motivations for reading, and their relations to reading frequency and reading performance* (Reading Research Report No. 63). Athens, GA: Universities of Georgia and Maryland, National Reading Research Center.

CHAPTER 3

Readers in Elementary Classrooms: Learning Goals and Instructional Principles That Can Inform Practice

Sarah J. McCarthey, James V. Hoffman, and Lee Galda

I N THE PAST, RESEARCH INTO TEACHING has focused on students' on-task behavior as a primary indicator of effectiveness. An effective teacher is portrayed as one who successfully maximizes the time students spend working on academic tasks. The teacher selects, organizes, and introduces tasks into the classroom context that are aligned with the educational goals in general and the assessment measures in particular. The teacher motivates students to engage in these tasks and supports the students to successfully achieve them. New knowledge is gained as a direct result of student time spent on tasks. Studies that have employed the time-on-task perspective have relied on low-inference behavioral indices to assess levels of student engagement. These indices track student behaviors such as sustained activity, visual focus, and work produced. It is argued that these behavioral indices are proximal indicators of cognitive attention, activity, and learning. Growth in achievement over time, as demonstrated by performance on standardized tests, is the standard for judging teaching effectiveness.

The engagement perspective for literacy challenges us to think differently about effective teaching practices in the elementary grades. Because of its conceptual, motivational, strategic, and social dimensions, literacy no longer can be viewed through a narrow behavioral lens such as time-on-task. Research into engaged literacy typically involves a variety of assessment strategies that tap not only the reader's thinking but the reader's motivations, strategies, and reflections as well. The social context for engagement is seen as a resource system for the reader to access and use. Researchers interested in studying the nature of engaged reading and the instruction that supports it, must consider the social context as an integral resource system rather than as a confounding or extraneous variable in a traditional research design. The engagement perspective does not necessarily negate the findings from research that has assumed a time-on-task perspective; it simply requires that we broaden the lens we use to examine teaching–learning processes.

In this chapter, we explore the practical implications of recent research into the teaching of literacy that has assumed an engagement perspective. We offer a "principled" conception of effective instructional practices at the elementary level based on a synthesis of this research. Our intent is to focus on issues of practice, not on research design or methodology. These described principles are offered not as components, or as isolated strands of an effective reading program, but as overarching (and sometimes overlapping) areas of, and conditions for, literacy activity in the classroom. We see these principles, in some sense, as conversation points regarding the literacy program. They are set in the terms and the frames that teachers often use to talk about what they do and what their students do during reading instruction. We begin with a restatement of the engagement perspective that is at the heart of our work and expound on eight general goals and principles related to this conception.

THE ENGAGED READER: SKILLED, CONNECTED, AND REFLECTIVE

For purposes of instruction, we argue here that the engaged reader can best be viewed as skilled, connected, and reflective. The engaged reader is *skilled*: in the use of the alphabetic code system to support word identification; in the use of strategies to represent text with understanding, interpretation, and expression; and, in adapting reading strategies to specific goals and text characteristics. The engaged reader is *connected*: to the imaginative, aesthetic, and artistic self and interpretive community; to his developing knowledge base and texts; and to personal interests, beliefs, and values. The engaged reader is *reflective*: on the processes of engaged reading and on personal progress and development.

A Developmental Perspective

While this view of engagement is described in terms of the "mature" reader, it is highly compatible with a developmental perspective on reading acquisition. In other words, the engaged reader is not seen as some idealized goal for which we strive but may never reach. Engaged reading may occur at all levels of development—from the emergent reader immersed in the reading of an "old favorite," to a fifth-grade reader's expository selection search for information to support a research project. Proficiency levels and expertise may vary but the fundamental processes of engagement are the same.

Interdependence of Oracy and Literacy

Along with a focus on the developmental perspective, we support a view of oracy (speaking and listening) and literacy (reading and writing) as highly interdependent processes. Dolores Durkin (1966), through her research into "early" readers, offered convincing evidence that writing skills emerge concurrently with reading. Marie Clay (1987) has demonstrated the remarkable ways in which emergent writing and talking are supportive of one another in their development. Shirley Brice Heath (1983), through her studies of language use in rural settings, has helped us understand the complex ways in which literacy and oracy are related to cultural processes. Research into vocabulary acquisition clearly shows that vocabulary entering through one of the receptive language systems typically finds its way into the expressive forms of language use. Oracy and literacy are further connected through shared (although sometimes reciprocal) processes. David Pearson and Robert Tierney (1984), for example, argue convincingly for learning to "write like a reader" and to "read like a writer."

In many cases the language systems are so interactive that our classification systems seem to misrepresent how language is used. Consider, for example, a joint book-reading experience by a trio of kindergarten students. Is this speaking? listening? reading? The processes are highly interactive. A growth experience in any language-processing area has the potential to lead to growth in one or all of the other areas. Beyond the relationships among language processes, one can look at the interplay of language and thought as a theoretical basis for the importance of connections. This is particularly true when one assumes an engagement perspective for literacy that includes motivational and social aspects, best captured through an "activity perspective."

An Activity Perspective

The eight principles we offer are activity-directed. The notion of "activity" as envisioned through these principles deserves some attention before the principles themselves are explored and discussed. There is a narrow and highly negative connotation for the term *activity* in education that places it in the category of "busy work," or "cutesy stuff" that teachers may use to fill the instructional day. These kinds of activities are judged more on their power to attract sustained attention from the students than on their substance. Another tradition, far richer in terms of its historical and philosophical reference points, regards activity as the heart of the educative process. Dewey (1900) was perhaps the first of the educational philosophers to explore the central role that activity plays in the educational process. For Dewey, the value of teaching and schooling is to be found in the direct experiences of the learners in classrooms. Activity is the basis for experience—in life and in classrooms. Activities that structure experience in the context of schooling should stretch the learner. Activities that structure experience should correlate and build on one another. Dewey (1938) writes, "Intelligent activity is distinguished from aimless activity by the fact that it involves selection of means—analysis—out of the variety of conditions that are present, and their arrangement—synthesis—to reach an intended aim or purpose" (p. 84).

Psychologists as well as educational philosophers have examined the place of activity in learning. Although Vygotsky (1978) did not use the term *activity* with any specialized meaning, those Russian psychologists who continued his work did. In fact, activity theory has been one of the defining movements in Russian psychology for the past 40 years. Russian psychologists, such as Leont'ev (1981), continued Vygotsky's work on the social construction of mind. Activity is used to refer to internally motivated, goal-directed behavior that is socially negotiated with language as the primary medium of communication. It is through problem solving mediated by language that expanded models of thinking are internalized and generalized to new contexts. Schools offer a particular context for activity that is no less "real" than out-of-school kinds of activity. Schools differ only in the ways in which they offer intentional support for learning through the teacher's involvement in the creation, formulation, and range of possible problem solutions offered to the learner. In determining effective teaching from an activity theory perspective, we must consider such factors as internal motivation, problem solving, social interaction, and the differentiated forms of support offered by the teacher.

EFFECTIVE READING INSTRUCTION GOALS AND PRINCIPLES

The value of the eight goals and principles comes in the attention they bring to specific kinds of activity structures that are part of the instruction. The specific principles suggest standards for success and focus across the literacy program. Within each area, we describe the challenge that the engagement perspective brings to the teaching of reading in contrast to traditional forms of instruction. Our intention is not to be exhaustive, but illustrative of the possibilities associated with an engagement perspective in and around these principles.

Attention to Print: Learning How Sounds and Symbols Map onto One Another

Whatever differences exist among scholars regarding the processes of reading and the kind of instruction that best supports its acquisition, there is no disputing the fact that children acquiring literacy in an alphabetic language must internalize the code for mapping sounds to symbols. Gough and Hillinger (1980) have described the important phases of literacy acquisition in a child's development of phonemic awareness, through a "code" stage of reading and eventually into the discovery of the alphabetic principle (the "cipher" stage).

Phonemic Awareness. The first phase of development is phonemic awareness. This refers to the language user's ability to manipulate consciously the discrete sound units within a language. Early demonstrations of this ability are associated, for example, with the recognition and exploration of rhyme. Later, and more advanced stages, are associated with an ability to segment, synthesize, and substitute the sounds of language. Demonstrations of this ability and awareness often are seen in the naturally occurring language play of children. Under more formal, test-like situations, these abilities can be elicited through simple word play tasks (e.g., "How many sounds do you hear in the word *bat*?" or, "I'm going to say some sounds and I want you to put them together to make a word: /s/ /i/ /t/"). As Adams (1990) has pointed out, performance of very young children on phonemic awareness tasks like these is highly predictive of subsequent success in reading. While phonemic awareness refers specifically to an oral language ability, there is some evidence that this ability is associated with languages that are based on an alphabetic script. Further evidence shows that children who are more engaged with this script (e.g., through parental interactions, independent play) develop phonemic awareness more rapidly.

Learning the Alphabetic Code. Gough and Hillinger (1980) described the second phase of reading as "code" reading. At this stage children recognize familiar words as units, relying on a general word configuration or "aspectual" analysis (e.g., they recognize the word "mother" because they recognize the letter M at the beginning). Eventually the code recognition strategy fails due to the limitations on visual memory. This early code type reading, however, does provide the basic database that can be used to break through to the discovery of the alphabetic principle and to what Gough and Hillinger describe as a "cipher" reading stage. This breakthrough is dependent on two factors: (1) the database from visual memory regarding the grapheme system for the language developed through "code" reading; and (2) a well-developed system of phonemic awareness. These two abilities set the stage for the basic discovery of the alphabetic principle. It is only at this point that readers can generalize their reading strategies to identify words they have never before seen.

   While the details of the acquisition process are under careful scrutiny by scholars, and this description is very simplistic in its representation, the pattern seems a reasonable one to describe the acquisition of the alphabetic principle. Once the discovery is made, the learner continues to develop greater automaticity in decoding to the point that the reader is free from "effort" at the recognition level and can turn full attention to the processing of meaning.

Practices That Nurture Learning About the Alphabetic System. Historically, instruction focused on acquiring the alphabetic principle has emphasized repeated practice with a small set of words. These words, learned as "sight words," were then subjected to scrutiny through phonic analysis. Students learned about the code through highly familiar word contexts. Recent trends toward the use of quality children's literature as an integral part of beginning reading instruction have been viewed by some as abandoning the goal of developing students' understanding of code. The popular press is filled with the writing of alarmists arguing that the introduction of quality literature (and the associated loss of severe vocabulary control) is the first step toward the total destruction of all basic education standards. Studies conducted at the NRRC directed specifically at the introduction of quality literature into beginning reading programs do not support this hypothesis. Adopting an engagement perspective, James Hoffman and colleagues (1994) have found, to no one's surprise, that quality literature is highly motivating to both students and teachers. Students prefer to learn with these texts and given the opportunity will choose these texts over traditional "readers." Teachers report that the motivational support associated with this quality literature increases students' willingness to engage in learning activities and supports creative thinking and response.

Does the intrinsic motivation associated with quality literature divert the student's and/or teacher's attention away from decoding goals? We found no evidence to support this hypothesis. In fact, we found evidence that the motivation associated with quality literature can be used to enhance the quality of code instruction. One particular study documented the differences in the content of teaching and the quality of students' learning in a traditional versus literature-based context—specifically related to code learning and use. A first-grade teacher in this study exhibited all of the characteristics associated with traditional, direct skills instruction. She presented skills systematically and sequentially, in small groups and with the whole class. She was explicit in her teaching and reteaching. She achieved high levels of student on-task performance, and her students achieved success in the tasks as they were presented. However, these students were limited in their willingness and/or ability to apply this knowledge to independent reading of connected texts. They were unable to describe to the researchers or to their peers the ways in which they might use this new skill to address the decoding problems they faced.

In contrast, another first-grade teacher emphasized the teaching of decoding skills in the context of quality literature experiences. In place of a plan for systematic and sequential teaching of skills, she adopted a plan for skills teaching that was sensitive to developmental issues and responsive to the "noticings" of the students. Challenging the criticism that skills instruction in a literature-based program is totally left to induction, this teacher was highly direct and explicit in the attention she drew to features of the code and how students might use this knowledge to enhance their reading ability. Instruction regarding the code was frequent and spread across the entire instructional day. Six recurring routines in this classroom provided for concentrated instruction:

- *Morning message.* This was a shared writing experience offered each morning by the teacher. The teacher composed the message on the overhead while the students read along. The teacher constantly challenged the students to use their knowledge (based on complete and partial language cues) to assist in the composing process.
- *Warm-ups.* This was a time when students read with the teacher from large charts containing rhymes and chants. Regularly, the teacher challenged the students to "notice" patterns in the print and to use this knowledge to decode text. Through "mini-teaches" the teacher introduced new patterns that perhaps the students had never before seen. New charts were added daily and old ones revisited.
- *Old favorite.* Books familiar to the students were read aloud chorally and individually. Students were constantly challenged to notice new things about how the written code is used to represent oral language. Vowel patterns, consonant combinations, inflections—everything was talked about and analyzed.
- *New book.* The introduction of a new piece of literature into the classroom came primarily through the "read aloud" of a new book by the teacher. While the primary focus for this first experience was on comprehension and response, the students were often encouraged to notice aspects of how the author used and represented language in print.
- *Guided reading.* The teacher met with the students in small groups or individually to read texts and apply the strategies taught in other settings. This was a rich context for the teacher to assess the degree to which students were gaining control over the code and its uses.
- *Readers/writers' workshop.* Sometimes alone, sometimes in small group settings, the students were encouraged to explore the texts that filled their classroom and to create new ones. They were reminded about specific strategies for using the knowledge of print to unlock the code.

The students in the literature-based instructional context became, over time, much more adept at using print for their own purposes; they became independent and motivated. These findings at the "case" level were supported through the larger study of teachers in classrooms using literature. The students who were instructed using literature were similar in terms of skill levels (as measured by isolated skills tests) to those students in previous years who had been exposed to traditional forms of skills instruction and vocabulary control. However, the students who had been instructed using literature were more skilled in reading connected text and more willing to engage with text that was outside of the traditional instructional menu (Hoffman et al., 1994; McCarthey, Hoffman, et al., 1994).

In a 2-year study of literacy learning in first and second grades, Lee Galda, Tony Pellegrini, and Betty Shockley Bisplinghoff (1996) found that talking about literature provided many opportunities for explicit instruction (sometimes from the teacher, sometimes from peers) and valuable practice. The invented spelling encouraged during writing workshop, along with time and a collaborative atmosphere, allowed these children to form, test, and alter hypotheses about code.

The results of these studies do not offer support for the hypothesis that students automatically will infer understanding of the code based solely on exposure to literature. The findings suggest that the explicit attention to and description of the code by the teacher is a necessary feature of effective instruction. Skeptics should note that the number of times explicit references to code features were made in the literature-based classroom studied was more than triple the number of references made in the "traditional" skills-based classroom. Further, while the references to code were offered only in "reading instruction" in the traditional classroom, references to code in the literature-based classroom were offered throughout the day and across a variety of curricular contexts. Our description here focuses on the possibilities for teaching code in the context of literature. Hoffman and McCarthey (1996) caution that many of the first-grade teachers in their study were not aware of alternative strategies to traditional skills instruction. These teachers, therefore, attempted to import their old practices into the new context—a strategy that did not meet with a great deal of success. Clearly, demonstrations and support for how to teach skills in the context of literature are a necessary part of effective teaching (Allington, 1980, 1983).

Encouraging the Development of Fluent Reading

The skilled reader knows much more about the written text than sound–symbol relationships. The skilled reader brings to the act of reading a wealth of language knowledge and draws on those strategies that have served in the acquisition of oral language (Goodman, 1986). A language user who is learning to read already knows about the syntactical structures and constraints of her first language and she already knows about the semantic base of a first language in context. Both of these types of knowledge provide an enormous support system for processing and sense making. In reading "connected" text, the challenge is the orchestration of developing knowledge about the code to complement existing knowledge of the syntax and semantics.

Readers who are able to move beyond the discovery of the alphabetic code to fluent reading are readers who learn to be strategic in the use of all the cue systems available—semantic, syntactic, and grapho-phonic (Routman, 1991). Fluency development is displayed most directly in oral reading performance. The accuracy and rate of reading reveal something of the level of successful coordination and use of the cue systems by the reader. A qualitative analysis of the patterns in miscues provides an even greater source of information about the learner's reliance on the various cue systems to construct meaning. Fluency development is demonstrated in more subtle ways as the reader begins to interpret text orally in a manner that reflects natural expression. The phrasing patterns, the points of word emphasis, the rising and falling pitch suggest a deepening level of processing by the reader (Zutell & Rasinski, 1991).

Our conception of fluency is not limited to an oral reading context. Fluency in processing is a part of silent reading as well. In silent reading, fluency is measured most directly through measures of rate and is developmental in nature. Ronald Carver (1990) has shown how the development of reading rate (which is part of "typical" reading) grows over time in relation to skills acquisition and internal standards for comprehension. Research has shown that fluency grows as a function of the amount of practice spent in reading connected text and in response to the quality of direct instruction (or models) of fluency offered. Richard Allington (1980, 1983) has argued that attention to the development of fluency is one of the "neglected" goals of traditional instruction in reading. Indeed, the data on the sheer amount of reading that "typical" students do in a "typical" day in connected texts are alarming. Some studies suggest that the average amount of time spent in connected reading for primary-grade students is less than 10 minutes *per week*. In terms of instructional models for fluency building, the picture is no less bleak. Classroom research suggests that "round-robin" reading continues to dominate instructional practice in reading despite the many demonstrations of its negative impact on student growth (Hoffman & Clements, 1983).

Practices That Nurture the Development of Fluency. Stahl, Heubach, and Crammond (1997) have proposed a model for fluency instruction using an engagement perspective that incorporates many findings from basic research in the area. Their approach, directed toward the development of fluency among primary school students, is based on five goals:

1. Lessons are comprehension-oriented even when smooth and fluent oral reading is being emphasized. This is important, they argue, because students need to be aware that the purpose of reading is to construct meaning, and that the practice they are undertaking will make them better comprehenders of text, not simply better word callers.
2. Children read material at a challenging level. Based on the findings from their research, Stahl and Heubach raise questions regarding traditionally accepted standards for determining "instructional level" (i.e., 95%–98% accuracy). They

suggest that practice in text that is more challenging contributes to the development of fluency, if sufficient instructional support is offered.

3. Children should be supported in their reading through repeated readings. This was found to be a critically important part of the fluency-building model. Varying forms of repeated reading support were offered to students, including echo reading, home reading, choral reading, and so on. The amount and form of the support offered should vary in relation to the reader's developing control over the text.

4. Children engage in partner reading. Partner reading is a support context that proved particularly effective in promoting fluency. It provides an opportunity for students to read connected text within a socially supportive context. Partner reading is an effective alternative to round-robin reading and offers extended opportunities for engagement. Also, partner reading gives the teacher an opportunity to monitor student progress.

5. Children increase the amount of reading that they do at home as well as at school. Even small differences in the amount of home reading practice have been shown to effect significant growth in reading ability. Within this goal, Stahl and Heubach identify several strategies for increasing time spent in reading in school and at home. For home reading, the rereading of basal stories read at school and the reading of trade books from a "take-home" library are encouraged. They encourage increased use of choice reading time during the instructional day for in-school reading.

Stahl et al. (1997) worked with classroom teachers to revise the traditional basal reading lessons from a more traditional directed reading activity (DRA) format to a model that combines elements of shared reading, partner reading, and choice. The evaluation of the results of this model suggests that a fluency-oriented model of instruction produces significant positive effects on not only fluency but also word recognition, comprehension, attitude toward reading, and students' view of themselves as readers.

Because the engagement perspective emphasizes the motivational and affective dimensions of reading, Stahl et al. (1997) also examined the development of student attitudes toward reading as they participated in this program. Drawing on interviews with the students, they found positive attitudes at all ability levels and for children of both genders. The students expressed particular satisfaction with the choice reading and partner reading components of the plan. Interestingly, the students were extremely articulate in relating the program features to specific aspects of their personal growth in skills and attitudes.

Choral reading was one powerful way to develop fluency in another first-grade classroom, studied by Lee Galda, Betty Shockley, and Tony Pellegrini (1995). As children in this classroom came to know some big book texts that their teacher read aloud, they began to read chorally, either during whole-class reading time or with partners and small groups during independent reading time. This allowed struggling readers to practice reading with the support of their more fluent peers. Choral reading was sometimes the first step toward the oral retelling of favorite stories, another way in which to become fluent in the language of stories and poems.

Some argue against instructional models that encourage the development of fluent reading through direct modeling, repeated practice, and partner reading because they are too behavioral in focus. Research conducted with the engagement perspective suggests that such models can become highly motivating. Shared reading that emphasizes expression and interpretation is highly engaging to students. This is particularly the case when the text offers rich and interesting language. Dr. Seuss, Bill Martin, Jr., and other children's authors and literacy educators have given us many demonstrations of texts and contexts that support the development of fluency. Stories that are highly predictable and filled with rhyme, rhythm, and humor provide a rich and motivating context for growth.

The development of fluency is a particularly troubling and challenging aspect of literacy acquisition for the student who speaks English as a second language. These students bring to the task of learning to read limited knowledge of English-language rhythms and syntax. In contrast to students who speak English as a first language and find they can use their structure knowledge as a support for success, students who speak English as a second language may experience interference in the acquisition of fluency. When instruction in the student's first language is impossible, it is imperative that direct instruction in fluency be offered. Irene Blum and her colleagues (1995) have demonstrated the benefits of using books with audiotapes to extend literacy instruction into the homes of second-language learners. Books shared with the students in school as part of the instructional plan were audiotaped and sent home with the students for repeated and extended practice. Parental training and support were offered. The results indicate substantial benefit from the opportunity to practice rereading books with audiotapes at home. The support provided by the audiotapes enabled students to read fluently texts of increasing difficulty. Also of interest was the positive effect on these students' reading motivation and behaviors.

While fluency, like code knowledge, may develop "naturally" through reading, it is important to realize that there are specific instructional strategies that can enhance growth for those who require additional support.

Flexible Use of Reading Strategies

Flexibility in reading is a concept filled with misconceptions. One misconception is associated with our image of the engaged reader. For many of us, the image of the engaged reader is something like the adult relaxing in an easy chair with a book, or a child snuggled in bed reading with a flashlight. While these are viable images of engaged reading, they are tied primarily to recreational or leisure kinds of reading experiences. In fact, the engaged reader uses many different types of texts for many different purposes. Automaticity in decoding and fluency are a part of all these types of reading experiences, but the actual demands of the task for the reader may be quite different as a function of the context. The reader working with a HyperCard text program on a computer, the reader using an encyclopedia to locate a specific piece of information, the reader scanning the sports page to find a favorite team's box score, the reader reading a story in preparation for discussing it with peers, the reader studying a chapter in a physics text using a study guide to get ready for a test . . . are all engaged with text. These are very different kinds of tasks, however, and underlying each is a distinct set of behaviors, understandings, and strategies that enable the reader to achieve success.

A second major misconception in this area is that flexible readers simply adjust their rates of reading to the difficulty of the text and their purposes for reading. Thus, the flexible reader slows down when the text gets difficult and/or the purpose is to "study" the content, and then speeds up when the text gets easy and/or the purpose is just to get the general idea. This, again, is a flawed notion. The flexible reader reflects on her purpose for reading, assesses the text structure, and then selects the appropriate reading strategies or combination of strategies. The reader may skim, scan, study, or "read" every word, or employ some combination of these. As Ron Carver (1990) has shown repeatedly, the notion that somehow the speed of reading is adjusted to reflect task demand is inappropriate, if not impossible.

A third major misconception in this area relates to the old adage, First you must "learn to read" (this occurs in the primary grades), and then you "read to learn" (this type of reading begins in earnest in the intermediate grades). Following this misconception, reading instruction in the elementary school, particularly in the primary grades, has tended to use narrative texts as the primary vehicle for practice. Narratives are motivating and offer an easy transition for the language learner from the oral narratives of early childhood into early reading. In this context of narrative, the developing reader learns the strategies and constructs in processing this kind of text. However, if narrative is the exclusive diet, then the strategies associated with flexible reading may not be developed. There is no basis for assuming that students who learn to read through a steady diet of narrative texts will make an easy shift into reading across a variety of text types or genres. Nonnarrative texts must be a part of the reading environment from the start. It is through frequent demonstrations with all kinds of texts that the developing reader learns to appreciate the multiple functions that reading serves in our lives and also is introduced to the flexible reading strategies that lead to success.

Setting aside these misconceptions, we find a powerful place for the concept of flexibility in engaged reading. The appropriate conception of flexibility emphasizes the reader's skill at adjusting her reading strategies to the task demands.

These task demands include consideration of the reader's goals, the text structure, and the social context.

Practices That Nurture Flexibility. Creating a classroom environment where a variety of text types are available is the first step in building a context that nurtures flexibility, but only a first step. The second step is for these texts to be used in functional ways following demonstrations of engagement by the teacher and class as a whole. Newspapers, magazines, and journals are important features of the literate environment in the classroom. Teacher "read alouds" should include not only stories but informational texts as well. Book displays should include informational texts that help the students extend their inquiry beyond the walls of the classroom. Technology and electronic texts should be a part of every classroom as well. Linda Labbo (1996) has shown the many ways in which computer technology can be used effectively in early childhood settings to support literacy acquisition.

Guthrie, Schafer, Wang, and Afflerbach (1995) have shown the importance of instruction in text search strategies as part of the Concept-Oriented Reading Instruction (CORI) model. One dimension of the CORI model—"Search and Retrieve"—is directed toward the skills and strategies associated with flexible reading. In the Search and Retrieve component the students are guided to learn how to search for subtopics related to their general interests and to search for informative sources. In one study, teachers modeled for students strategies for searching the index and table of contents to find specific information about such topics as life on the moon, craters, and space travel. Students were given an opportunity to apply these strategies in small cooperative group settings. Successful students applied these strategies in a variety of complex learning tasks involving multiple text sources.

Teaching reading flexibility is also a major component in the transactional strategies model developed by Michael Pressley and his colleagues (1994). In one investigation of transactional strategies, using the Students Achieving Independent Learning (SAIL) model, students were taught to adjust their reading to their specific purpose and to text characteristics (e.g., Is the material interesting? Does it relate to the reader's prior knowledge? What genre does the text fit? How difficult is the text?). The students were instructed to predict upcoming events (in narrative text) or information (in expository text), alter expectations as the text unfolded, generate questions and interpretations while reading, visualize represented ideas, summarize periodically, and attend selectively to the most important information. All of these processes were taught through direct explanations provided by teachers, teacher modeling, coaching, and studied practice, both in groups and independently. Here again successful learning was achieved.

Flexibility in reading is taking on new dimensions as we move to increased use of an electronic medium for text. Through the work of David Reinking and Janet Watkins (1997), we have some indication of the potential for teaching flexibility by using HyperCard-type programs. They engaged elementary school students in one of the most traditional kinds of academic tasks (i.e., writing a book report) using a HyperCard program that involved multimedia presentations. Students were taught how to program in HyperCard up to scripting level. They learned how to use all of the HyperCard tools for drawing, copying, and pasting graphics, creating buttons and text fields, linking cards, and so forth. The lessons were specifically designed to prepare students to create multimedia book reviews.

Another interesting aspect of this research, in particular in terms of its relationship to flexibility, is the student being placed in the role of authoring text. In this way the student comes to understand the nature of the text structure. These understandings can then become internalized into flexible reading strategies. The book reviews (i.e., the databases) were made available for use in central locations in the classrooms and school. Their data suggest that students were more engaged in learning and using the technology related to multimedia book reviews than in other academic activities in the classrooms.

If fluency is the "ignored" goal in reading instruction, then flexibility must be regarded as the "absent" goal. There are both tremendous need and opportunity for us to explore this area.

Engagement with Quality Literature: Challenging and Nurturing the Imaginative, Creative, and Artistic Senses

In a transmission model of reading instruction, teachers provide information to students and drill them on isolated skills. Students read from basal textbooks in round-robin fashion and fill out worksheets to display their understanding of the "facts" of the story. Teachers are in control of classroom discourse, asking low-level comprehension questions (to which they know the answers) and evaluating students' answers. As familiar as this routine may be to many of us, this model has failed to excite students to become lifelong readers and critical thinkers. Why? First, students are generally bored by the lifeless texts that draw from controlled vocabulary lists and feature characters and settings that do not resemble their own experiences (Goodman, 1989). Second, students have few opportunities to provide their own interpretations of these texts. And third, comprehension questions fail to encourage the diversity of responses students have toward literature, nor do they challenge students to analyze or evaluate the texts in meaningful ways.

Some attempts have been made to address these problems by having teachers build students' background knowledge and by introducing literature written by children's book authors rather than basal companies. However, efforts to connect students' experiences and background knowledge to texts have not considered the diversity and richness of students' experiences and interpretations. Bringing in children's literature has not succeeded in motivating students when teachers simply "basalize" the literature, focusing on skills instruction and directing students to complete large numbers of comprehension questions.

In contrast, adopting an engagement perspective suggests that reading is not only a constructive process, but a social process as well. That is, reading does not occur just within a child's head, but rather through interactions with particular texts and other people. Vygotsky (1978) suggested that reading is a higher psychological process that takes place within a social context.

Reader response theories, advocated by Langer and Rosenblatt (1983), have suggested that reading is a transaction between the reader and the text. To facilitate students connecting to the imaginative, aesthetic, and artistic senses, discussion of high-quality literature has become a priority in current research and practice. Conversations about text can help students construct meaning, explore new ideas, take alternative perspectives, and evaluate the quality of the literature. Other forms of response such as writing and sociodramatic play are equally important for encouraging students to understand, interpret, and connect texts to life experiences and other texts. How can teachers provide opportunities for students to respond to texts?

Practices That Facilitate Student Response. A recent study found that students' independent reading activities were sparked and sustained by social interactions with friends and family members. In fact, instruction in reading did not increase the amount or breadth of reading unless the teacher provided opportunities for students to develop interpersonal relationships (Raphael & Hiebert, 1996). Classroom teachers have been experimenting with a variety of ways to encourage social interaction among students. For example, journals in which students write their emotional and cognitive responses to the literature and ask questions about the texts are important ways for teachers to find out what students are understanding about the literature. One important means of giving students opportunities to respond to literature is through teacher-led or peer-led discussions. Students can develop sophisticated understandings of text through discussion groups and learn to address important themes, synthesize information, and use a range of responses.

Janice Almasi (1995) studied both teacher-led and peer-led discussions of narrative text to describe the nature of students' sociocognitive conflicts and what students learned in different formats. Peer-led discussions provided opportunities for more conversations and higher-quality discussions than did the teacher-led discussions. A greater amount of student talk, in turn, led to the ability to recognize and resolve cognitive conflicts.

One form of student-led discussions that has gained in popularity in the intermediate grades is the use of small discussion groups, what Taffy Raphael and Susan McMahon (1994) have called "Book Clubs." Book Clubs consist of four components:

1. The *reading* component focuses on daily reading of a literature selection. Different formats such as the teacher reading aloud, students reading silently, or students reading with a partner are used at different times.
2. The *writing* component features students writing entries into logs such as critiquing, examining feelings, sharing personal stories, or responding to "think sheets" designed to elicit specific types of responses such as comparing and contrasting features of the book.
3. *Community* share is the daily time for whole-class discussions about the book and for the teacher to model good discussion strategies.
4. *Instruction* includes support in each of the other components.

Generally, students bring what they have written to the small, heterogeneously organized groups. What ensues is an open-ended discussion based on students' written work that allows students to clarify issues within the book, express their personal feelings, make connections from their own lives to the literature, or debate the merits of the particular piece of literature.

Two cautions are noteworthy to consider as teachers consider discussion groups. First, discussion groups are not automatically successful; students may not keep on task, may argue among themselves, or may keep some students from contributing. Teacher modeling of discussion, attention to group composition, and teacher encouragement of inclusion of all students are important factors in promoting successful groups.

Additionally, without high-quality texts that have the potential to elicit a range of interesting interpretations, discussion groups may not be successful. Teachers will need to consider the type and quality of the literature that they and their students select. For example, few classrooms include literature that features characters from an ethnic minority playing a significant role or involve students in discussions of ethnic identity at a deep level (Tomlinson, 1995). Since literature has the power to shape students' values, it is important for teachers to select literature that reflects the diverse nature of the culture. Arthur Applebee (1977) has found that the achievement of fourth- and eighth-grade students of diverse backgrounds can be increased if students have opportunities to read literature that they find interesting and relevant to their own lives. Research also has found that students respond more positively to literature when they can identify with the characters and events and when they can feel pride in their own heritage. Multiethnic literature can help children become aware of both unique qualities of groups and common features across them (Au, 1993; Harris, 1992; Purves & Beach, 1972; Tomlinson, 1995).

Responses need not be limited to written responses; often drawings or enacting scenes from the literature can provide opportunities to connect with the literature. Researchers have characterized many cognitive, linguistic, and social competencies required by children in this type of play, including the following:

1. *Role playing*. Communicating and adopting role-appropriate behavior
2. *Make-believe transformation*. Using symbols to stand for objects through language or actions
3. *Social interaction*. Agreeing through language and actions to interact with other players to connect with the play theme
4. *Oral communication*. Organizing and structuring play and making pretend statements

These kinds of experiences can become the basis for building important connections between the language systems that are engaging for students. In Betty Shockley's first-grade classroom, children regularly responded to the stories they read with improvisational drama, and sometimes even opera. These re-enactments helped them make these stories their own. They also provided important oral language practice as well as work in sequence of events and group dynamics (Galda et al., 1995).

Writing in response to literature has become an increasingly important way for students to express their understanding and interpretation of texts. Michael Pressley, Joan Rankin, and Linda Yokoi (1996) surveyed 83 primary-grade teachers who had been nominated as effective in promoting literacy in their classrooms. When questioned regarding the integration of writing into reading instruction, 88% responded in the affirmative. Similarly, 88% reported the integration of reading with listening and 75% with speaking. Most of the teachers (86%) reported that students wrote stories increasingly with each grade level. A similar percentage reported using journal writing. Dictations (individual and whole class) were used by the kindergarten and first-grade teachers to support story writing and story response. The findings from this survey of teachers have been corroborated by a recent study by Rose Marie Codling and Linda Gambrell (1997). They found through extensive interviews that 70% of the third-grade students and 93% of the fifth-grade students think of stories they have read when writing their own stories. This research suggests that writing in response to literature has become a central feature of classroom practices.

Effective practices derived from an engagement perspective combine the "what" with the "how." In other words, the content of the literature students read is as important as the ways teachers engage students. Responding to high-quality texts through a variety of means can promote student understanding and interest and lead to multiple interpretations and critical thinking about the books read. Responses to literature and the use of engaging texts can lead to nurturance of students' imagination and aesthetic sense. Classrooms that provide opportunities for students to read, discuss, enact, and write about their interpretations are likely to facilitate lifelong, engaged, and critical readers.

Developing Concepts and Acquiring Strategies
That Nurture Independent Learning Through Texts

Since John Dewey (1938) suggested that participation in a democratic society requires more than learning facts, many educators have grappled with how to create an inquiry-based curriculum. An inquiry-based curriculum is derived from the identification of relevant problems from the concrete world. Through "real-world" experiences, students can gain information that is crucial to developing concepts about how the world operates.

Obstacles that have prevented the development of an inquiry-based curriculum have included segmenting the curriculum and school day into small parts so that subject areas are taught separately; emphasizing reading skills or strategies outside a particular content; and presuming that students cannot engage in "higher-level" thinking until they have mastered less abstract ideas. The engagement perspective has challenged many of these assumptions and suggested that reading is a tool to foster growth in content knowledge. Further, integrating reading into content areas such as science and social studies throughout the day can facilitate higher-level thinking even with young children (Stahl, Hynd, Glynn, & Carr, 1996).

Approaches that foster engagement and inquiry in which students learn to read through purposeful use of a variety of texts have been identified at several levels. Guthrie and his colleagues (1996) developed Concept-Oriented Reading Instruction, which involves students observing and personalizing real-world problems, learning a variety of cognitive strategies for exploring problems, interacting socially, and communicating their understanding to genuine audiences. Fifth graders who were taught science and reading with this approach showed substantial growth in reading achievement. Students reported choosing to read more frequently and widely than students in basal classrooms. They reported that choices were driven by intrinsic rather than extrinsic motivation; and they gained in higher-order cognitive strategies such as searching for information, comprehending informational text, constructing conceptual knowledge, and transferring knowledge to solve new problems. Features of the classroom context that were engaging to students included opportunities for observations, developing concepts, and interacting with others.

James Hoffman and colleagues (1996) have described a first-grade classroom in which students were involved in inquiry projects throughout the day. Students were encouraged to make connections across subject areas and to study topics in depth. Even the more reluctant readers became involved when they could choose their own topics after the teacher introduced topics through picture books. Jerry Harste (1994) has organized an entire school around inquiry-based curriculum involving multiple sign systems such as art, music, mathematics, drama, and language.

Practices That Foster Connecting Knowledge and Inquiry. In the development of CORI, Guthrie and his colleagues (1996) selected themes and designed a framework for units in third and fifth grades to be taught for 16–18 weeks each semester. The framework had four phases:

1. *Observe and personalize.* Students had opportunities to observe concrete objects and events in their natural world (e.g., trees, flowers, insects). Next, students brainstormed and stated questions they wanted to explore with additional observations, data collection, and discussion. Students kept journals wherein they recorded their observations and personalized their interest by written questions. These were displayed throughout the classroom.
2. *Search and retrieve.* Students were encouraged to choose subtopics for more in-depth learning and to search for a variety of resources to answer their questions. Such resources as books, pictures, reference books, and videotapes offered explanations and information that led to other questions for exploration. Strategies for searching such as forming goals, categorizing, extracting, and synthesizing were taught explicitly through teacher modeling, guided practice, and teamwork.
3. *Comprehend and integrate.* Teachers taught students strategies for comprehending and integrating information using a variety of trade books, both informational texts and novels. Emphasis was on identifying topics, determining important details, and summarizing sections of the texts.
4. *Communicate to others.* Students became experts on the topics they researched and they wanted to express their understanding to others. They developed synthesis projects to explain their findings to an audience. Students used a variety of forms such as reports, charts, class-authored books, dioramas, charts, and informational stories to communicate their findings.

These strategies resulted in developing students' motivation to learn and increased their abilities to use strategies within content areas.

A first-grade teacher, Pam, studied by Hoffman and his colleagues (1996), successfully adapted her reading instruction to reflect the advantages of integrated curriculum inquiry. Pam's emphasis was on inquiry into topics of interest to her and her students (e.g., space, China, Brazil). Choice was a central feature of the inquiry units. For example, when studying a space unit, students decided which area (e.g., flight, the solar system, or Jupiter) they would explore in more depth.

Although the unit began as part of the science period, students incorporated their interest in space into language arts, library, and stations.

When children were not as familiar with the topics, Pam spent a significant amount of time building their background knowledge by introducing books and talking about them. Then, students chose a topic to study in depth. For example, after Pam brought in both informational and narrative books about China, two students chose to research the Chinese New Year; several others investigated Chinese food and made fortune cookies complete with fortunes written by the children. Another group of students, who were interested in Chinese literature, read Chinese fairy tales and rhymes, then wrote their own play, using puppets, that they presented at the Chinese Fair.

Throughout the inquiry units students were involved in consulting different resources to answer the questions they had selected as research topics. For example, after reading the book *Itchy Itchy Chicken Pox*, students called a veterinarian when a question arose about whether dogs could get chicken pox. To contact the veterinarian, students had to learn the important reading strategy of using a telephone book. Pam further supplemented inquiry by helping students focus on information-gathering strategies. Within the context of the inquiry units students learned to read for a purpose, how to skim for necessary information, and how to consult different kinds of resources (e.g., experts, telephone books, encyclopedias, or "Eye Witness" books). Pam frequently reminded students, especially her emergent readers, to view pictures as important sources of information and include visual discoveries in their "notes." Using a variety of genres within the context of inquiry allows students to find information, be involved in research, and employ a number of sophisticated reading strategies.

Instead of organizing the curriculum around traditional disciplines such as math, science, and language arts, Jerry Harste (1994) and a group of teachers have established an inquiry-based curriculum around children's questions. Students are encouraged to choose a topic, explore their relationship to the topic, and use the disciplines as heuristics for finding out about the topic. For example, a student studying the sun could get different types of content knowledge from various disciplines. From biology, the student could learn about the relationship of the sun toward plant and animal life. History could provide information about past beliefs and practices, while literature could provide myths that explained the role of the sun in different cultures. Multiple sign systems such as art, music, and language became research tools and means of communicating information to others.

Despite the obstacles that have prevented many teachers from implementing inquiry-based curriculum suggested by Dewey (1938), researchers and practitioners have worked together to identify successful inquiry-oriented practices and develop challenging, integrated curricula. Each example described in the previous section illustrates teachers involving students in inquiry-oriented curriculum that crosses traditional subject area boundaries. Students read to solve concrete, real-world problems. Through modeling of strategies within particular content and topics, teachers can encourage students to develop deep knowledge about important topics. Even young children can learn research techniques and ways to communicate with others when provided the opportunity to pursue topics of interest. Reading can serve as a tool for gaining information and concepts within real-world contexts.

Motivation for Reading: Pursuing Personal Interests

In a transmission model of instruction, teachers select the materials to be read and assign tasks to be completed. They establish the classroom routines, and students are expected to follow instructions. Students' personal interests and values are of little importance. Further, textbooks tend to represent children's experiences as white, middle-class, and unproblematic, while the interests of diverse cultural and ethnic groups are ignored. Current research has suggested that how much children read is directly related to how motivated they are to read. Students are motivated to read when they have opportunities to engage in reading and when they see their own experiences represented in books (Csikszentmihalyi, 1978).

How do we assist students in becoming motivated to read? Motivated reading occurs when readers have a "flow experience" or a continuing impulse to learn—that is, readers become completely absorbed in an activity (Wigfield & Guthrie, 1997). Such reading is characterized by intense involvement, curiosity, and a search for understanding. When readers become completely absorbed, they are likely to continue their engagement in other contexts. For example, if students become excited about reading in school, they are more likely to want to read at home as well. One of the primary ways to encourage students to become motivated is to catch their interest. Interest is established in an activity by having some control over the task or environment.

Practices That Facilitate Connections to Personal Interests and Motivations. Practices that facilitate interest and intrinsic motivation include three features: community, challenge, and choice (Deci, Vallerand, Pelletier, & Ryan, 1991).

Establishing classroom contexts that encourage social interaction and knowledge sharing among teachers and students enhances students' interests and aids in building a community of learners. Julianne Turner (1995) found a reciprocal relationship between students' interests and classroom environments. Students must engage in tasks that develop interest in literacy at the same time that the learning environment must offer opportunities that invite students' participation.

One way to encourage social interaction is to reduce the teacher's traditional role as the authority and develop relationships where teachers and students share the authority for knowing. In a knowledge-sharing model, teachers acknowledge multiple points of view and do not privilege their own opinions as the sole source of truth. Teachers establish a condition of "deep responsiveness" in which they encourage students' questions and respond to students' ideas. The community of learners invites, listens, responds to, and acts upon students' thoughts, feelings, interests, and needs. Practices that facilitate developing a community of learners include encouraging students to express themselves; structuring classroom activities that are student-centered; providing students with opportunities to share their work with others; and allowing students choices about topics to learn, criteria for evaluation, and order and pacing of tasks (Oldfather & Dahl, 1995). Mary Ng and John Guthrie (Ng, Guthrie, McCann, Van Meter, & Alao, 1996) found support for this model in their recent study of intrinsic motivation. When fifth-grade students felt they belonged to the classroom and the context was "interpersonal" in nature, they were motivated to participate in literacy learning.

Two multicultural classrooms that were exemplary of "honored voice" are described by Betty Shockley, Barbara Michalove (classroom teachers), and JoBeth Allen (university researcher) (1995). They worked together to develop appropriate instruction for students, many of whom were having difficulties learning to read. In these classrooms, children had real reasons for reading and writing, were supported for risk taking, were responsible for their own learning, and felt they belonged to a literate community. Tasks such as writing to pen pals or reading to other classes were reasons for writing and reading that held students' interests. All students were involved in teaching, challenging, and supporting one another. Using other competent students as resources supported students in taking risks. These features kept students interested in literacy tasks because they had a supportive context. Student choice about what they read and with whom they read contributed to a sense of responsibility. A sense of belonging was developed by giving students choices and a stable learning environment; for example, they had reading workshops at the same time every day. These key features of the classrooms contributed to formerly low-achieving students developing interests in reading and writing and becoming successful learners.

A second feature of connecting reading to students' interests and values is providing students with authentic, challenging tasks. Authentic tasks are opportunities for using literacy for functional, communicative, and aesthetic purposes. For example, experiences with quality literature that encourage students to read for purposes of learning new ideas and enjoyment are important.

Julianne Turner (1995) found in her study of tasks in different types of classroom settings that students were more strategic when tasks provided opportunities for problem solving and critical thinking. "Open" tasks were those in which students themselves could choose relevant information or decide how to solve a problem. Tasks such as partner reading (in which students shared the oral reading of a story), composition of texts on self-selected topics, and reading self-selected trade books facilitated students' interest and motivation. Complexity and challenge were features of the task that promoted interest on the part of the students. For example, tasks that were complex in nature in which a student could plan, organize, and monitor projects provided challenge to students.

A third feature of connecting reading to students' interests and values is through the provision of choice in classrooms. When students are allowed to make decisions about their academic work, they are more likely to be interested in and committed to those decisions. Linda Gambrell, Codling, and Palmer (1996) found that children believe that the most interesting books and stories are ones that they have selected themselves. Even "reluctant readers" will be more likely to read when they can select materials that are of interest to them. Jane West and Lee Galda (1996) found that students experienced greater enjoyment when they could choose with whom they read, where in the classroom they would sit, and how they would carry out the task. This body of research suggests that students should be allowed to decide what they read, in which activities they participate related to the materials, and the contexts in which they read and complete activities.

In successful classrooms described by Lesley Morrow (1996), students had opportunities to make choices about several aspects of literacy instruction. First, they could choose the kind of activity they wanted to complete. Activities included reading a book alone, reading to a friend, listening to a taped story, telling a "feltboard story," being read to, checking out books to take home, or writing a story. Once children had selected the type of literacy activity, they could then select the particular book they wanted to read, the content of the story they wanted to tell, or the topic of the piece they wanted to write. Further, students could choose whether to work alone or with a partner, and then decide with whom they wanted to work. The amount and nature of the choices were important components in promoting student achievement.

While connecting to students' interests is an important goal of instruction, several cautions need to be mentioned in relation to the features of community, challenge, and choice. First, setting up communities that promote student interaction does not suggest that teachers abdicate their roles. Students do not necessarily enter classrooms with the skills to make informed decisions; teachers will need to provide much support for students. Second, in the past teachers may have required students to complete tasks that were "too easy" (i.e., tasks that were "close-ended" and involved repetitive exercises). In the other direction, teachers could err by giving students tasks that were "too hard" without the necessary support for students to be successful. Careful consideration of students' developmental levels and the nature of the task can alleviate this potential pitfall. Third, building a curriculum around individual students' interests could be taken to an extreme, resulting in individuals pursuing their own interests without regard for the benefits of the classroom community. Further, the press from administrators and policy makers to "cover the content" cannot be disregarded. Teachers will need to find a balance in considering students' interests and values and addressing the concerns of the larger educational community.

Creating classroom communities, providing challenging tasks, and allowing students to make choices characterize effective practices that connect to students' interests and motivations. Connecting to students' interests and values ultimately can produce motivated, engaged readers.

SELF-MONITORING THE PROCESSES OF SENSE MAKING

Awareness of Reading Strategies

Young children learn a great deal about reading and writing, such as awareness of print conventions, before entering school; however, traditional school experiences have done little to build on students' existing knowledge. Thus, many students remain confused about the purposes or processes of reading within the school environment; they see reading as a procedure or time of the day rather than a meaningful cognitive activity. Developing engaged readers, by contrast, involves helping students to become both strategic and aware of the strategies they use to read.

Many researchers have tried to foster strategic reading through both direct and indirect methods. For example, Paris, Cross, and Lipson (1984) taught third and fifth graders explicit strategies prompted by metaphors, such as, "Be a reading detective," and followed up by providing feedback and opportunities to apply the strategies in different contexts. Jerry Duffy and Laura Roehler (1989) trained teachers to give detailed explanations of strategies. Students displayed increased awareness of strategies after exposure to these direct methods. As theories about the role of social context have gained in importance, researchers have developed instructional methods that involve peers in the identification and sharing of strategies. Annemarie Palincsar and Anne Brown (1984), for example, developed reciprocal teaching in which students were taught to use predicting, questioning, clarifying, and summarizing, and then, in turn, they taught these skills to their peers. Peer support also was used by Stevens, Madden, Slavin, and Farnish (1987) in their cooperative grouping model. Modeling, peer tutoring, and cooperative activities were features that provided opportunities for students to discuss content and processes of reading. These studies suggest that specific methods can enhance students' ability to monitor their processes and that the social context plays a major role in supporting students' understanding of strategies.

Practices That Support Reflection on Reading Processes. Judith Langer and Arthur Applebee (1986) have suggested five important components of instruction that support the development of metacognitive strategies: ownership, appropriateness, structure, collaboration, and transfer of control. Students need to develop a sense of ownership over what they read and write. Instruction needs to be designed that is appropriate to the developmental level of the learner, while the structure of the task needs to fit students' needs. Promoting collaboration among peers is essential for students to share the strategies they are learning with each other. The ultimate goal of instruction is to transfer control to students—they need to be responsible for regulating their own learning (Corno, 1986).

An important aspect of instruction that aids students in developing metacognitive strategies is dialogue. Children's ability to talk about language is an indicator of their metacognitive processes. Thus, students need many opportunities to talk about their ideas and strategies. Lee Galda, Betty Shockley, and Tony Pellegrini (1995) found multiple opportunities for students to talk with one another in Shockley's classroom. The more students talked with each other in diverse groups, the more they used language that was positively related to literacy development. Shockley's first-grade classroom was characterized by the following opportunities for students to interact:

- *Oral sharing* time not only allowed students to talk about their home experiences, but provided a forum for students to retell familiar stories, rehearse stories they would write about later, and increase awareness of the language they were using.
- *The writing workshop* allowed students to become aware of various cognitive strategies as students helped each other sound out words, spell, and compose stories. Discussing students' stories promoted attention to detail and awareness of the role of the audience, and helped children internalize the writing strategies of others.
- *The reading workshop*, in which students read self-selected books, allowed students to become aware of and practice reading strategies with other students. Students often helped each other decode words, shared aspects of the story, or alternated reading aloud with a partner.
- *Whole-class reading* focused on the teacher reading a Big Book or other book aloud. Students talked not only about events and characters, but also about strategies for understanding print. The dramatic re-enactments that often followed the story provided students with opportunities to transform their understanding of the story and to use dialogue in meaningful ways.
- *Project centers* provided another opportunity for meaningful use of oral language to monitor students' own understanding of texts. Students chose to do dramatic readings, plays, or other relevant activities that provided opportunities to think aloud through talk.

All of these features of the classroom allowed students opportunities to learn from one another and to become aware of the purposes and processes of making sense of print. Within each of the activity areas, students used oral language to enhance their own understandings of print and to become increasingly able to regulate their own learning.

In a second-grade classroom studied by Michelle Commeyras and Georgiana Sumner (in press), dialogue was again a central feature of classroom interaction. In this classroom the focus was on students' questions about literature. Students were quite willing to generate many questions when given the opportunity and they expressed a desire to communicate to others what perplexed them about literature. However, privileging certain kinds of questions or assuming there was a hierarchy to questions (such as Bloom's taxonomy) stifled students' questions. This study suggests that teachers need to establish supportive contexts in which students can pose questions that are important to them about texts. Questions are another form of talk that allows students to monitor their own understanding of the material.

As theory and research have moved to embrace a social model of learning, classroom talk clearly plays an increasingly important role in the development of self-monitoring strategies. No longer are researchers and teachers suggesting that reading is a process that occurs within an individual's head; instead, decoding, comprehending, and monitoring of one's own processes are enhanced through social interaction. The teacher and peers are central to helping students make the internal reading processes external, thus allowing students increased control over processes. However, there is an important caution when considering teacher and student dialogue—just any classroom talk will not necessarily facilitate students' self-monitoring. Talk must be focused on the task, appropriate to students' developmental levels, and facilitative rather than restrictive. When students' ways of talking do not match the teacher's because of differences in cultural backgrounds, miscommunication and alienation can occur. (See Kathryn Au's book *Literacy Instruction in Multicultural Settings*, 1993, for further discussion about cultural mismatches.) For teachers, being sensitive to students' backgrounds and thoughtful about participation structures is essential to enhance opportunities for all students to engage in meaningful literacy activities.

Reflection on Development and Progress

Goal Orientation and Motivation. All human activity is goal-directed—which is not to say that all human activity is necessarily rational (i.e., conscious and deliberate). Some goal-directed activity is innate (e.g., breathing). Other goal-directed activity is dysfunctional (e.g., drug abuse). In the case of literacy, however, there is a more socialized and rational base for goal-directed activity. Literacy is both a means and an end. Individuals seek entertainment or information through reading. Individuals also seek to improve their reading ability as a means of gaining greater access to entertainment and information. Most current theories of motivation suggest that individuals will put effort toward reaching goals that they perceive as achievable and desirable. If we can provide developing readers with a record of where they have been, with details on where they are, with some sense of the steps on the path that lies ahead, and with some assurance that they can achieve these steps given reasonable amounts of effort, we can enhance motivation.

Current theories of the motivation process suggest that the following factors exert a strong positive influence on activity:

- The value an individual places on a task or goal determines whether the individual will expend the effort necessary to accomplish it.
- Goals are most likely to be pursued if they are personally relevant and important.
- Individuals are more willing to engage in activities, even those that are not of inherent interest, if the ultimate goal is of personal value.
- Students who perceive a task as important will engage in the task in a more planned and effortful manner.
- An individual's sense of personal competence at achieving a goal directly influences that person's decision to pursue the goal.
- A cooperative learning environment is more likely to support students' motivation toward a goal than is a competitive environment.
- The teacher can enhance motivation by encouraging students to adopt a learning-oriented (How can I do this task? What will I learn?) rather than a performance-oriented stance (How will I look? What will others think about me?).
- Goal specificity, challenge, and proximity are important determinants of engagement in achievement tasks. (Oldfather & Wigfield, 1996)

In what ways can and should these understandings regarding motivation inform our plans for instruction? One clear point of contact between these findings and practice comes through a consideration of plans for assessment.

Practices That Encourage Reflection on Goals and Progress. An effective reading program can encourage reflection on the part of the developing reader by offering a plan for assessment that is grounded in a developmental perspective of literacy acquisition and is designed to yield performance data useful in documenting progress toward learning goals. Traditionally, assessment plans for reading have relied exclusively on norm-referenced, standardized tests that are informative to neither teachers nor pupils. Assessment schemes that rely exclusively on criterion-referenced tests suffer from the same limitations. It is only through the development and application of authentic and ongoing performance assessment plans that teachers and pupils are informed in a meaningful way. By using portfolios and other alternative strategies, the pupil becomes a part of the learning/assessment process. Short-term and long-term goals are negotiated and motivation is fostered.

Research into the use of portfolio assessment as the basis for a comprehensive assessment plan in the reading/language arts area has demonstrated the superiority of portfolio over traditional models. Through the adoption of portfolios, students and teachers share in the responsibility for documenting growth not only in skill, but also in the process of setting short-term and long-term goals. Portfolios require that students reflect on themselves as learners and engage in planning for focusing future effort. Peter Afflerbach (1996) explains that portfolios can document complex and interrelated aspects of students' growth and achievement. Further, he finds that a portfolio can accommodate an expanded range of reading outcomes and time frames associated with an engagement perspective on reading.

Portfolios serve many purposes, depending on the needs of the classroom or school in which they are used. Portfolios can serve as repositories for the history of students' development and accomplishment in engaged reading tasks and outcomes. Portfolios can be used to display, to parents, administrators, teachers, and the students themselves, the range of students' accomplishments related to complex tasks of engaged reading. Portfolios can help students develop reflective and critical perspectives on their own work across the school year, familiarize students with the techniques of assessment, and contribute to students' independence in assessing their own performance.

Although ample documentation exists of the positive contribution of portfolio assessment strategies on students' motivation and growth, concerns have been raised over the practical issues involved in the use of such plans. Stakeholders in education who are outside the immediate classroom context for learning may regard the assessment aspects of portfolios with suspicion. These data may be regarded as highly subjective and not very useful in making comparisons of individual student performance to commonly recognized standards for achievement. On what basis should policy makers and program leaders make their decisions when the "objective" data from standardized testing are not available? Some research suggests that the feasibility of maintaining two parallel systems of assessment (i.e., the internal one for teachers, students, and parents, which is portfolio based; and the external one for administrators, policy makers, and the public, which is "test" based) is impossible in the real world. At the philosophical level, the two systems are at loggerheads, with the latter showing total disregard for the motivational aspects of reading development. At the practical level, the demands of maintaining two systems—one not valued outside the classroom and the other not valued within the classroom—can prove overwhelming.

Sheila Valencia and Kathryn Au (1996) have studied the use of portfolios in different contexts, with both research sites addressing such issues as how well portfolios document literacy learning that is both authentic and aligned with the curriculum, teachers' ability to interpret and evaluate portfolio evidence from more than one site, and what teachers learn about literacy instruction and assessment as a result of cross-site collection. They found that as teachers closely examine students' work, they clarify important learning outcomes and learn to interpret student performance on multiple forms of evidence. Teachers were found to be capable of high levels of agreement in evaluating students (across research sites) based on portfolio evidence. Agreement levels were influenced by the presence of a strong "rubric" for evaluation.

James Hoffman and colleagues (1996) reported work with a group of teachers in a major metropolitan school district, who had joined to "do away with" standardized testing at the first-grade level. Working collaboratively, school-based and university-based educators designed an alternative assessment plan. The Primary Assessment of Language Arts and Mathematics (PALM) model focuses on three strategies for data collection:

1. *Ongoing (curriculum-embedded) assessments,* which involve the careful inspection, interpretation, and documentation of students engaged in classroom tasks
2. *Taking-a-closer-look assessments,* which involve the selective use of informal assessments for particular purposes and for particular students
3. *Demand assessments,* which involve the administration of standardized tasks across a number of classrooms and the interpretation of performance of individual students in relation to the participating group

The data collected through these strategies become part of a portfolio that contains not only work samples but also a developmental checklist documenting student progress over time. Results of an evaluation study of this model indicate that a carefully designed performance assessment plan with a portfolio base can provide data useful to both internal and external audiences. The PALM model yields data that are useful to teachers and students to encourage reflection and goal setting. It also yields data that can be used on a normative basis to compare a student's or group of students' academic progress with that of a referent group. Based on the results of this study, the school district has moved to implement the PALM model as a substitute for standardized testing. Further, the district is now piloting the use of the model throughout the primary grades.

Retrospective interviews with teachers implementing the model suggest two cautions. First, use of a portfolio system requires considerable staff development and a supportive climate. Second, implementation and maintenance of a portfolio system require considerable effort beyond that typically associated with traditional forms of assessment. The motivation for the teacher must be more than just to derive a score on a student at the end of the year. The motivation must be tied to better ongoing instructional decision making by the teacher, and enhanced reflection by learners regarding their progress toward their literacy goals.

CONCLUSION

The eight goals presented here suggest a new way of thinking and talking about learning to read. We envision learners who are skilled, connected, and reflective practitioners of the craft of reading. The instructional principles that match these goals describe the kind of instruction that leads to engaged reading. Examples of effective instruction leading to these goals are many—only some have been presented here. There is no one way, no easily followed map that leads teachers and students toward engaged reading. Rather, there are a number of effective practices and many ways of working toward these goals. Effective practice is always contextual, depending on the needs and strengths of the students, the teacher, and the larger instructional community.

With no map, how can we begin to implement the engagement perspective in the teaching of reading in our elementary classrooms? What is it that teachers, teacher educators, parents, and others interested in reading can do to ensure the development of engaged readers? We can begin by framing questions that allow us to step back and assess teaching practices, using the descriptors of engaged reading discussed in this chapter as a guide.

We might begin with a consideration of activity. Activity, as we have defined it, is internally motivated, goal-directed behavior that is socially negotiated through language. Relevant questions that reflect an activity perspective might include the following:

- Are students engaged in tasks that are interesting to them?
- Is there a clear, important goal they are trying to accomplish?
- Have students helped to establish the goals and frame the tasks?
- Are students working together to attain their goals?
- Are there opportunities, structure, and the emotional climate necessary for effective social interaction?
- Are students effectively using language to learn and to express themselves?

The eight goals and instructional principles, likewise, can shape questions to ask as we assess the effectiveness of practice. With respect to *skill*, we might ask:

- Are students appropriately adept in their use of the alphabetic system?
- Are there extended opportunities for interactions with connected text?
- Are students developing as fluent, meaning-oriented readers?
- Are students learning varied, effective reading strategies and applying them in a variety of contexts?
- Are students provided with a variety of texts and tasks that require the use of varied strategies?

With respect to *connections*, we might ask:

- Are students provided with literature that stimulates imaginative, aesthetic responses?

- Do students have opportunities to demonstrate their aesthetic involvement with appropriate texts?
- Are students provided with challenging texts that allow them to build concepts and knowledge important to their learning goals?
- Are students provided with choices in the texts they read, how they read, and with whom they read?
- Are students eager to select books?
- Are the interests of students effectively balanced with the curricular requirements of the educational community?

With respect to *reflection*, we might ask:

- Are students aware when they have difficulties making sense of what they are reading?
- Are students able to adjust their strategies to regain the sense of text?
- Are students able to adjust their stance as readers to suit their purposes for reading and the demands of the text?
- Are students provided with opportunities to reflect on the reading process?
- Are students provided with opportunities to assess their own learning?
- Are students able to accurately assess their strengths and weaknesses as readers?

These questions are just the beginning. We look forward to the time when every teacher in schools across the United States can answer yes to each of these questions. At the same time, we are confident that the way teachers engage students in reading will be quite different in each case. Teaching is a highly personal activity that, like literacy, involves skill, connectedness, and reflection. As ever more teachers use an engagement perspective to guide their practices, other questions and reflections will emerge. Ultimately, it is the questions that we ask that motivate the most meaningful changes. These changes, in turn, can lead to successful practices that allow all of our children access to effective literacy and the desire to attain it.

REFERENCES

Adams, M. J. (1990). *Beginning to read: Thinking and learning about print*. Cambridge, MA: MIT Press.

Afflerbach, P. (1996). Engaged assessment of engaged reading. In L. Baker, P. Afflerbach, & D. Reinking (Eds.), *Developing engaged readers in school and home communities* (pp. 191–214). Mahwah, NJ: Erlbaum.

Allington, R. L. (1980). Poor readers don't get to read much in reading groups. *The Elementary School Journal, 84*, 423–440.

Allington, R. L. (1983). Fluency: The neglected reading goal in reading instruction. *Reading Teacher, 36,* 556–561.

Almasi, J. F. (1995). The nature of fourth graders' sociocognitive conflicts in peer-led and teacher-led discussions of literature. *Reading Research Quarterly, 30,* 314–351.

Applebee, A. (1977). The elements of response to a literary work: What we have learned. *Research in the Teaching of English, 11,* 255–271.

Au, K. H. (1993). *Literacy instruction in multicultural settings.* Fort Worth, TX: Harcourt, Brace, Jovanovich.

Blum, I. H., Koskinen, P. S., Tennant, N., Parker, E. M., Straub, J., & Curry, C. (1995). Using audiotaped books to extend classroom literacy instruction into the home of second language learners. *Journal of Reading Behavior, 27*(4), 535–563.

Carver, R. P. (1990). *Reading rate: A review of research and theory.* San Diego, CA: Academic Press.

Clay, M. (1987). *What did I write?* Portsmouth, NH: Heinemann.

Codling, R. M., & Gambrell, L. B. (1997). *The motivation to write profile: An assessment tool for elementary teachers.* (ERIC Document Reproduction Services No. ED 402 562)

Commeyras, M., & Sumner, G. (in press). Questions children want to discuss about literature: What teachers and students learned in a second-grade classroom. *Elementary School Journal.*

Corno, L. (1986). The metacognitive control components of self-regulated learning. *Contemporary Educational Psychology, 11,* 333–346.

Csikszentmihalyi, M. (1978). Intrinsic rewards and emergent motivation. In M. Lepper & D. Green (Eds.), *The hidden costs of reward: New perspectives on the psychology of human motivation* (pp. 205–216). Hillsdale, NJ: Erlbaum.

Deci, E. L., Vallerand, R. J., Pelletier, L. G., & Ryan, R. M. (1991). Motivation and education: The self-determination perspective. *Educational Psychologist, 26,* 325–346.

Dewey, J. (1900). *The school and society.* Chicago: University of Chicago Press.

Dewey, J. (1938). *Logic: The theory of inquiry.* New York: Holt.

Duffy, G. G., & Roehler, L. R. (1989). *Improving classroom reading instruction: A decision-making approach.* New York: Random House.

Durkin, D. (1966). *Children who read early.* New York: Teachers College Press.

Galda, L., Pellegrini, A., & Bisplinghoff, B. (1996). *Literacy in transition: Home and school influences.* (ERIC Document Reproduction Services No. ED 403 540)

Galda, L., Shockley, B., & Pellegrini, A. (1995). *Talking to read and write: Opportunities for literate talk in one primary classroom* (Instructional Resource No. 12). Athens, GA: Universities of Georgia and Maryland, National Reading Research Center.

Gambrell, L. B., Codling, R. M., & Palmer, B. M. (1996). *Elementary students' motivation to read* (Reading Research Report No. 52). Athens, GA: Universities of Georgia and Maryland, National Reading Research Center. (ERIC Document Reproduction Services No. ED 395 279)

Goodman, K. S. (1986). *What's whole in whole language?* Portsmouth, NH: Heinemann.

Goodman, K. S. (1989). Access to literacy: Basals and other barriers. *Theory into Practice, 28,* 300–306.

Gough, P. B., & Hillinger, M. L. (1980). Learning to read: An unnatural act. *Bulletin of the Orton Society, 20*, 179–196.

Guthrie, J. T., Schafer, W. D., Wang, Y. Y., & Afflerbach, P. (1995). Relationships of instruction on reading: An exploration of social, cognitive, and instructional connections. *Reading Research Quarterly, 30*(1), 8–25.

Guthrie, J. T., Van Meter, P., McCann, A. D., Wigfield, A., Bennett, L., Poundstone, C. C., Rice, M. E., Faibisch, F. M., Hunt, B., & Mitchell, A. (1996). Growth of literacy engagement: Changes in motivations and strategies during Concept-Oriented Reading Instruction. *Reading Research Quarterly, 31*, 306–332.

Harris, V. J. (1992). Multiethnic children's literature. In K. D. Wood & A. Moss (Eds.), *Exploring literature in the classroom: Content and methods* (pp. 169–201). Norwood, MA: Christopher Gordon.

Harste, J. C. (1994). Multiple ways of knowing. *Language Arts, 71*, 337–349.

Heath, S. B. (1983*). Ways with words: Language, life and work in communities and classrooms*. Cambridge: Cambridge University Press.

Hoffman, J. V., & Clements, R. (1983). Reading miscues and teacher verbal feedback. *The Elementary School Journal, 84*, 423–440.

Hoffman, J. V., McCarthey, S. J., Bayles, D., Elliot, B., Ferree, A., Price, D., & Abbott, J. (1996). *Literature-based reading instruction: Problems, possibilities, and polemics in the struggle to change* (Reading Research Report No. 67). Athens, GA: Universities of Georgia and Maryland, National Reading Research Center. (ERIC Document Reproduction Services No. ED 400 524)

Hoffman, J. V., McCarthey, S. J., Abbott, J., Christian, C., Corman, L., Curry, C., Dressman, M., Elliot, B., Maherne, D., & Sthale, D. (1994). So what's new in the new basals? A focus in first grade. *Journal of Reading Behavior, 26*, 47–73.

Hoffman, J. V., Worthy, J., Roser, N., McKool, S., Rutherford, W., & Strecker, S. (1996). *Performance assessment in first grade classrooms: The PALM model* (Yearbook of the National Reading Conference). Chicago: National Reading Conference.

Labbo, L. D. (1996). A semiotic analysis of young children's symbol making in a classroom computer center. *Reading Research Quarterly, 31*(4), 356–385.

Langer, J. A., & Applebee, A. N. (1986). Reading and writing instruction: Toward a theory of teaching and learning. In E. Rothkopf (Ed.), *Review of research in education* (Vol. 13, pp. 171–194). Washington, DC: American Educational Research Association.

Langer, J. A., & Rosenblatt, L. M. (1983). *Literature as exploration*. New York: Modern Language Association of America.

Leont'ev, A. N. (1981). The problem of activity in psychology. In J. V. Wertsch (Ed.), *The concept of activity in Soviet psychology*. Armonk, NY: Sharpe.

McCarthey, S. J., Hoffman, J. V., et al. (1994). Engaging the new basal readers. *Reading Research and Instruction, 33*(3), 233–256.

Morrow, L. (1996). *Motivating reading and writing in diverse classrooms: Social and physical contexts in a literature-based program*. Urbana, IL: National Council of Teachers of English.

Ng, M. M., Guthrie, J. T., McCann, A. D., Van Meter, P., & Alao, S. (1996). *How do classroom characteristics influence intrinsic motivations for literacy?* (Reading Research Report No. 56). Athens, GA: Universities of Georgia and Maryland, National Reading Research Center.

Oldfather, P., & Dahl, K. (1995). *Toward a social constructivist reconceptualization of intrinsic motivation for literacy learning* (Perspectives in Reading Research No. 6). Athens, GA: Universities of Georgia and Maryland, National Reading Research Center. (ERIC Document Reproduction Services No. ED 384 009)

Oldfather, P., & Wigfield, A. (1996). Children's motivations for literacy learning. In L. Baker, P. Afflerbach, & D. Reinking (Eds.), *Developing engaged readers in school and home communities* (pp. 89–113). Mahwah, NJ: Erlbaum.

Palincsar, A. S., & Brown, A. (1984). Reciprocal teaching of comprehension-fostering and comprehension-monitoring activities. *Cognition and Instruction, 1,* 117–175.

Paris, S. G., Cross, D. R., & Lipson, M. Y. (1984). Informed strategies for learning: A program to improve children's reading awareness and comprehension. *Journal of Educational Psychology, 76,* 1239–1252.

Pearson, D., & Tierney, R. (1984). Toward a composing model of reading. In J. Jensen (Ed.), *Composing and comprehending* (pp. 33–45). Urbana, IL: National Conference on Research in English.

Pressley, M., El-Dinary, P. B., Brown, R., Schuder, T. L., Pioli, M., Green, K., & Gaskins, I. (1994). Transactional instruction of reading comprehension strategies. *Reading and Writing Quarterly, 10,* 5–19.

Pressley, M., Rankin, J., & Yokoi, L. (1996). A survey of instructional practices of primary teachers nominated as effective in promoting literacy. *Elementary School Journal, 96*(4), 363–384.

Purves, A. C., & Beach, R. (1972). *Literature and the reader.* Urbana, IL: National Council of Teachers of English.

Raphael, T., & Hiebert, E. H. (1996). *Creating an integrated approach to literacy instruction.* Fort Worth, TX: Harcourt, Brace, Jovanovich.

Raphael, T. E., & McMahon, S. I. (1994). Book club: An alternative framework for reading instruction. *The Reading Teacher, 48*(2), 102–116.

Reinking, D., & Watkins, J. (1997). *A formative experiment investigating the use of multimedia book reviews to increase elementary students' independent reading* (Reading Research Report No. 73). Athens, GA: Universities of Georgia and Maryland, National Reading Research Center.

Routman, R. (1991). *Invitations: Changing as teachers and learners K–12.* Portsmouth, NH: Heinemann.

Shockley, B., Michalove, B., & Allen, J. (1995). *Creating parallel practices: A home-to-school and school-to-home partnership* (Instructional Resource No. 13). Athens, GA: Universities of Georgia and Maryland, National Reading Research Center.

Stahl, S. A., Heubach, K., & Crammond, B. (1997). *Fluency-oriented reading instruction* (Reading Research Report No. 79). Athens, GA: Universities of Georgia and Maryland, National Reading Research Center.

Stahl, S. A., Hynd, C. R., Glynn, S. M., & Carr, M. (1996). Beyond reading to learn: Developing content and disciplinary knowledge through texts. In L. Baker, P. Afflerbach, & D. Reinking (Eds.), *Developing engaged readers in school and home communities* (pp. 139–163). Mahwah, NJ: Erlbaum.

Stevens, R. J., Madden, N. A., Slavin, R. E., & Farnish, A. M. (1987). Cooperative integrated reading and composition: Two field experiments. *Reading Research Quarterly, 22,* 433–454.

Tomlinson, L. (1995). *The effects of instructional interaction guided by a typology of ethnic identity development: Phase I* (Reading Research Report No. 44). Athens, GA: Universities of Georgia and Maryland, National Reading Research Center.

Turner, J. C. (1995). The influence of classroom contexts on young children's motivation for literacy. *Reading Research Quarterly, 30*, 410–441.

Valencia, S. W., & Au, K. (1996). *Portfolios across educational contexts: Issues of evaluation, teacher development, and system validity* (Research Report No. 73). Athens, GA: Universities of Georgia and Maryland, National Reading Research Center.

Vygotsky, L. S. (1978). *Mind in society: The development of higher psychological processes.* Cambridge, MA: Harvard University Press.

West, J., & Galda, L. (1996). Family literacy: Creating home–school connections. *New Advocate, 9*(2), 169–173.

Wigfield, A., & Guthrie, J. T. (1997). Reading engagement: A rationale for theory and teaching. In J. T. Guthrie & A. Wigfield (Eds.), *Reading engagement: Motivating readers through integrated instruction* (pp. 1–13). Newark, DE: International Reading Association.

Zutell, J., & Rasinski, T. V. (1991). Training teachers to attend to their students' oral reading fluency. *Theory into Practice, 30*(3), 211–217.

CHAPTER 4

Instructional Considerations for Literacy in Middle and Secondary Schools: Toward an Integrated Model of Instruction

Cynthia Hynd

ASPECTS OF ENGAGEMENT DESCRIBED IN the foregoing chapters—motivation, strategy use, cognition, and social influence—change as students move from elementary school to middle school and then to high school. For example, career choice affects high school students' motivations more than it affects elementary school students' motivations. Societal demands and socioeconomic status play a part in high school students' career decisions and, thus, also influence their motivations. As students learn more, their thinking about concepts related to those fields and their strategies for reading become more refined. James Booth and William Hall (1994), at the University of Maryland, found that as students grow older, they increasingly understand concepts, even abstract ones; students are better able to see underlying principles; and their ability to monitor their understanding increases. In addition, students develop deep interests in certain disciplines while they decide that other disciplines are not as interesting to them. Peer-group influences become more intense and, although these influences can support amount and quality of reading and academic learning, they also can lead to the diminishment of reading and learning. Students may have more opportunities to ask for their classmates' academic help on weekends and evenings, but may choose socializing over learning. Also, social pressures can lessen the amount of pleasure reading students do. Harter, Whitesell, and Kowalksi (1992) say that intrinsic motivations decline as students' progress through school, and extrinsic motivations, increase.

The organizational structure of schools also differs. Elementary school students moving into middle school go to different classes with different subject matter teachers, often for the first time. To counter the loss of subject matter integration, while still maintaining the benefits of providing students with teachers who have more content expertise, many middle schools adopt a model in which science, social studies, English, and math teachers form a team. These teams plan thematic units in common and/or monitor their students' progress in all classes. When students enter high school, they may lose the benefits of the team approach. On the other hand, their teachers are often more immersed in their disciplines, and students can experience working with teachers with a great deal of subject matter knowledge. Thus, there is a tension between integration and specialization that is not felt in earlier grades.

The differences in student instruction at various levels of schooling have implications for change as students progress through the grades. This chapter provides a vision of instruction that illuminates and integrates motivational, strategic, cognitive, and social influences on reading, and aims to provide information that can be used to produce truly engaged middle and secondary school readers. Toward this end, eight principles are described for instruction in middle and secondary schools based on research using the engagement framework.

THE COMPLEX AND INTERACTIVE NATURE OF MOTIVATION AND KNOWLEDGE DEVELOPMENT

Motivation, strategy use, and knowledge level are interdependent, developmental, and increasingly tied to a particular discipline. When a student reads a science textbook, for instance, the knowledge she already has about science helps determine the kinds of strategies she will use and how motivated she feels to read. In turn, her level of motivation helps determine the kinds of strategies she uses and plays a part in the amount and quality of knowledge she learns. Her strategy use will determine knowledge level and motivation as well. As one increases, so do the others; that is their developmental and interactive nature.

What distinguishes middle and secondary schools from elementary schools is that the disciplines, such as science and history, become more separated as the grades advance. The reason for this separation is that each discipline has developed its own traditions for both research and instruction. As an outgrowth of the specialized knowledge one must have to be an "expert" in a domain, the various domains develop their own arcane language, ways of conducting research, and ways of disseminating knowledge. Students become more immersed in disciplinary traditions as they continue schooling—concurrently their knowledge about each discipline increases, while their sense of interdisciplinary connection diminishes.

How Knowledge Develops

Alexander (1995) proposed that learning in subject domains, such as science and history, occurs on three developmental levels. These levels are necessarily tied to domains because of the differences in the nature of knowledge across domains. *Acclimated* learners are in the beginning stages of learning their subject matter, and thus knowledge is low and not very coherent. The student's low knowledge means that she will have to rely on strategies to help her learn from text. However, these strategies may not be executed efficiently or effectively. Many students in middle and high school classes operate at this level. A beginning student of history may read history texts as if they were merely a collection of facts to learn, and be unable to distinguish important information—bias from objectivity, or secondary from primary sources. He may like learning about World War II but not believe that history learning overall is important or especially interesting. His knowledge is low, his interest is topical rather than general, and his strategic efforts—to gather a list of unrelated facts and remember them—are inefficient.

Competent learners, in contrast, have more extensive and coherent knowledge about a subject matter. They are beginning to understand key concepts or principles that define the domain and hence are more motivated by learning goals that are domain-related rather than merely topical or situational in nature. Competent learners are more likely to choose and use appropriate strategies effectively and are able to operate more independently than students who are acclimated learners. High school students taking an advanced history class may know many "facts" of history, but they also are aware that historians make interpretations based on existing evidence. When they read, they know they should try to analyze text critically, situate it in a time frame, corroborate it with other sources, and evaluate the author's credibility. Students may try these strategies because they have a profound general curiosity about history and a more specific interest in the topic they are reading.

Proficient learners have vast stores of subject matter knowledge and are expected to contribute new knowledge. They are driven largely by internal goals. Proficient learners need little instructional support and, in fact, provide help for others. Advanced graduate students and professionals are often at this level. Immersed in the discipline, they understand what it means to a historian or scientist, and they act accordingly. Their reading strategies are goal-driven and highly efficient. Historians not only read critically, as described above, but do so with ease and efficiency.

Motivation for Learning

An integrated view of knowledge development and motivation was proposed by McCombs (1996). She defined motivation using an integrative framework combining skill, will, and social support strategies that consider the learner, the instruction, the learning materials, and the larger context for learning. She emphasized that for a student optimally to gain content knowledge, he must have strategic knowledge (e.g., knowledge of how to map cause/effect relationships) that will enable him to learn from a particular type of material (e.g., a history textbook), know that this is a situation where the strategic knowledge will be helpful, be in a situation where the strategic knowledge can be employed (e.g., a collaborative group), and want to engage in the activity (e.g., be personally interested in the topic).

Furthermore, motivation for learning is situated because it varies depending on the task, the content, the context, and the goals (Paris & Turner, 1994). If a student were to read a history textbook to learn what happened in the Gulf of Tonkin, for example, he would be faced with a task (read to find out what happened) and a content (the Gulf of Tonkin). Because he is in a class (the context) where the teacher expects him to remember factual information to pass an objective test, and because he embraces this context without particularly liking the topic he is studying, he may decide that he should memorize enough of the facts to pass the test with a "C" (the goal).

Optimal contexts for motivated learning, according to McCombs (1996) and Paris and Turner (1994), are classrooms that offer information that students choose to learn because of personal interest, that challenge students to expand their thinking, that allow students some control over how they learn, and that provide opportunities for helpful collaboration.

Presented in the next sections are principles that illuminate the specific elements of engagement and help us further to understand their interaction.

INTRINSIC, SOCIAL, SELF-EFFICACY, AND UTILITARIAN MOTIVATIONS FOR LITERACY AND LEARNING

Motivation is an important element for engaged reading. Several research studies have helped us understand the motivations of middle and high school students. Oldfather (Oldfather, 1993, 1994; Oldfather & Dahl, 1995) worked with a group of students as they progressed from a fifth/sixth-grade class through high school. Operating from the belief that students develop their understandings of the world and themselves from their social interactions, she engaged these students in studying their own motivations as they interacted with others in the classroom. Students reported being motivated by classroom environments that were respectful and responsive, that allowed self-expression, that focused on meaning rather than correctness, and that allowed students to have choices. She referred to students' need for self-expression and respect as *honored voice*, or the feeling that students have important things to say.

Students, however, did not always feel motivated. When they did not, it was because they believed they were denied the opportunity to direct their own learning or believed they were incompetent to perform the task requested. Some students were able to overcome their negative feelings and participate in the required activity, even to the point of becoming motivated. These students searched for meaning in their activities and tried to keep positive, open minds. Other students participated in the required activity, but never became motivated. Possibly they relied on ineffective motivators such as compliance to help them complete the task. Some students, however, never completed the task or completed it halfheartedly. These students were unable to overcome their negative feelings and most often reported that the feelings stemmed from their perceived inability to perform the tasks effectively.

Intrinsic Motivation

This research supports earlier quantitative work by Adele Gottfried (1985), who found a correlation between students' perception of competence and anxiety and their level of intrinsic motivation. If students' perception of competence fell, or if their anxiety rose, their intrinisic motivation waned. Guthrie, Alao, and Rinehart (1997) discussed the possibility that as students progress through school, there is more emphasis on grades in individual subjects. Thus, students have the opportunity to compare themselves with others more often, and their self-perceptions of their competence may falter as a result of those comparisons. When that happens, intrinisic motivation decreases. Also, in the move to middle school and later to high school, anxiety rises because of the unfamiliarity of new environments.

Hynd and her colleagues at the University of Georgia and Guzzetti and her colleagues at Arizona State University (Hynd, Guzzetti, McNish, Fowler, & Williams, 1997; Hynd, McNish, Lay, & Fowler, 1995; Hynd, McNish, Qian, Keith, & Lay, 1994) asked students about their motivations in a number of high school physics classrooms. Students who reported being motivated by a profound interest in physics and who believed that physics was relevant to their everyday and future lives were the most likely to exert the effort to overcome their intuitive but nonscientific understandings of physics principles. These students read more widely, talked to their teachers and parents, and thought deeply about physics applications both in class and out of school. Many of them saw that they would use physics in their future careers. For example, one student became so distraught that he had misunderstood a basic physics principle that he went to the library and read about the topic, talked extensively with his father (an engineer), and discussed his understandings with his teacher after school. "I really need to know this stuff. I'm going to be an engineer," was his explanation for his behavior. Students who did not learn physics principles that went against their everyday understandings believed that physics was an important subject, wanted to do well in school, but were not as likely to be interested or see the relevance of physics in their lives. Therefore, intrinsic motivation and relevance seemed important elements in these students' learning.

What Is the Role of Grades in High School?

Grades take on more importance in high school than in elementary and middle school. Grades count toward graduation, and As and Bs count when students try to get into colleges. Wigfield and Guthrie (1997) described grades as extrinsic motivators for elementary school students. That is, the motivation for grades stems from the need for a reward; therefore, motivation for grades is not as effective as motivation based on interest, which is intrinsic. However, nearly all of the advanced physics students, whether they learned the physics principles or not, said they desired good grades and would work for them even when they were not very interested in the topics they studied. Their desire for grades was largely instrumental. They saw those grades as moving them forward in life from high school into college and believed that the grades would allow them to pursue their career interests. Students also believed in their ability to do well in school and pursued good grades so they would not let themselves or their parents down. Thus, getting good grades in physics had a utilitarian influence on their lives and was more related to their inner need to feel competent than merely meeting an externally imposed expectation. This observation is suggested by previous research. Connell and Ryan (1984) discussed, for example, the idea that children internalize extrinsic reward systems to self-regulate their achievement activities.

We have learned that successful high school students, and to an extent middle school students, are motivated by social interaction with teachers and peers, have a keen interest in the discipline and topics that they study, have a feeling of their competence, and see the relevance and utility in learning. Students' motivations are complex; that is, students often report a number of motivations rather than just one. Further, they compensate for each other at times, and act in concert at other times. For example, when a student's interest in a topic is low, then the usefulness of learning the information may help sustain his learning, or his feelings of connectedness with others may result in his developing an interest in topics introduced to him by his friends and teachers. As students advance, it becomes more important how relevant and useful information is, because students are beginning to decide what they will choose as career goals.

HOW AND WHEN TO USE EFFECTIVE READING STRATEGIES TO OBTAIN DISCIPLINARY KNOWLEDGE

Strategies are activities that help students identify, understand, and remember important information and key concepts. Looking at an index to search for a topic, for example, is a strategy to help students identify information. Rereading, breaking down complex text into more manageable units, and reading appropriate background materials are strategies that aid students' understanding. Identifying and remembering a key word in a definition is a strategy to help students remember the definition. Ideally, students should know what strategies to use and how and when to use them. Further, they should constantly evaluate their strategies and change them appropriately. If students were regularly to do this, they would be self-regulated learners. As Alexander (1995) noted, self-regulation most often happens when students' content and disciplinary knowledge is high.

Pressley and colleagues (1994) stated that most researchers' ideas about strategies include the need for students to have *procedural knowledge*; that is, students should know how to perform a strategy; *declarative knowledge*; that is, they should have some knowledge of the content in which they are to use the strategy; and *metacognition* or self-awareness; that is, they should know when to apply the strategy, know whether they are applying it effectively, and monitor their understanding of the content as a result of the strategy. In his model, Pressley also included motivation and found that students needed to be motivated to learn in order to use a strategy well.

Often, however, students do not use strategies effectively. Dreher (1995) found that sixth-grade students, all competent readers, had difficulty using search strategies to locate information about a familiar topic in a text, even when they had participated in instruction on how to access topics by using the table of contents and the index. Students also had difficulty writing a report using multiple sources. Although they chose their own questions on a topic they found interesting, they changed topics rather than persist in looking for information to answer these questions in their papers. Students primarily used one source rather than several, copied information, and wrote content-free conclusions. Dreher discussed other research showing that students who know *about* strategy use do not always use what they know, and suggested that students needed systematic, guided practice in strategy use *while they are engaged in answering their content area questions*. Her suggestion is supported by the work of Guthrie, Van Meter, McCann, Anderson, and Alao (1996). They found that strategy lessons and practice helped younger students to use multiple sources as they learned about topics in science.

In Dreher's (1995) study of students' search strategies, the students appeared to have procedural knowledge (they could tell someone abstractly how they should search for information), declarative knowledge (they were familiar with the topic), and motivation (they were given choices and said they were interested), but not metacognition. They did not know when to apply the strategies they had learned and did not evaluate whether they were using effective strategies.

Types of Strategies for Learning Content and Disciplinary Information

Researchers often disagree about whether the strategies we teach students should be specific to a discipline or general. If strategies are general, then students can be taught a strategy and apply it to several subject matter areas. If strategies are specific to a discipline, then students should be taught different strategies for science, history, and English.

Teaching with Analogies

Shawn Glynn and his colleagues (Glynn, 1994, 1996, 1997; Glynn, Law, Gibson, & Hawkins, 1994) at the University of Georgia report that teachers can improve students' understanding of topics by using analogies and by teaching analogy use to students. He also presents a model for the use of analogies. According to Glynn, teachers and textbook authors use analogies all of the time when they use phrases such as, "It's just like . . . ," "It's the same as . . . ," and "It's no different than . . ." But when analogies are used unsystematically, they can lead to confusion and misunderstandings. In his model, the concept and its analog are introduced, relevant features of both are identified and compared, differences are noted, and conclusions are drawn. For example, Bohr's model of the atom (target concept) could be compared with a bookcase (analog), because there are energy levels in the atom just as there are shelves in a bookcase. Each shelf can contain many books just as each energy level contains electrons and neutrons (similarity). But the shelves on the bookcase are linear, while the energy levels of the atom surround the nucleus (this is where the analogy breaks down). Each of these steps in the explanation of the analogy is important for student understanding.

In these examples of strategy use, we see their interaction with knowledge and motivation. One influences the other in a reciprocal fashion. Teachers who understand this interactive nature will be more likely to provide contexts for learning that encourage growth in all areas simultaneously rather than isolating strategy instruction from students' motivated learning experiences. Teachers who teach their students strategies and guide students in practicing the strategies while engaged in meaningful learning activities will be more likely to ensure that students develop the procedural, disciplinary, and metacognitive knowledge that enhances strategy use.

HOW FEATURES OF TEXTS AFFECT STUDENTS' LEARNING

As we consider students' reading engagement, we need to consider the text. Texts are an important and ubiquitous part of the learning environment and the focus of much research. There is increasing evidence that the way ideas are presented in texts affects the quality and quantity of the information students gain from reading. Hence, the quality of texts affect the quality of a reader's engagement. This evidence comes from student interview data, quantitative research, and classroom observation. Teachers who listen to their students' concerns and know how certain texts help or hinder a student's understanding are more capable of picking effective texts for classroom use. They also are better able to help their students overcome difficulties with texts that are not well written.

Level of Information

Several researchers have documented the ways in which textbooks in the disciplines are inappropriately written. Specifically, texts in science and history leave out information that may be crucial to students' development of coherent ideas about the information they are to learn. Further, textbook authors often assume that students already know information that they do not (Beck, McKeown, Omanson, & Pople, 1984; Beck, McKeown, Sinatra, & Loxterman, 1991). Britton and Gulgoz (1991) documented that to be understood, texts often require inferences that cannot be made without adequate background information. Thus, students who do not already have high levels of knowledge cannot really benefit from reading these texts. Glynn and his colleagues (1994) point out that texts often use analogies ineffectively. Although analogies in subjects such as science can be very helpful in tying one's background knowledge to new information (e.g., comparing the earth's crust and core to the parts of a hard-boiled egg), they can be misleading if texts fail to explain the differences between the targeted concept and the analog (e.g., students may think that the core of the earth is solid).

Quality of Writing

Studies of high school students show that they react negatively to poorly written texts (Hynd, McNish et al., 1994; Hynd et al., 1995; Hynd et al., 1997). Students become very frustrated with their textbooks when the texts do not help them understand, with advanced students experiencing more frustration than less advanced ones. On the other hand, well-written texts motivate students to read. Well-written texts fully elaborate complex ideas, make ties with students' existing knowledge, use relevant examples, highlight important ideas, explain difficult vocabulary, and use plain rather than arcane language. If texts do not meet these conditions, students often give up on the notion that texts can help them learn. The frustration comes through in one advanced physics student's words about her textbook:

> Well, I know they use words that are, like, confusing . . . uh difficult words to understand. Like, in a lot of those texts that you gave us to read, I mean, it was just simple words, something anybody can understand. And that's why I liked them a lot. Because I learned something from them. I mean some of the things in here they talk about, I mean, they don't explain it, or they don't use words that everyone can understand, and a lot of new words they throw at you all at once, and it's just like, wait a

minute, now I've got to go back and figure out what this meant and then, so I'll know what the next thing meant.

Another student compared reading her physics textbook with trying to construct a house with no foundation, because she lacked the foundational knowledge to make sense of the text's language. Still another reported her frustration at trying to make up a missed class lesson by reading her textbook and working the assigned problems. Without the teacher's support, she could not understand a key principle in physics and did poorly on the test.

Most evidence to date suggests that well-written texts enhance learning. Britton, Schneider, Colomb, Sorrells, and Stimson (1996) found that students increased their learning when they read texts rewritten either to untangle difficult concepts or to highlight their important points. Isabel Beck and her colleagues (Beck et al., 1991; Beck, McKeown, & Worthy, 1995) found that students' comprehension improved when texts were revised to be more coherent—to have more ties between ideas. She also found that making texts more active and lively (giving them "voice") enhanced comprehension.

Further, well-written texts can help students learn more than they can from lecture, discussion, demonstration, hands-on activities, and other instructional activities (Hynd, Alvermann, & Qian, 1993; Hynd, McWhorter, Phares, & Suttles, 1994; Hynd et al., n.d.). In one study, students who engaged in peer-group discussions learned less than control groups, while those who read texts gained, even on tests delayed for 2 weeks.

For students whose existing conceptions are challenged by new information, texts with a refutational style are more effective at getting students to understand and learn the new information, and are better liked than texts that merely explain the new ideas. In refutational style, commonly held ideas are acknowledged, but students are told that the new ideas presented in the text explain phenomena in a more accurate and useful way. Students' existing ideas are refuted and the new ideas are explained. Also, narrative formats for science texts work well at motivating students to read about difficult ideas, especially if students have a hard time seeing the applicability of scientific principles to real-life situations.

Computerized Texts

Displaying texts on the computer is another way of improving texts so that they are more understandable. According to Reinking (1996), computerized texts have the potential to overcome many problems encountered with poorly written materials and single texts. In a hypertext environment, where readers can make links across different texts based upon a semantic network, students' access to multiple texts is instant and seamless. A student can even add her own text to the network. In addition, a computer may be programmed to adapt to an individual reader's needs. For example, the computer can modify a text based on a reader's reading rate and accuracy in answering questions. A study found that secondary students who were poor readers performed as well as good readers on comprehension questions when they read these adapted texts (L'Allier, 1980). Computers also can provide a pronunciation or a context-specific definition of words, an animated illustration of the content of the text, a map of the text's structure, a helpful analogy, or an easier, less technical version of the text. The sequence and the amount of reading can be controlled by a computer. As mentioned previously, a computer also can be programmed to intersperse questions in text and require mandatory review when questions are answered incorrectly. Therefore, computerized texts have the potential to transform reading for middle and secondary school students. David Reinking (1996) recommends that parents, teachers, and schools look for ways to overcome equipment deficiencies, lack of knowledge, and inertia so that the benefits of computerized texts can be experienced.

How Multiple Texts Can Promote Motivation and Critical Thinking

Although educators often recommend the use of multiple texts in subject area learning (Guthrie et al., 1997; Ravich, 1990), teachers in subject matter classes often use only one textbook. Forty-five percent of history teachers and approximately 90% of science teachers in high schools use a single textbook in their classes (Patrick & Hawke, 1982; Yore, 1991).

The reasons for using more than one text are compelling. As already noted, in science, single textbooks often do not address students' levels of concept knowledge, levels of vocabulary knowledge, or need for elaborate and relevant explanations. Teachers can have students read more than one text to give them richer avenues for understanding. Multiple texts can offer students choices based on their personal interests and thus are more motivating to students (Guthrie, McGough, Bennett, & Rice, 1996). Finally, multiple texts can provide opportunities for students to think critically about the process of constructing and interpreting knowledge in various disciplines. Making sense of the conflicting information across different texts can help students understand how knowledge is developed. To make this point, let us examine the example of history.

In history, teaching students to engage in historical analysis with a single textbook is difficult. This difficulty, in large part, is due to the traditional format of most history textbooks. While textbooks in other fields, such as psychology, often refer to the research efforts of professionals in the field and may even report conflicting findings, history textbooks rarely present such information. Rather, the tradition is to present the information as a story. Thus, the reader never sees the hidden activity of the historian in constructing the telling of the story.

When historians read, they engage in critical reading strategies such as sourcing (noting the author's expertise), contextualization (noting the time period in which the text was written and reflecting on the social, economic, and political conditions that existed), and corroboration (comparing and contrasting the text with others) (Wineburg, 1991). Given the way history textbooks are written, high school students have little opportunity to engage in such strategies. When several texts are taken in concert, however, a teaching opportunity is present, especially when the texts contradict each other, present different information, or present the viewpoints of different groups of people.

Stahl and his colleagues (Stahl, Hynd, Britton, McNish, & Bosquet, 1996; Stahl, Hynd, Montgomery, & McClain, 1997) examined texts that represented a traditional, revisionist, and postrevisionist view of the discoveries of Christopher Columbus. The traditional text included the idea that Christopher Columbus's discoveries required great courage and brought the world closer together. The revisionist view presented the Native American perspective that Columbus was greedy and cruel, and denigrated the culture of a peace-loving and prosperous people, bringing disease and pestilence to an area that was not, to the people living there, "the New World." The postrevisionist view argued that Christopher Columbus was merely a product of his time and was neither more cruel nor more courageous than other explorers. These texts, and others like them, present opportunities for history teachers to help students engage in sourcing (Who wrote the texts, where did they appear, and what expertise did the authors have?), contextualization (In what time period were they written, what was the climate in which they were written?), and corroboration (How do they compare and contrast?). As students look at these elements, they can learn that history is interpreted differently by different groups at different time periods because of sociocultural and political conditions.

Without instruction, however, students may not gain much from the use of more than one text. VanSledright and Kelly (1997) examined trade book use in a fifth-grade history class, finding that trade books were more motivating to students than regular textbooks. Yet, students still had difficulty making judgments about the reliability and validity of what was written. Reading various accounts of the same event did not help the students question the interpretations of events about which they read nor did students even note the differences across texts. In a study of multiple texts in an advanced high school world history class, Steve Stahl found the same results (Stahl et al., 1996). Students focused on information in common across the various texts rather than the way historical evidence was interpreted by different authors. Rather than questioning the texts and their authors (Beck et al., 1995; McKeown & Beck, 1994; Wineburg, 1991, 1994), students engaged in understanding history as "a fact compendium" (Greene, 1994; VanSledright & Kelly, 1997). Therefore, teachers in middle and high schools need to help their students become critical thinkers by guiding them to read the way historians do—to source, contextualize, and corroborate texts and to question the author's expertise.

POWER RELATIONS INHERENT IN SOCIAL INTERACTIONS

Thus far, I have discussed the interactive nature of strategy use, knowledge, and motivation for learning from text, and have discussed some text features that encourage or discourage engaged reading. This section and the next one will highlight the importance of social interaction in learning; this section will present the perspective that issues of power and authority play out in those social interactions. Understanding these issues helps us to think more critically about our goals, our materials, and our methods of instruction.

Social constructivists argue that learning takes place through social interaction (Bloome, 1986; Dyson, 1989). In fact, everything we know, including language, history, and science, is constructed through this interaction. For example, historians interpret important events through a social lens. They operate within certain time periods, have certain political affiliations, belong to certain cultural groups, and hold certain beliefs that determine how they select and interpret historical evidence. Therefore, Native Americans interpret Columbus's "discovery" of America differently from traditional historians. Scientists, although they wish to understand reality, are influenced by the way in which previous knowledge has been categorized and described, by political considerations, and by their measurement devices developed under the same constraints. Although Galileo reasoned that the earth was not the center of the universe, his ideas were not accepted until the social and political climate changed. Thus, the scientific "facts" we learn are socially constructed. We give students certain kinds of reading experiences in schools because curriculum experts have determined what literature should be used. Hence, the kinds of reading students do in school is socially constructed.

Critical theorists argue that people in positions of power and authority determine what is accepted as knowledge and what literature gets read. In their view, people in power seek to maintain that power, thereby disenfranchising and exploiting those who are not powerful. Their theory explains that Galileo's understanding of the universe was not accepted because people in power had a stake in maintaining the current scientific understandings.

Critical theorists also argue that, for inequities to change, disenfranchised groups must consciously seek to unseat those in power. Thus, women's groups have had to unleash massive campaigns to get the right to vote. African Americans have fought for African American literature to be read in schools, and Native Americans have had to struggle to get their perspectives portrayed in history books. Critical theorists believe that teachers and students need to analyze literature, history, science, and, indeed, all educational activity by asking questions about power and authority. This type of analysis will help them become critical consumers of texts and participate as more knowledgeable citizens.

Issues of power are prevalent in middle and high school classrooms, as well as in higher academia. At the University of Georgia, Alvermann and Commeyras

(1994) noted that the language of texts often conveys power relations where males supersede females. In fact, many studies of male and female characters in children's literature and other school materials show inequitable power relations (Barnett, 1986; McDonald, 1989). Even when authors and publishers have attempted to create gender-equitable literature, students maintain gendered views of themselves and the world. Alvermann and Commeyras (1994) and Brodkey (1992) have argued that stereotypical representations of males taking precedence over females should be the focus of class discussions, so that previously invisible inequities can be interrupted or changed. In practice, however, that interruption presents difficulties. Alvermann, Commeyras, Young, Randall, and Hinson (1996) were unsuccessful in their attempts to alter gendered interpretations of text in middle and high school classes during discussion. The middle school teacher veered away from discussions of sensitive issues because of the possibility of disapproval from parents and school administrators. In the high school class, students became contentious in their discussions, with females and males forming opposing, solidified groups.

Similar to Alvermann and her colleagues' effort to change students' perceptions of gender, Louise Tomlinson (1995, 1996) attempted to change students' perceptions of race. She taught teachers to use Bank's typology to classify literature based on the level of ethnic identity development it illustrated. The idea is that teachers can classify books according to the way that ethnic identity is typified in them and then use that classification as a basis for choosing important books for students to read. There are six levels in Bank's typology. A person at Level 1 in ethnic identity development may have low self-esteem and a negative view of her culture. As her level of ethnic identity development rises, she may at first feel separate and threatened by others (Level 2). Later, she will learn to feel more self-accepting (Level 3), function in more than one culture (Level 4), have positive attitudes toward other ethnic and racial groups (Level 5), and finally have a global view of race and culture that is fully accepting (Level 6). Tomlinson found that although teachers understood the typology, they could not easily use it to foster the development of higher levels of ethnic identity.

SOCIAL INTERACTION AS A POWERFUL FORCE
IN LITERACY AND LEARNING

Social interaction is an important consideration in schools and is necessary for literacy and learning (Vygotsky, 1978). The context of the social interaction, its content, and students' existing levels of knowledge and motivation, however, determine whether learning takes the form teachers wish it to take. In other words, students learn from each other and from the teacher. *What* they learn from each other and the teacher interacts with motivation, strategy use, existing knowledge, and the context and quality of the interaction.

Students' Perceptions of the Role of Social Interaction

In a study of a high school integrated curriculum project (Hynd et al., n.d.), social support was perceived by students as the most important part of their positive perceptions during their year-long experience. Students often felt motivated by their teachers to achieve. However, they more often described positive interactions that were purely social in nature (friendships with teachers and other students) than interactions that promoted literacy and learning. Despite numerous observations by researchers of literature discussions where students engaged in lively interchanges about their multiple interpretations of texts, and despite the fact that these students regularly worked on group projects, students mentioned the friendships they developed with classmates as the reason for finding the integrated curriculum project motivating rather than their intellectual stimulation.

Students in advanced physics classes exhibited intense and frequent social interaction as they participated in group lab investigations and discussed physics principles in both formal and informal settings. Yet, only a few students reported that they relied on other students to learn physics principles. At times, social interaction appeared to be debilitating to their understanding of targeted principles. For example, one student talked two others into believing that a high powered rifle would *not* project a bullet according to the same principles as a less powerful projectile. All three students still held nonscientific ideas about projectiles until the end of the unit on projectile motion, even after laboratory investigations, live and videotaped demonstrations, class discussions, verbal explanations, reading, and talking to their parents outside of class. Thus, their social interaction was powerful and very engaging, but it did not help them to learn what they were expected to learn. In laboratory investigations, interactions often revolved around reading directions and completing the task rather than conceptual understanding, producing minimal learning from such activities. (Students reported enjoyment of lab activities, however.) In lower-level physical science classes, students in one class repeatedly said that, to learn, they had to ignore their peers, while students in another class only occasionally reported learning from their friends.

Why Are Social Interactions Sometimes Less Than Helpful?

Three possibilities follow: (1) The content to be learned may go against normal reasoning and, therefore, may not be conducive to "discovery" through discussion. The counterintuitive nature of the principles discussed in physics surely played a role in the difficulty the students had in understanding projectile motion after discussing their strongly held, nonscientific beliefs. Their beliefs seemed reasonable, while the scientific theory did not. (2) The structure of the task may keep students focused on lower-level routines. This was certainly the reason that students did not have meaningful discussions about laboratory investigations. Most of their mental energy went into completing the assignment. (3) Students' goals for discussion may conflict with the teacher's goals for discussion. Teachers often expect students to come away from discussions with certain preordained understandings of texts and the ideas in them. Students may not have this goal, but rather may view discussions as opportunities to make friends, take a side, explore power relationships, or engage in self-expression free of constraint. Only marginally are these discussions tied to the text or the assigned topic.

Our studies of social interaction in middle and high school classrooms seem to contradict findings pointing to the effectiveness of social interaction with younger students (e.g., Gambrell & Almasi, 1996). There may be no definitive word about the effectiveness of group discussions, however, especially in relation to the link between group interactions and achievement. Studies of cooperative learning (e.g., Johnson, Johnson, & Stanne, 1985; Slavin, 1996), which examine the interactions within groups who have been given highly constrained tasks and structures, document the positive effects on achievement of learning in groups. However, even that work suggests that certain types of groups are not effective. Achievement is reduced with certain participation structures (independent or competitive) (Johnson et al., 1985) or when all students are low functioning (Mulryan, 1994). Further findings indicate that the positive effects for cooperative group learning of fourth, fifth, and sixth graders appeared only when there were frequent high-quality group experiences. Frequent low-quality group interactions were associated with negative student outcomes. High-quality experiences were positively associated with ability scores. Finally, students' perceived status determines power relations in group interactions. Students with perceived high status dominate group interactions. They are more influential and are more likely to be thought of as leaders. Low-status students can suffer (Dembo & McAuliffe, 1987). The picture also is not clear concerning studies of elementary school students' open-ended literacy discussions. Laurie MacGilivray (in press), for example, uncovers the emergence of disturbing stereotypes of gender and power in the discussions of younger children about their reading and writing.

It may be, however, that the link between social interaction and achievement *appears* to lessen as students get older. Revolving around this question is the changing nature of middle and high schools and the students who populate them. For one, expectations for achievement may change, with increasing grade levels being associated with higher stakes for students' performance on traditional measures of achievement. Teachers at higher levels, believing that "knowledge is power" and being disciplinary experts, may care more that students learn the kind of in-depth disciplinary information deemed necessary to score well on graduation tests and entry tests into college. Therefore, they may be more dismayed when students veer off the topic or develop understandings that go against accepted beliefs. The expectation is that students will learn disciplinary knowledge, and the fear is that discussion may not be the most efficient avenue for that learning. There is a shift in view from a reliance on intrinsic motivators such as interest and enjoyment in learning to a reliance on more extrinisic motivators such as test scores. This shift in view is, arguably, an outcome of an education that is divided into distinct disciplines where a student's future in a discipline is largely incumbent on test scores and grades.

What Makes Discussions Worthwhile to Students?

Alvermann and colleagues (1996) did a multicase, multisite study of high school students' discussion of texts in content area classes that helps illuminate under what conditions discussions are helpful to students. Students had well-formed ideas about what it took to make a discussion work. They preferred working in small groups with others they knew and liked, and believed that contributing was important for everyone in that it helped the group stay focused on the topic. They also believed that the way teachers presented tasks and the content of their discussions were important. Open-ended tasks fostered more meaningful discussion than tasks that could be divided into components and completed independently, and liking the topic was crucial to students staying focused on the task. They used group discussions as opportunities for listening and learning from others, for voicing opinions, and for clarifying meaning. Just as in a study by Janice Almasi and Linda Gambrell (1994) with fourth graders, this study found that students did better in peer-led groups than in teacher-led groups, and preferred to be in charge of exploring meaning.

These investigations point to the power of social interaction in learning. Students feel motivated by group interaction. However, student goals for interaction and teacher goals for interaction sometimes conflict. The following implications for instruction are suggested: (1) the best tasks for group discussion are those that are open-ended and subject to multiple interpretations; (2) the best groups for discussion are those that are friendly and motivated by the topic; (3) because their motivation is important, students should be asked for ideas for topics of discussion; (4) middle and high school students can evaluate their discussions and should have the opportunity to do so; (5) teachers may experience difficulty in getting students to overcome inequitable relationships through discussion; and (6) teachers may need to take a more prominent role in guiding discussion or have students engage in another learning activity if they have a specific direction they want the discussion to take. Even though teachers need to take a more active role, they should not stop soliciting their students' ideas. On the contrary, teachers need constantly to appropriate students' understanding into their instruction. Otherwise, instruction may not mesh with student understandings and learning will not take place.

THE NECESSITY OF INNOVATIVE PROGRAMS
CONTAINING PERSONALLY SIGNIFICANT GOALS,
CHALLENGING TEXTS, AND SUPPORTIVE SOCIAL CONTEXTS

This final section discusses new types of programs that use, with middle and high school students, what we now know about engagement. As students grow older, they become more capable of developing complex mental concepts and of monitoring their own learning. Students are better able to self-regulate. At the same time, there are many reasons why students become less engaged in literacy and learning as they age. In high school, students learn that knowledge in each subject area becomes more specialized and they may feel that some areas are no longer relevant to their lives. In addition, Harter and colleagues (1992) suggest that as they progress through the grades, students have more opportunities to evaluate their work compared with others and may develop negative perceptions as a result, leading to loss of intrinsic motivation.

If the goal of schooling is to produce life-long, engaged learners who are productive members of society and critical consumers of information, then we need to look at innovative ways to engage students, while still preparing them for the rigors of the disciplinary expertise they will use in their careers. In one such innovative project, Ruby Thompson and Gloria Mixon (1997) from Clarke–Atlanta University sought to engage middle school students in reading by teaching parents to read books with their children. Their rationale was that parents offered more powerful modeling, and could provide more regular practice, give more immediate feedback, and provide more valuable reinforcement, than could teachers. Although they solicited the participation of 15 parents, only six attended and completed the sessions. They found that these six parents were capable of responding to the texts and of eliciting responses from their children. In addition, they found that parents and children reported enjoying the reading. A major drawback to their project, however, was that parents reported not having enough time. Parents also suggested that they should be allowed to choose their own books to read with their children, because they were not always interested in the books they had to read. That observation attests to the power of choice and autonomy.

David O'Brien and Deborah Dillon (1997) from Purdue University began an innovative program to help high-risk high school students become engaged in literacy. They developed the program based on the following principles: (1) students should be challenged, but allowed to succeed; (2) students should be given choice in what they learn and how they learn it; (3) students should have authentic purposes for engaging in literacy tasks; (4) instructional tasks should be interesting, yet flexible; and (5) students must be considered as unique individuals. Following these principles, they used computers and related technology with traditional reading and writing tools to help students read, discuss, and write. The students read newspapers, magazines, or their own peer-authored stories. They generated reports and multimedia projects shared with peers, parents, and guests. O'Brien and Dillon found that these students very rarely chose an activity that looked like a traditional school task. They were enthusiastic, however, about reading CD-ROM murder mysteries and writing stories that dealt with their lives and the popular culture. Students showed their engagement in literacy through their sustained interest and investment of time and energy. They showed their lack of engagement through "pretending" to read and write (e.g., playing with the fonts on the keyboard instead of typing). When they were engaged, they often constructed projects that "assaulted school culture with their popular culture." Thus, they exemplified the assertion that needs should be matched between the student and the culture of the school. The students' reactions to the various tasks illuminated the need for relevance.

Finally, Hynd and her colleagues (n.d.) studied an existing high school integrated curriculum program. In this program, ninth-grade students took classes from a team of three teachers who taught biology, world history, and English. These three teachers planned units with thematic ties across them, scheduled classes in longer blocks, engaged students in reports and projects across classes, taught the students similar strategies, and monitored students' progress carefully and often. In one thematic integration, for example, students learned about the Greeks in world history, read *The Odyssey* in English, and studied the contribution of Greek scientists in biology. Students in all classes were taught note-taking skills and how to make concept cards to help them study and remember unit information. They kept a common notebook, and they received a report of their progress bimonthly. Students in this program reported being much more highly engaged in these three classes than in their other school classes and described how the integration of information across classes generally made information easier to learn and more interesting.

However, teachers in the program reported significant difficulties in enacting a true integration. For one, there were curricular concerns. Teachers were not free to change the topics that had to be "covered," so they ended up changing the sequence of topics and settling for lower-level integrations than they would have liked. Other concerns were disciplinary in nature. Because the disciplines are traditionally separated in high school, the teachers came from different instructional traditions. Further, they rarely had the opportunity to observe each other's classes, and although they communicated constantly, the constraints of their schedules and class sizes restricted their ability to learn each other's instructional styles. Also, they were not generalists, but specialized in the topics they taught. Thus, they had difficulty seeing the possibilities for integration that they might have seen had they understood more about the other teachers' fields. In becoming a part of the team, teachers were less likely to be involved with others in their own discipline, making it more difficult to form ties within their fields and feeling somewhat ostracized by their colleagues who taught the same subject matter. Finally, there were interpersonal concerns. They worried that their philosophies and practices did not always agree. For example, the science teacher adopted a more impersonal stance with students than the other two teachers did, and they all worried about the effect of this difference on their students.

These challenges to integration are unique to middle and high school settings. In elementary schools, one teacher can integrate three or four subjects because the students stay in one class the entire day. Teachers are likely to have been educated as generalists, so they are more likely to have some knowledge of the curriculum across subject matters and can integrate teaching techniques more flexibly. Also, the curriculum is not as rigid as it is in high school classes and can be integrated more easily. Guthrie's (Guthrie, Van Meter, McCann, Anderson, & Alao, 1996) study of an integrated curriculum in third- and fifth-grade classes attests to the power of integrating reading, writing, and science. In his studies, students gained in motivation, strategy use, and knowledge over students in classes that were not integrated.

Although middle and high schools present unique challenges to educators, it behooves us to keep developing innovative programs aimed at increasing engagement and learning. These programs offer students a chance to become readers and thinkers. In developing such programs, educators should focus on providing students with ways to see the relevance of their activities to their everyday and future lives. Educators should give students some choice in the way activities are completed and offer students well-written materials that help them truly understand the topics they are studying. An atmosphere for social interaction should be provided that is focused and allows students to express themselves. Students should be provided with ample opportunities for engagement in reading.

REFERENCES

Alexander, P. (1995). Superimposing a situation-specific and domain-specific perspective on an account of self-regulated learning. *Educational Psychologist, 30*(4), 189–193.

Almasi, J., & Gambrell, L. (1994). *Sociocognitive conflict in peer-led and teacher-led discussions of literature* (Reading Research Report No. 12). Athens, GA: Universities of Georgia and Maryland, National Reading Research Center.

Alvermann, D. E., & Commeyras, M. (1994). *Gender, text, and discussion: Expanding the possibilities* (Perspectives in Reading Research No. 3). Athens, GA: Universities of Georgia and Maryland, National Reading Research Center.

Alvermann, D. E., Commeyras, M., Young, J. P., Randall, S., & Hinson, D. (1996). *Interrupting gendered discursive practices in classroom talk about texts: Easy to think about, difficult to do* (Reading Research Report No. 54). Athens, GA: Universities of Georgia and Maryland, National Reading Research Center.

Alvermann, D. E., Young, J. P., Weaver, D., Hinchman, K. A., Moore, D. W., Phelps, S. F., Thrash, E. C., & Zalewski, P. (1996). Middle- and high-school students' perceptions of how they experience text-based discussions: A multicase study. *Reading Research Quarterly*, *31*, 244–267.

Barnett, M. A. (1986). Sex bias in the helping behavior presented in children's picture books. *The Journal of Genetic Psychology*, *147*, 343–351.

Beck, I. L., McKeown, M. G., Omanson, R. C., & Pople, M. T. (1984). Improving the comprehensibility of stories: The effects of revisions that improve coherence. *Reading Research Quarterly*, *19*, 263–277.

Beck, I. L., McKeown, M. G., Sinatra, G. M., & Loxterman, J. A. (1991). Revising social studies text from a text-processing perspective: Evidence of improved comprehensibility. *Reading Research Quarterly*, *26*, 251–276.

Beck, I. L., McKeown, M. G., & Worthy, J. (1995). Giving a text voice can improve students' understanding. *Reading Research Quarterly*, *30*, 220–239.

Bloome, D. (1986). Reading as a social process in a middle school classroom. In D. Bloome (Ed.), *Literacy and schooling* (pp. 123–149). Norwood, NJ: Ablex.

Booth, J. R., & Hall, W. S. (1994). *Relationship of reading comprehension to the cognitive internal state lexicon* (Reading Research Report No. 14). Athens, GA: Universities of Georgia and Maryland, National Reading Research Center.

Britton, B. K., & Gulgoz, S. (1991). Interactive learning environments and the teaching of science and mathematics. In M. Gardner, J. G. Greeno, F. Reif, A. H. Schoenfeld, A. DiSessa, & E. Stage (Eds.), *Toward a scientific practice of science education* (pp. 111–140). Hillsdale, NJ: Erlbaum.

Britton, B. K., Schneider, M., Colomb, G., Sorrells, R., & Stimson, M. (1996). *Improving instructional text: Tests of two revision methods* (Reading Research Report No. 58). Athens, GA: Universities of Georgia and Maryland, National Reading Research Center.

Brodkey, L. (1992). Articulating poststructural theory in research on literacy. In R. Beach, J. L. Green, M. L. Kamil, & T. Shanahan (Eds.), *Multidisciplinary perspectives on literacy research* (pp. 293–318). Urbana, IL: National Conference on Research in English and National Council of Teachers of English.

Connell, J. P., & Ryan, R. M. (1984). A developmental theory of motivation in the classroom. *Teacher Education Quarterly*, *11*, 64–77.

Dembo, M., & McAuliffe, T. (1987). Effects of perceived ability and grade status on social interaction and influence in cooperative groups. *Journal of Educational Psychology*, *79*(4), 415–423.

Dreher, M. J. (1995). *Sixth-grade researchers: Posing questions, finding information, and writing a report* (Reading Research Report No. 40). Athens, GA: Universities of Georgia and Maryland, National Reading Research Center.

Dyson, A. (1989). *Multiple worlds of child writers: Friends learning to write*. New York: Teachers College Press.

Gambrell, L., & Almasi, J. (Eds.). (1996). *Lively discussions!* Newark, DE: International Reading Association.

Glynn, S. M. (1994). *Teaching science with analogies: A strategy for teachers and textbook authors* (Reading Research Report No. 15). Athens, GA: Universities of Georgia and Maryland, National Reading Research Center.

Glynn, S. (1996). *Effects of instructions to generate analogies on students' recall of science text* (Reading Research Report No. 60). Athens, GA: Universities of Georgia and Maryland, National Reading Research Center.

Glynn, S. (1997). *Learning from science text: Role of an elaborate analogy.* Athens, GA: Universities of Georgia and Maryland, National Reading Research Center.

Glynn, S., Law, M., Gibson, N., & Hawkins, C. (1994). *Teaching science with analogies: A resource for teachers and textbook authors* (Instructional Resource No. 7). Athens, GA: Universities of Georgia and Maryland, National Reading Research Center.

Gottfried, A. E. (1985). Academic intrinsic motivation in elementary and junior high school students. *Journal of Educational Psychology, 77*(8), 631–645.

Greene, S. (1994). The problems of learning to think like a historian: Writing history in the culture of the classroom. *Educational Psychologist, 29,* 89–96.

Guthrie, J. T., Alao, S., & Rinehart, J. M. (1997). Literacy issues in focus: Engagement in reading for young adolescents. *Journal of Adolescent & Adult Literacy, 40*(6), 438–450.

Guthrie, J. T., McGough, K., Bennett, L., & Rice, M. E. (1996). Concept-Oriented Reading Instruction: An integrated curriculum to develop motivations and strategies for reading. In L. Baker, P. Afflerbach, & D. Reinking (Eds.), *Developing engaged readers in school and home communities* (pp. 165–190). Mahwah, NJ: Erlbaum.

Guthrie, J. T., Van Meter, P., McCann, A., Anderson, E., & Alao, S. (1996, January). *Does Concept-Oriented Reading Instruction increase motivation, strategies, and conceptual learning?* Paper presented at the annual meeting of the American Educational Research Association, New York.

Harter, S., Whitesell, N. R., & Kowalksi, P. (1992). Individual differences in the effects of educational transitions on young adolescents' perceptions of competence and motivational orientation. *American Educational Research Journal, 29,* 777–808.

Hynd, C. R., Alvermann, D. E., & Qian, G. (1993). *Prospective teachers' comprehension and teaching of a complex science concept* (Reading Research Report No. 4). Athens, GA: Universities of Georgia and Maryland, National Reading Research Center.

Hynd, C., Guzzetti, B. G., McNish, M. M., Fowler, P., & Williams, W. (1997). *Texts in physics class: The contribution of reading to the learning of counterintuitive physics principles.* Athens, GA: Universities of Georgia and Maryland, National Reading Research Center.

Hynd, C., McNish, M. M., Lay, K., & Fowler, P. (1995). *High school physics: The role of text in learning counterintuitive information.* (Reading Research Report No. 10). Athens, GA: Universities of Georgia and Maryland, National Reading Research Center.

Hynd, C. R., McNish, M. M., Qian, G., Keith, M., & Lay, K. (1994). *Learning counterintuitive physics concepts: The effects of text and educational environment* (Reading Research Report No. 16). Athens, GA: Universities of Georgia and Maryland, National Reading Research Center.

Hynd, C., McWhorter, Y., Phares, V., & Suttles, W. (1994). The role of instructional variables in conceptual change in high school physics topics. *Journal of Research in Science Teaching, 31,* 933–946.

Hynd, C., Stahl, S., Glynn, S., Carr, M., Britton, B., Sanders, T., Tiller, D., & Wayne, M. (n.d.). *Observational analysis of an integrated curriculum.* Manuscript submitted for publication.

Johnson, R. T., Johnson, D. W., & Stanne, M. B. (1985). Effects of cooperative, competitive, and individualistic goal structures on computer assisted instruction. *Journal of Educational Psychology, 77*(6), 668–677.

L'Allier, J. J. (1980). *An evaluation study of a computer-based lesson that adjusts reading level by monitoring on task reader characteristics.* Unpublished doctoral dissertation, University of Minnesota, Minneapolis.

MacGilivray, L. (in press). Princesses who commit suicide. *Journal of Literacy Research.*

McCombs, B. L. (1996). Alternative perspectives for motivation. In L. Baker, P. Afflerbach, & D. Reinking (Eds.), *Developing engaged readers in school and home communities* (pp. 67–87). Mahwah, NJ: Erlbaum.

McDonald, S. M. (1989). Sex bias in the representation of male and female characters in children's picture books. *Journal of Genetic Psychology, 150,* 389–401.

McKeown, M. G., & Beck, I. L. (1994). Making sense of accounts of history: Why young students don't and how they might. In G. Leinhardt, I. Beck, & C. Stainton (Eds.), *Teaching and learning in history* (pp. 1–26). Hillsdale, NJ: Erlbaum.

Mulryan, C. M. (1994). Perceptions of intermediate students' cooperative small-group work in mathematics. *Journal of Educational Research, 87*(5), 280–291.

O'Brien, D. G , & Dillon, D. R. (1997). *Promoting the engagement of "at-risk" high school students: Perspectives from an innovative program.* Athens, GA: Universities of Georgia and Maryland, National Reading Research Center.

Oldfather, P. (1993). *Students' perspectives on motivating experiences in literacy learning* (Perspectives in Reading Research No. 2). Athens, GA: Universities of Georgia and Maryland, National Reading Research Center.

Oldfather, P. (1994). *When students do not feel motivated for literacy learning: How a responsive classroom culture helps* (Reading Research Report No. 8). Athens, GA: Universities of Georgia and Maryland, National Reading Research Center.

Oldfather, P., & Dahl, K. (1995). *Toward a social constructivist reconceptualization of intrinsic motivation for literacy learning* (Perspectives in Reading Research No. 6). Athens, GA: Universities of Georgia and Maryland, National Reading Research Center. (ERIC Document Reproduction Services No. ED 384 009)

Paris, S. G., & Turner, J. C. (1994). Situated motivation. In P. R. Printrich, D. R. Brown, & C. E. Weinstein (Eds.), *Student motivation, cognition, and learning* (pp. 213–237). Hillsdale, NJ: Erlbaum.

Patrick, J. J., & Hawke, S. (1982). Social studies curriculum materials. In *The current state of social studies: A report of Project Span* (pp. 105–185). Boulder, CO: Social Science Education Consortium.

Pressley, M., El-Dinary, P. B., Brown, R., Schuder, T. L., Pioli, M., Green, K., & Gaskins, I. (1994). Transactional instruction of reading comprehension strategies. *Reading and Writing Quarterly, 10,* 5–19.

Ravich, D. (1990). *The American reader: Words that moved a nation.* New York: Harper-Collins.

Reinking, D. (1996). *Electronic literacy* (Perspectives in Reading Research No. 4). Athens, GA: Universities of Georgia and Maryland, National Reading Research Center.

Slavin, R. (1996). Research on cooperative learning and achievement: What we know; what we need to know. *Contemporary Educational Psychology, 21,* 41–49.

Stahl, S. A., Hynd, C. R., Britton, B. K., McNish, M. M., & Bosquet, D. (1996). What happens when students read multiple source documents in history? *Reading Research Quarterly, 31,* 430–458.

Stahl, S., Hynd, C., Montgomery, T., & McClain, V. (1997). *In 1492, Columbus sailed the ocean blue: Reading multiple historical documents in a high school history class* (Technical Report). Athens, GA: Universities of Georgia and Maryland, National Reading Research Center.

Thompson, R., & Mixon, G. A. (1997). *The reading engagement of inner city African American parents: Implications for middle grades children's reading at home.* Manuscript in preparation.

Tomlinson, L. (1995). *The effects of instructional interaction guided by a typology of ethnic identity development: Phase I* (Reading Research Report No. 44). Athens, GA: Universities of Georgia and Maryland, National Reading Research Center.

Tomlinson, L. (1996). *Applying Banks' typology of ethnic identity development and curriculum goals to story content, classroom discussion, and the ecology of classroom and community: Phase I* (Instructional Resource No. 24). Athens, GA: Universities of Georgia and Maryland, National Reading Research Center.

VanSledright, B. A., & Kelly, C. (1997). *Reading American history: How do multiple text sources influence historical learning in fifth grade?* (Reading Research Report). Athens, GA: Universities of Georgia and Maryland, National Reading Research Center.

Vygotsky, L. S. (1978). *Mind in society: The development of higher psychological processes.* Cambridge, MA: Harvard University Press.

Wigfield, A., & Guthrie, J. T. (1997). Relations of children's motivation for reading to the amount and breadth of their reading. *Journal of Educational Psychology, 89*(3), 420–432.

Wineburg, S. S. (1991). On the reading of historical texts: Notes on the breach between school and academy. *American Educational Research Journal, 28,* 495–519.

Wineburg, S. S. (1994). The cognitive representation of historical texts. In G. Leinhardt, I. Beck, & C. Stainton (Eds.), *Teaching and learning in history* (pp. 171–208). Hillsdale, NJ: Erlbaum.

Yore, L. (1991). Secondary science teachers' attitudes toward and beliefs about science reading and science textbooks. *Journal of Research in Science Teaching, 28,* 55–72.

CHAPTER 5

Opportunities at Home and in the Community That Foster Reading Engagement

Linda Baker

STUDENTS' EXPERIENCES IN SCHOOL are powerful influences on the development of engaged reading, but school is not the only influential setting in the lives of children and adolescents. Families and communities are critical during the early childhood years. They help prepare children for school, and they also play an important role once children begin school in supporting and extending opportunities to learn. Bronfenbrenner (1979) proposed an influential model of human development that emphasized the importance of studying the various contexts in which children develop and the important interconnections among them. This perspective informs the present chapter as it examines children's literacy-related experiences at home and in the community as well as the home–school connections that affect the development of reading engagement. We show that the experiences individual children have within these settings vary considerably depending on the social and cultural contexts in which they live.

Consider the differences in perceptions of reading that children might bring to school with them in the following two situations. Parents in Baltimore were asked what they thought would be the best way to help their children learn to read. A low-income, African American mother of a preschooler responded:

> She'll pick a book on her own and she pretend she read but when I sits there and read with her I points to the word as I read along with her so she'll know how to identify the word that I am reading. I would think that soon, when she get in kindergarten, Amina she will be able to read.

Engaged Reading: Processes, Practices, and Policy Implications. Copyright © 1999 by Teachers College, Columbia University. All rights reserved. Prior to photocopying items for classroom use, please contact the Copyright Clearance Center, Customer Service, 222 Rosewood Dr., Danvers, MA 01923, USA, tel. (508) 750-8400.

A middle-income parent of a first grader responded:

> Reading with them and enforcing how much fun, how pleasurable reading is, not to approach it as a chore like "you *have* to learn to read." I read to her when she was very little . . . the inflection in my voice, my enthusiasm, the colors in the book . . .

These interview responses, which will be discussed further in a subsequent section of the chapter, were acquired during a 5-year longitudinal study called the Early Childhood Project. This NRRC project was designed to explore the contexts in which young urban children from various sociocultural groups become literate. Findings from the study will be used to illustrate key points throughout the chapter (for details, see Baker, Serpell, & Sonnenschein, 1995; Baker, Sonnenschein, Serpell, Fernandez-Fein, & Scher, 1994; Baker, Sonnenschein, et al., 1996; Serpell et al., 1997; Sonnenschein, Baker, Serpell, Scher, Goddard-Truitt, & Munsterman, 1996, 1997). Other NRRC research also will be highlighted as we consider conditions that foster reading engagement at home and in the community, and as we explore ways to promote connections between home and school that enhance student engagement. We begin by considering some methodological issues in the study of home influences.

STUDYING THE INFLUENCE OF HOME AND FAMILY

Research on home influences is not new, but the kinds of questions researchers ask have shifted over time. Early research on the role of the home in reading development focused mainly on family characteristics such as socioeconomic status and parental educational level (see Scott-Jones, 1991; White, 1982, for reviews). This led to conclusions like, "Children read better if their parents have a lot of money." But this is correlational information; it does not tell us what *causes* better reading. Clearly, money itself is not responsible.

A second wave of research, recognizing the limitations of status variables as indicators of the home literacy environment, focused more on characteristics of the environment itself, such as availability of books and educational materials (e.g., Durkin, 1966; Morrow, 1983). This led to conclusions like, "Children read better if there are lots of books in the home." This correlation, too, does not tell us what causes the advantage. If books sit unread on a bookshelf, they obviously will not do much good.

More recent still is the trend toward direct observation of the literate practices within the home, such as what goes on when an adult and child share a storybook (Heath, 1983; Teale, 1984) and what goes on during the course of daily life (Purcell-Gates, 1996). The former focus leads to conclusions like, "Children read better if their parents talk with them about the meaning of the story and ask them challenging questions." Sometimes these conclusions, too, are based on correlations. However, they come much closer to giving us practical information about ways to enhance children's early literacy development. Moreover, controlled experiments can be conducted to find out if the kinds of questions parents ask actually cause better reading. For example, one group of parents can be instructed in effective strategies for reading with their children, and a second group not given special instruction. Children in the two groups are compared both before and after a specified period of home reading activity. Such experiments have suggested a causal connection between parent behaviors and children's reading development (e.g., Whitehurst et al., 1994).

This changing emphasis is leading to a better understanding of the family's role in literacy development and how this role varies across different socio-cultural communities. When we think about ways to intervene to help improve children's chances of becoming successful and engaged readers, this change is especially important. We have much more hope of changing patterns of parent–child interactions around literacy events at home than we do parents' occupational status (Baker et al., 1994; Sonnenschein, Brody, & Munsterman, 1996). More-over, ethnographic studies focusing on daily routines have made it clear that the literacy-related interactions characteristic of families from nonmainstream socio-cultural groups also may be adaptive for particular aspects of literacy develop-ment (Heath, 1991; Taylor & Dorsey-Gaines, 1988).

Although research on home and family influences has not focused explicitly on engaged reading, we can infer a number of features of students' lives outside of school that are likely to foster engagement. The following list outlines a num-ber of features that have been shown through research to affect reading achieve-ment, motivations for reading, and/or amount of leisure reading (for reviews, see Baker, Scher, & Mackler, 1997; Guthrie & Greaney, 1991; Morrow, 1989; Scott-Jones, 1991).

HOME AND COMMUNITY FEATURES ASSOCIATED WITH READING ENGAGEMENT

- Adult reading material of various types is abundant.
- Children see adults reading frequently.
- Books for children are readily available.
- Children are read to regularly or read on their own regularly.
- Children are provided with space and opportunity for reading.
- Children go to the library and check out books regularly.
- Children and adults engage in frequent conversation.
- Children engage in language play through songs, rhymes, and word games.
- Parents take children on frequent outings.

- Children have access to technologies such as computers and television.
- Parents hold and express positive ideas about reading.
- Parents value literacy as a source of entertainment.
- Parents provide reading guidance and encouragement.
- Social interactions around reading are plentiful and pleasurable.
- Home literacy and school literacy are connected.

Notice that the experiences are not limited to those involving books and other print materials. Taking children on trips to the zoo, museum, or even the local park can provide them with valuable knowledge that will help them better understand material they read. Notice also the focus on not only what parents do but what they believe. Parental beliefs, values, and expectations have been acknowledged only recently as playing an important role in children's development (Goodnow & Collins, 1990; Serpell et al., 1997). As we shall see, parents' perspectives on how children learn to read are related to the opportunities they make available for their children in the home, their children's success in mastering important emergent literacy skills, and children's motivations for reading.

Recognizing that many of the studies of home influences were limited in their scope of inquiry, Baker, Sonnenschein, and Serpell (Baker et al., 1994) designed the Early Childhood Project to explore the contexts of early literacy development of a socioculturally diverse group of children, using both quantitative and qualitative techniques, over an extended period of time. The sample is described briefly here; specific findings are discussed in sections that follow. The study began in 1992–93 when 41 prekindergarten children enrolled at public elementary schools in Baltimore and their primary caregivers (usually mothers) were recruited. The families represented four sociocultural groups: (1) low-income African American; (2) low-income European American; (3) middle-income African American; and (4) middle-income European American. All but 10 of these families were from low-income communities. A second group of participants was recruited in 1994–95, when all children were in first grade. The expanded sample of about 68 families is more balanced with respect to income level. The project included a broad array of measures of home experiences, parental beliefs, and children's competencies, collected over a period of up to 5 years.

HOME READING EXPERIENCES

Storybook Reading

If you were asked, "What should parents do to help prepare their preschool child for learning to read in school?" you would probably say they should read to their child. Storybook reading in the home has long been considered among the most important things parents can do to prepare their child for literacy (Anderson, Hiebert, Scott, & Wilkinson, 1985). Virtually every educational advice book and article written for parents includes the recommendation, "Read to your child." Even books written at the turn of the twentieth century stressed the value of storybook reading (Huey, 1908). In the Early Childhood Project, frequency of storybook reading in kindergarten, as reflected through parental reports, was related to measures of children's orientation toward print. That is, children who were read to more frequently knew the names of more letters, had greater knowledge of print-related concepts such as where one begins reading in a storybook and where a word begins and ends, and had greater knowledge of the functions and uses of print materials, such as knowing that a coupon was used in a grocery store (Baker, Fernandez-Fein, Scher, & Williams, 1998; Sonnenschein, Baker, et al., 1996). Moreover, frequency of early storybook reading predicted word recognition in grade 3, even after controlling for the effects of maternal education (Baker & Mackler, 1997).

Observations of parents reading to their young children illustrate that children acquire literacy-related skills through social interaction (Sulzby & Teale, 1991). Parents provide support for their child's emerging competencies and tailor their interaction to the child's needs. Storybook readings with very young children usually involve frequent conversation between parent and child; the story itself may not even be read completely. As the child grows older, there is an increasing focus on the story, with the parents reading larger and larger segments of text without interruption. Another change in interaction involves giving children increasing responsibility for the activity, encouraging them to talk about the story, predict what will happen next, and even read the printed text. Shared storybook reading is a social activity that helps set the stage for the social interaction involving books that is a characteristic of older engaged readers (Guthrie et al., 1996).

Parents differ in the ways they read books with their children. Some of these differences seem to be important in helping children learn concepts about print and vocabulary. For example, children benefit more from storybook reading when there is lots of discussion about the story's meaning and when parents relate aspects of the story to the child's own experiences (Scarborough & Dobrich, 1994; Sulzby & Teale, 1991). Pellegrini, Galda, Perlmutter, and Jones (1994) studied shared book reading as a context for vocabulary development. Low-income mothers and their preschool children were videotaped reading informational texts such as toy advertisements and trade books. Children's learning of vocabulary from the texts was better if mothers encouraged children to talk about the material as they were reading it together.

Many people believe that shared storybook reading helps children develop an understanding of the relations between letters and speech sounds (phonemes), an important precursor to independent reading. With repeated joint storybook reading experience, it is thought, children come to pay closer attention to the print, noticing correspondences between the words that are being read and the letters on the page (Goodman, 1986). However, parents usually do not provide children with explicit information about print (Phillips & McNaughton, 1990). In the Early Childhood Project, kindergarten children were observed during a joint book reading session with the person they were most likely to read with at home, usually either the mother or an older sibling. All verbalizations were coded as to whether they dealt with print. Examples were, "N is also in your name," and "What's that word? Spell it." This kind of talk occurred very infrequently, although it was more common with certain types of books, such as rhyming, alphabet books, or predictable language books (Baker et al., in press; Munsterman & Sonnenschein, 1997). It may be that books with a more explicit educational focus are more useful for fostering the skills involved in early reading than are conventional storybooks. Indeed, frequency of experience with ABC-type books in prekindergarten was a much stronger predictor of word recognition skills in grade 3 than was experience with storybooks (Baker & Mackler, 1997).

Parents' descriptions of their children's early efforts to participate in shared storybook reading often reflect amusement but also suggest awareness of the value of such behaviors. A low-income, African American mother in the Early Childhood Project wrote of her 4-year-old son, "He likes to listen to you when you read to him and then he likes to tell you the words you told him, so that makes it likes he's reading the book to you, but he's just memorizing the words" (Baker et al., 1995). The extent to which parents encourage, support, and value such behaviors is likely to play a major role in stimulating children's desire to become engaged readers.

Although storybook reading clearly is important, some recent syntheses of research findings suggest that it may not be as effective as everyone assumes (Bus, van Ijzendoorn, & Pellegrini, 1995; Scarborough & Dobrich, 1994). Storybook reading does seem to make a difference in children's language development, their knowledge about print, and their early reading achievement. However, these effects are small from a statistical perspective because storybook reading accounts for only 8% of the variance in children's reading. Many different factors go into determining whether a child will be a successful reader, such as motivation, language ability, cognitive functioning, instruction, and other relevant home experiences. These additional factors together likely account for the remaining 92% of the variance in reading achievement. There clearly is more to what is important in preparing children for reading than storybook reading alone.

Other Print-Related Experiences

Children growing up in a literate society see print all around them in the environment, on product packaging, on billboards, on television, as well as in books and magazines. They learn the meaning of print—its functions and uses—by observing how print is used by others and through their own playful explorations (Neuman & Roskos, 1997; Purcell-Gates, 1996). Storybook reading is an activity that is more common among middle-income families than low-income families (Chaney, 1994; Heath, 1983; Raz & Bryant, 1990). However, preschool children from diverse sociocultural groups have a variety of experiences at home, extending beyond conventional storybook reading, that help prepare them for literacy. An absence of storybook reading does not mean that children are not exposed to literate practices. Other types of literacy events occur in the homes of lower-income and minority children, such as reading the mail or looking at an advertising flyer. These experiences, too, provide young children with opportunities to learn about the functions and uses of print (Baker et al., 1994; Goldenberg, Reese, & Gallimore, 1992; Sonnenschein, Brody, & Munsterman, 1996; Teale, 1986).

The following diary excerpt from a low-income mother in the Early Childhood Project reveals her preschooler's interest in print and her self-initiated efforts to learn about it:

> Then I decided we would take a nap. Unfortunately, Jessica decided she didn't want to. But while we were laying down, she was looking at my shirt. She was having me tell her the letters on it. She was having me tell her what they were and she was saying them as she was pointing to them. I would say them, then she would say them. And she went back and said the ones she knew.

Children also have opportunities to explore reading and writing through play. Pretend play is a common activity for most preschool children. Through pretend play children come to understand the physical and social world, including literate practices (Neuman & Roskos, 1997). Playing school quickly becomes a favorite activity once children are exposed to schooling. The mother of a first grader in the Early Childhood Project wrote in her diary that her son was starting to get into reading a lot. She credited his older sister in helping her son to read. He particularly liked reading to his sister because she played school with him and made a game out of reading (Baker, Scher, & Mackler, 1997).

The print that surrounds us on billboards, flyers, road signs, and stores typically is referred to as environmental print. What do children learn from this print that they encounter as part of their daily lives? Many preschool children learn the logos of familiar products and places. They can tell you that a bottle says "Coca-Cola" because of the distinctive way the words are written and the characteristics of the soda bottle itself. But if you print "Coca-Cola" on a plain sheet of paper, those same children likely will have trouble reading the words. Four-year-old Kerry, who eats Cheerios regularly at home, was shown a box of Cheerios and asked what it said on the box. She responded enthusiastically, "Cheerios!" When asked, "Where does it say Cheerios?" she pointed to the small print at the bottom of the package that read, "Toasty oat cereal." Environmental print is valuable in orienting the child to print and to the notion that print is meaningful and serves a specific function, but it does not seem to play a direct role in helping children learn to read. They need to know the letters of the alphabet before they will pay attention to the individual letters in the logo (Ehri, 1984; Harste, Burke, & Woodward, 1982; Sonnenschein, Baker, et al., 1996).

Independent Leisure Reading

Even before they begin formal schooling, many children choose to spend time looking at books independently (Baker, Scher, & Mackler, 1997). Their actions suggest they value literacy as a source of entertainment. Children from diverse income and ethnic groups are reported by their parents to engage regularly in this activity (Baker et al., 1994; Marvin & Mirenda, 1993; Raz & Bryant, 1990), although data from the Early Childhood Project indicate more frequent independent experiences with books by middle-income preschoolers than low-income preschoolers. Individual differences appear quite early, moreover, with some beginning readers engaging in frequent voluntary reading and others showing little inclination for such pursuits (Cunningham & Stanovich, 1993). In the Early Childhood Project, parental reports of the frequency with which their second graders chose to read material not assigned by their teachers were correlated with the children's self-reported motivations for reading (Scher & Baker, 1997).

The amount of reading experience a child has at home becomes an increasingly powerful predictor of reading achievement from kindergarten to fifth grade, as Rowe (1991) demonstrated. For the younger children in his study, the strongest predictors were being read to and reading to others, whereas for the older children, the strongest predictors were reading alone and talking about books with family and friends.

Unfortunately, the amount of time students spend in leisure reading decreases considerably as they grow older, with distressingly low levels of voluntary reading reported by middle school and high school students (Mullis, Campbell, & Furstrup, 1993). Because the amount and breadth of reading a student does outside of school is associated with reading achievement (Anderson, Wilson, & Fielding, 1988; Guthrie, Schafer, Wang, & Afflerbach, 1995), it is important that we understand the factors responsible for the decline and that we seek ways to increase leisure reading. Providing students with space and opportunity for reading at home is important, as is ensuring access to reading materials. Motivational factors clearly play a role also. In their study of African American, inner-city students in the middle grades, Thompson and Mixon (1997) found that other leisure-time pursuits were preferred to reading, such as watching television, listening to music, and playing games. Many students perceived reading as boring. When students did read for pleasure, they usually selected culture-specific popular magazines. Few students had personal book collections.

Public Libraries

An important community resource for promoting engagement in reading is the public library. Research has shown that library use is a powerful predictor of reading achievement and motivation (Guthrie & Greaney, 1991). Low-income preschoolers visit the library less frequently than middle-income preschoolers (Baker et al., 1994; Marvin & Mirenda, 1993; Raz & Bryant, 1990), and when older low-income students do go to the library, it is often for the purpose of completing school assignments rather than to get materials for pleasure reading (Thompson, Mixon, & Serpell, 1996). Parents living in the inner city may not take their young children to the public library because of genuine concerns about safety (Britt & Baker, 1997). Inner-city libraries often are plagued by budgetary problems and so do not offer the appealing milieu of suburban libraries that are rich in books as well as in multimedia technologies. The culture of the public library is different from the school library; children and adolescents perceive the public library as a place where they can engage in literacy activities of their own choosing (Alvermann, Young, & Green, 1997).

FAMILY DISCUSSIONS

Communication Styles

Children learn how to use language to communicate through their daily interactions with family and friends. The patterns of communication and social routines that children learn in the home may facilitate or impede their communication and literacy learning in school, depending on whether the patterns are similar or different. Heath (1983) compared patterns of language at home and at school in different communities in the Piedmont Carolinas, focusing on the use of questions. In the homes of children growing up in an African American, working-class community, parents used questions to elicit information they genuinely wanted to know. In contrast, teachers used questions requiring the students to display knowledge. Because it was clear to the students that the teachers already knew the answers, these questions seemed odd to the students and they resisted responding. The communicative demands of the classroom clashed with the rules guiding language use at home, creating a cultural mismatch. However, the communicative styles of parents in the middle-income community were similar to those of the teacher, and the students did not experience difficulty with questions in school. From the earliest years, these parents asked their children "known answer" questions, such as

"What color is your shoe?" and "What is that?" as they pointed to a picture of a cat in a storybook. Understanding the styles of communication used by families from diverse cultural groups can help teachers ease children's transition from home to school (Au, 1993).

Knowledge About Language

Growing up in an environment where parents and children regularly converse promotes the ability to think about language itself. This ability, known as metalinguistic awareness, plays an important role in literacy development. For example, children need to know the meanings of language terms like "word" and "sentence." Parents can help their children acquire metalinguistic awareness if they use terms that refer to language (Mason & Allen, 1986; Olson, 1984; Sulzby & Teale, 1991; Wells, 1986).

A particular kind of knowledge about language, called phonological awareness, is important in helping children learn to "break the code" in reading and writing (Ehri, 1991; Gough, Ehri, & Treiman, 1992). Phonological awareness involves knowledge about and sensitivity to the sounds that constitute language (i.e., phonemes). A simple kind of phonological awareness demonstrated by many preschoolers is the ability to recognize or produce words that rhyme with one another. Most children growing up in the United States have frequent experiences that can foster phonological awareness. They sing on a regular basis, listen to music frequently, and hear advertising jingles on TV and radio. They listen to caregivers reading books with rhyme and alliteration, and they play word games focusing on the sounds of the language (Baker et al., 1995; Chaney, 1994; Fernandez-Fein & Baker, 1997; Marvin & Mirenda, 1993).

Informal everyday interactions also can provide children with information about the sounds of the language. Consider the following experience of a low-income mother in the Early Childhood Project. She described how her 4-year-old daughter overheard her discussing angles with her husband as she was studying for the GED. The daughter came into the room to show them her right ankle. The mother explained that they were talking about angles not ankles, and that the words may sound alike but they are different (Baker et al., 1994; Baker et al., 1998).

Home experiences such as these have been shown to influence the development of phonological awareness as well as early reading competencies. Fernandez-Fein and Baker (1997) examined the frequency of relevant home experiences and the nursery rhyme knowledge of preschool children from diverse backgrounds in relation to rhyme sensitivity. Children who engaged in word games at home and who had good knowledge of nursery rhymes (reflecting at least in part frequent home experiences with these rhymes) scored higher on tests of rhyme detection and rhyme production. Moreover, nursery rhyme knowledge was a powerful predictor of word recognition in grades 1, 2, and 3 for a subset of these children who were followed longitudinally in the Early Childhood Project (Baker & Mackler, 1997). These relations held even after controlling for the effects of maternal education.

Other kinds of knowledge about language may be fostered by language play as well. For example, the creative verbal play that is highly valued in many black communities involves not only rhyming but also the use of metaphors and similes (Heath, 1983). This is a good example of a nonmainstream literate practice that prepares children to engage in a valued school literacy skill, using language in nonliteral ways.

Narrative Structure and Function

Language experiences that help children learn about the structure and function of narrative also are relevant for literacy development (Hemphill & Snow, 1996). These include storybook reading, oral storytelling, and mealtime conversation. Stories have regular and predictable structures that begin with an introduction of setting and main characters; then something happens that motivates the character to action; he or she responds to the action; there are certain consequences; and the problem is resolved at the end. Most of the books children encounter in the early years of schooling consist of stories following this predictable structure. Children understand material better when it is presented in a familiar format; reading and discussing stories with children will foster this familiarity (Doiron & Shapiro, 1988). Children from diverse sociocultural groups have frequent opportunities at home for learning about the structure and function of narrative (Baker et al., 1995; Heath, 1983).

THE WORLD BEYOND THE HOME

Out-of-school experiences that enrich children's general knowledge of the world are important in the development of reading engagement. Conceptual knowledge is critical to engagement, even at the earliest levels (see Chapter 2). Students acquire knowledge of the world not only through the information provided by books, but also through information available in the newer technologies of television and computers.

Television

Television serves as a tool for acquiring knowledge, which in turn promotes reading comprehension and interest in reading. In the Early Childhood Project, television viewing was the single activity most likely to be engaged in on a daily basis when children were in prekindergarten and kindergarten, by children from low-income and middle-income families, and by children of European American and African American descent (Baker et al., 1994). Television viewing continued to be the most common recurrent activity when the children were in grades 2 and 3 as well.

Statistics are abundant on the large amounts of television viewed by children in elementary and secondary schools. Opinions diverge as to the effects of frequent television viewing on reading achievement, but recent research suggests it may not be as detrimental as once assumed (Neuman, 1991; Reinking & Wu, 1990). In fact, moderate amounts of television viewing seem to be particularly valuable for children whose parents lack the financial resources to provide them with firsthand experience of different places, animals, and peoples (Searls, Mead, & Ward, 1985). Lest we are seen as painting a too-positive picture of television, we should mention that children who read more in their leisure time come from homes where there are rules about the amount of television viewing (Guthrie et al., 1995).

Computers

Computers are becoming increasingly common in many students' homes. For some preschoolers today, mastering the important skill of learning to write their name does not initially mean painstakingly forming each letter on paper using a crayon, but rather selecting each letter on the computer keyboard and seeing their name displayed on the monitor. Access to computer software, CD-ROMs, and the Internet considerably widens the horizons of students of all ages.

Reinking and Watkins (1997) introduced elementary school students and their parents to technology-based literacy activities. Students learned how to program in HyperCard to create multimedia book reviews. Parents volunteered to help out in the computer lab because of their interest in their children becoming computer literate. They embraced the project enthusiastically because of its goal of increasing independent reading. Engagement with technology at school carried over to increased literacy activities at home. For example, one girl used her computer skills at home to create a presentation about her teacher's trip to see a "boyfriend" on Valentine's Day, and then she presented it to the teacher and the class. This illustrates how technology can contribute to more meaningful literacy activities that connect home and school.

Outside Experiences

Children also acquire knowledge of the world through first-hand experience. The variety of experiences to which children are exposed by their families plays an important role in expanding the children's knowledge base. Children whose families provide them with rich and varied experiences have higher levels of reading achievement (Crain-Thoreson & Dale, 1992; Snow, Barnes, Chandler, Goodman,

& Hemphill, 1991). Trips to stores and libraries, visits with friends and relatives, participation in organized activities, and informal play all provide knowledge and experience that will serve children well in reading (Baker et al., 1995). Such experiences also contribute to motivations for reading. Children who become interested in a topic through their personal experiences likely will seek out books to learn more about the topic (Guthrie et al., 1996; Wigfield & Guthrie, in press).

FREQUENT OPPORTUNITIES FOR SOCIAL INTERACTION

Talking About Books with Friends and Family

Social interactions are important contexts for reading development and engagement (Alvermann & Guthrie, 1993; Baker, Afflerbach, & Reinking, 1996). This is true at school, as well as at home, and in the community. In an analysis of 1986 NAEP data, Guthrie and colleagues (1995) found that students who reported talking about things they read with friends and family at home read more frequently than those who did not at ages 9, 13, and 17. These social interactions were more powerful predictors of reading activity than the nature and extent of printed materials available in the home. Similar evidence of the importance of social interaction was obtained by Wigfield and his colleagues (Wigfield & Guthrie, in press; Wigfield, Wilde, Baker, Fernandez-Fein, & Scher, 1996). They found that students in grades 4, 5, and 6 often do not share reading activities with friends and family, but those who do so the most tend to read more frequently. This suggests that an effective strategy for increasing the amount of leisure reading that students engage in is to provide more opportunities for them to read with others.

Alvermann, Young, and Green (1997) adopted this approach in setting up book clubs at a local library where young adolescents could meet and talk about books. The students kept logs of their reading activity at home and kept journals where they recorded their reflections on their reading and the book club sessions. For the students, a powerful motivator to maintain participation in the clubs was the opportunity to meet with their peers and talk about books. Many students expressed the view that their school friends would think they were weird if they talked about books with them. New friendships were forged around literate activity in this informal nonschool-like setting.

Literacy Networks

The number of different people students interact with in literacy activities also affects reading development, as shown by Pellegrini, Galda, Shockley, and Stahl (1994) in a study of first-grade students' literacy networks. A literacy network might include the students' mother and older sibling for bedtime stories and two close friends for shared writing and reading in school. Pellegrini and colleagues speculated that the larger (i.e., more people) and more varied (i.e., people in different roles, such as teachers, parents, and friends) the social network, the greater the benefit. In their study, students who interacted with diverse people were better able to take the perspectives of others, seeing things from different points of view. They were also more metalinguistically aware, using mental terms such as "think" and linguistic terms such as "read" and "write," and they talked more about people and events not immediately present. As discussed earlier, these skills are associated with success in reading and writing.

Nurturing Environments

Children's earliest social interactions around books typically occur in infancy during shared storybook reading with parents. Storybook reading provides children with an opportunity to have a warm and supportive interaction with their parents and helps them view reading as a pleasurable activity (Baker, Sonneschein, & Cerro, 1997; Wigfield & Asher, 1984). Bus, van Ijzendoorn, and Pellegrini (1995) found that the quality of the relationships toddlers have with their caregivers is related to the frequency and nature of the storybook reading interaction.

In the observational study of shared book reading conducted as part of the Early Childhood Project, the social/affective features of the interaction also were analyzed. Features included the reader's expression while reading, physical contact with the child, appearance of engagement in the activity, sensitivity to the child's interest and engagement, and the child's appearance of engagement. The affective quality of the environment predicted children's motivation for reading in first grade and second grade. Thus, children who experienced reading in a comfortable and supportive social context at age 5 were more likely to recognize the value of reading, show interest in reading, and have positive concepts of themselves as readers in subsequent years (Baker, Scher, & Mackler, 1997; Munsterman & Sonnenschein, 1997).

Perhaps not surprisingly, the affective quality of the storybook reading was more positive when the reader was a parent rather than an older sibling (Munsterman & Sonnenschein, 1997). Pellegrini, Galda, Perlmutter, and Jones (1994) suggested that there may be more conflict when siblings engage in joint storybook reading, resulting in a cooler socioemotional climate for the interaction. Information collected within the Early Childhood Project indicates that low-income children are more likely to experience storybook reading with siblings, whereas middle-income children are more likely to experience it with adults (Sonnenschein, Brody, & Munsterman, 1996). Whether these different participation structures relate to subsequent differences in reading engagement is an important empirical question.

Family contributions to reading engagement extend beyond social interactions in literacy contexts such as shared book reading. Brody and colleagues (1994) demonstrated that families are less likely to provide an environment conducive to reading development when they have financial and interpersonal stresses. They assessed the effects of family relationships, parent psychological functioning, and financial resources in a sample of rural African American families. Parents with limited material resources were more likely to experience depression and hopelessness because of the stresses associated with financial concerns. This caused a disruption in the way the parents related to one another and supported one another in their child-rearing practices. This disruption interfered with the development of self-regulation in the family's young adolescents. They were less likely to set and attain goals, to plan actions and evaluate their consequences, and to persist in the tasks they undertook. These lower levels of self-regulation, in turn, limited the students' reading achievement.

LITERACY AS A SOURCE OF ENTERTAINMENT

Parental Perspectives on Literacy

The perspectives parents hold with respect to literacy affect the development of reading engagement in their children. In the Early Childhood Project, parents described in diaries the everyday activities of their children either as preschoolers or as first graders. The print-related experiences that were mentioned were categorized using a taxonomy adapted from the ethnographic work of Teale (1986) and Goldenberg, Reese, and Gallimore (1992) (see Baker et al., 1994; Baker et al., 1995). In a subsequent interview, parents were asked for their views about the most effective ways of helping their child learn to read (Baker, Sonnenschein, et al., 1996; Sonnenschein et al., 1997). The two sources of information together suggested three different perspectives on the nature of literacy:

1. Literacy is a source of entertainment; book reading itself is fun, and there are many other enjoyable activities in which literacy plays a role.
2. Literacy consists of a set of skills that should be deliberately cultivated; children should be given opportunities to practice their emerging competencies.
3. Literacy is an intrinsic ingredient of everyday life; by virtue of their participation in daily living routines such as shopping and food preparation, children come to see the functional value of literacy.

There were variations among sociocultural groups in the emphasis given to these perspectives. Middle-income parents showed greater endorsement of the perspective that literacy is a source of entertainment than did low-income parents, whereas low-income parents gave more attention to the perspective that literacy is a skill to be deliberately cultivated. Recall the responses of the two parents cited at the beginning of this chapter on how to help their child learn to read. The middle-income parent had more of an entertainment perspective, whereas the low-income parent focused more on the development of the skill of word recognition.

Similar sociocultural differences have been observed in other studies as well (Fitzgerald, Spiegel, & Cunningham, 1991; Goldenberg et al., 1992; Stipek, Milburn, Clements, & Daniels, 1992). Parents with low income and less education tend to emphasize drill and practice of reading skills over more informal opportunities for literacy learning. In contrast, middle-income parents adopt a more playful approach to literacy learning than do low-income parents. McLane and McNamee (1990) found that African American mothers of children in Head Start did not seem to be interested in or comfortable with their children's playful approaches to reading and writing. Instead they arranged reading and writing activities for their children that were much like school lessons.

Relations Between Parental Perspectives and Reading Engagement

The relations between parental perspectives and early literacy development have been explored in the Early Childhood Project (Baker, Sonnenschein, & Cerro, 1997; Scher & Baker, 1996, 1997; Sonnenschein et al., 1997; Sonnenschein, Baker, Serpell, & Schmidt, in press). Of interest was whether a child raised in a home that is predominantly oriented toward the view that literacy is a source of entertainment is more or less likely to develop reading-related competencies than a child raised in a home where literacy more typically is viewed as a set of skills to be acquired. A composite measure of the entertainment perspective was a better predictor of emergent competence in phonological awareness and knowledge about print than was a measure of the skills perspective (Sonnenschein, Baker, et al., 1996). An early emphasis on entertainment also predicted scores on the Woodcock Johnson Word Identification subtest in grades 1, 2, and 3, as well as on the Passage Comprehension subtest in grade 3. Finally, children whose parents responded in an interview that one of the reasons for reading was enjoyment, scored higher on a scale assessing motivations for reading in first grade (Baker, Sonnenschein, & Cerro, 1997; Scher & Baker, 1996).

Further support for a link between perspectives and engagement comes from a study by DeBaryshe (1995). She used an instrument assessing parental beliefs about reading aloud to young children to test a causal model of the relations between maternal beliefs, practices, and child outcomes. Additional measures included mothers' own literacy levels, maternal reports of the child's interest in reading, verbal interactions during parent–child book reading, maternal reports of the child's exposure to reading frequency, and measures of the child's language. Parents with high scores on the beliefs scale endorsed beliefs such as that book reading should be motivating and child centered, that a focus on meaning is more important than emphasizing code skills in the preschool period, and that children need daily exposure to book-related talk. The author hypothesized there would be causal pathways from maternal beliefs to reading frequencies and from maternal beliefs to storybook reading interactions; these pathways were in fact significant. She also hypothesized that beliefs would affect child interest indirectly through home practices. Unexpectedly, beliefs had a direct effect on child interest rather than an indirect effect.

Further research clearly is needed to better understand how parent beliefs mediate children's interest and engagement in reading. Perhaps the affective quality of the interactions, which DeBaryshe (1995) did not measure, is critical. This possibility is supported by evidence from the Early Childhood Project that affective aspects of book reading interactions predicted children's subsequent motivations for reading, but verbal interactions did not (Munsterman & Sonnenschein, 1997). Moreover, although parents who endorsed an entertainment approach reportedly engaged in more storybook reading with their children, frequency of storybook reading was not in itself correlated with children's motivation scores (Scher & Baker, 1996; Sonnenschein, Baker, et al., 1996). Nevertheless, results of these studies are important. They suggest that parents who emphasize basic skills, at the expense of enjoyable storybook reading focused on meaning, may convey a picture of reading as dull and lifeless that stays with the child long after school entry.

SOLID CONNECTIONS BETWEEN HOME AND SCHOOL

Communication Between Home and School

At the beginning of this chapter, we referred to Bronfenbrenner's (1979) view that human development occurs in an ecological context consisting of several layers of embedded systems or settings. He believed that it was important for there to be links between settings like home and school that promote mutual trust and shared goals. Bronfenbrenner also stressed the importance of two-way communication between the settings. We, too, believe that students are more likely to be engaged readers when parents and teachers have a shared understanding of students' needs and work together toward common goals (Baker, Allen, et al., 1996; Morrow & Young, 1996; Thompson, Mixon, & Serpell, 1996).

The need for open communication is apparent when we consider two common school practices: assigning homework to students and assessing students. Homework provides an important link between home and school, giving parents an opportunity to exert influence, offer help, and learn what is going on in school. However, simply advising parents to help their children with their homework is not sufficient; they are often unsure of the kinds of assistance they are to provide.

Moreover, research has shown that teachers differ in the nature of parental involvement they prefer (Baker, Sonnenschein, & Cerro, 1997). One teacher may want a parent to check her child's understanding of a book she read before writing a report on the book; another teacher simply may want the parent to help the child find a suitable book. It is important that there be clear communication of goals, expectations, and problems across settings.

Regarding assessment, parents typically are provided with some information about the tests their children receive in school, but they often do not really understand it. Afflerbach (1996) identified several reasons why effective communication of assessment information is critical. It can lead to: (1) increased parental support of instructional programs that are tied to assessments; (2) increased understanding of the links between home and school reading; and (3) increased interest in how student development in reading is measured.

Social and Cultural Differences in the Connectedness of Home and School

Although parents from different cultural groups all want their children to succeed in school, they have different views of their roles in the process. Lareau (1989) found that parents in working-class families believed teachers to be primarily responsible for education; relations between home and school were characterized by separation. In contrast, parents in middle-class families believed that education is a shared responsibility between teachers and parents; for them, relations between home and school were characterized by interconnectedness. The Early Childhood Project addressed home–school responsibilities specifically with respect to reading. Encouragingly, low-income parents of prekindergarten children were as likely as middle-income parents and teachers to express the view that school and home share the responsibility for helping children learn to read (Baker, Allen, et al., 1996).

Differences in perceptions of connectedness of home and school have been reported for students as well as parents. Some students do not see the relation between what they learn in school and what goes on outside of school. This is especially likely to occur when the cultural practices of the home and school communities differ. Recall, for example, the home–school mismatch in communication styles that created problems for some minority students until teachers accommodated the differences (Au, 1993; Heath, 1983). Teachers interviewed by McCarthey (1997) seemed to think that merely providing many literacy opportunities would result in students making connections between home and school. This did seem to occur for the middle-class, European American third and fourth graders in their classes, but not for the working-class students of color. The former students read fiction at home and school, shared their writing with the entire class, and brought items from home to show peers. The latter students did not participate in home literacy activities that matched the school activities, and they did not share items or stories from home, keeping their home and school lives separate.

Interest is increasing among researchers, educators, and policy makers in developing programs that build links between students' lives at home and in school. Parents are often unsure of how to help their children with literacy at home. Many low-income and minority parents, in particular, do not believe they have the resources to help (Edwards, 1994; Hannon, 1995; Morrow & Young, 1996). Several intervention programs have focused on teaching these parents how to share storybooks with their children, and there is some evidence that this approach has positive effects (Edwards, 1994; Whitehurst et al., 1994). However, the skills and interaction processes that are valued by educators may not necessarily be those that parents regard as important. Recall that many low-income and minority parents believe that effective assistance means emphasizing letter identification and spelling–sound correspondences. Care must be taken to ensure that family literacy programs make sense to parents. It is important that parents' beliefs and perspectives be respected.

Programs Involving Parents in Coordinating Home and School Reading

One obstacle to the development of reading engagement faced by many low-income students is a lack of access to books and other reading materials at home (Neuman, 1986). It is well established that students who read more at home are higher achievers. One effective intervention strategy is to provide students with books to take home from school and to encourage socially interactive book reading experiences at home. Unfortunately, schools in low-income neighborhoods often lack the resources to purchase books for this purpose, unless they receive outside assistance (Britt & Baker, 1997). We consider here several projects that were effective in their efforts to provide resources, resulting in greater student engagement.

Running Start is a motivational program, set up by the nonprofit organization Reading is Fundamental with corporate support, aimed at increasing first-grade students' opportunities for reading high-quality literature at home and at school. A major goal is to involve parents in their children's literacy development. Students are challenged to read or have someone read to them 21 books in a 10-week period; the prize for meeting the challenge is a book for the student to own. Gambrell (Gambrell, Almasi, Xie, & Heland, 1995; Gambrell & Morrow, 1996) evaluated the effectiveness of the program in an inner city populated predominantly by families of minority backgrounds. Participants in the Running Start program were compared with a similar group of students and parents on several measures of motivation and participation in literacy activities. Clear differences between groups were found. The Running Start students spent more time in independent reading, discussed books more with family members, took more books home from school, participated in more family reading activities, and showed higher levels of reading motivation. In other words, access to books and social interaction around books are important factors in promoting home and school engagement in reading.

Another successful program is especially valuable for students who do not speak English as their native language. A major challenge facing teachers in American schools is the increasing linguistic and cultural diversity of the students in their classrooms (Fitzgerald, 1995). Not only is there a mismatch between the cultures of home and school, but the students often do not have English books available in their homes, nor do they have anyone to read to them at home. Koskinen, Blum, and their colleagues devised a program where audiotapes of books that were read in the classroom were sent home with a tape recorder and a print copy of the book (Blum et al., 1995; Koskinen et al., 1995). Parents were encouraged to participate with their children in this "special reading homework." Because reading the same book repeatedly helps young readers develop fluency and accuracy, the students were encouraged to listen to the book and read along two to three times each day to themselves or someone in their family. The books available to the children accommodated a variety of reading interests and ability levels. First-grade students who were second-language learners benefited substantially in terms of fluency, reading accuracy, and motivation for reading. Parents and teachers reported that the students read more and showed increased confidence and independence in their reading.

Morrow and Young (1996) extended a successful school-based literature program to the home. Elements of the home program included engaging parents and children in storybook reading, writing journals, and using *Highlights for Children* at home as well as at school. Monthly meetings were held with teachers, parents, and students sharing ideas and working together. An evaluation of the program was conducted in an inner-city community populated predominantly by African American and Hispanic families. Students in first through third grades who participated in the program were compared with a similar group of students who did not participate. Participants demonstrated higher reading achievement and motivation for reading than nonparticipants.

Shockley, Michalove, and Allen (1995) attempted to build closer connections with families by blending the contributions of home and school. Children in Shockley's first-grade class chose books from the classroom library to take home with them each night. The child could read, or another family member could read to the child, or they could read together. Families were encouraged to engage in a natural conversation about the book and to record their responses in a journal. Shockley responded to each family's entry. She also created a class book based on family stories contributed by the families. She encouraged families to tell her about their child, and she asked them to reflect on how their child learned to read. Families were invited to attend meetings at the school. Parents reported that the opportunities to be actively involved with their children's reading and writing, and with their children's teachers, were very important to them. These activities helped create closer links between children's home lives and their school lives.

How Understanding Home Literacy Can Help Teachers Foster Reading Engagement

Teachers who are able to learn about the literacy resources and opportunities available to their students outside of the classroom are in a better position to design curriculum and participation structures that are consonant with the children's home experiences (McCarthey, 1997; Serpell, Baker, & Sonnenschein, 1995). McCarthey found that teachers in a school serving a culturally diverse population tended to have more information about the home lives of their middle-income students, in part because the students themselves were more willing to provide that information through their writing and class discussions. The teachers, who themselves had European American, middle-class backgrounds, designed curriculum and participation structures that were more congruent with middle-class home literacy experiences than with working-class experiences.

A hallmark of projects designed to promote stronger connections between home and school is that teachers make special efforts to learn about students' home lives. They talk with parents about ways of working together to enhance students' literacy (Moll & Greenberg, 1990; Morrow & Young, 1996; Shockley et al., 1995). Shared understandings are important in paving the way for the creation of effective partnerships (Serpell, Baker, Sonnenschein, Gorham, & Hill, 1996; Thompson et al., 1996). Moll and Greenberg created partnerships between classrooms and working-class, Mexican American communities in Tucson, Arizona, that drew on household "funds of knowledge" for curriculum development. Such knowledge might include tractor and automobile repair, household management, agriculture, construction, religion, and economics. Teachers visited homes to learn about these funds of knowledge, as well as the social networks that sustained them. Then teachers developed units of study based on family knowledge and experiences, often involving family members as resources, that engaged students in meaningful ways with literacy.

Effective approaches to strengthening home–school connections include recruiting parents as partners, placing real decision-making power with parents, and creating culturally compatible classrooms that reflect the language and culture of the students (Thompson et al., 1996). As Oldfather and Wigfield (1996) wrote, engaged reading can be promoted if school, family, and community members collaborate "to share personally and socially meaningful literate activities" (p. 109).

CONCLUSION

There are many opportunities and experiences available to students in the home and community that promote engagement. We have seen that students are more likely to be engaged readers when they are raised in environments rich in print, oral language, and opportunities for acquiring knowledge. They are more likely to be engaged readers when they grow up in environments that provide opportunities for nurturing social interactions around books and where caregivers view literacy as a source of entertainment. We also have seen that connections between home and school are important. Students are more likely to be engaged readers when they grow up in environments where the connections between home and school are strong and are based on mutual respect and reciprocity. Many different intervention approaches that involve parents in coordinating home and school reading can increase reading engagement. Teachers who are familiar with their students' home literacy practices are in a better position to foster reading engagement. In summary, current research has made it clear that the family and wider community are critical not only in preparing young children to learn to read but also in sustaining skills, motivations, and strategies for literacy learning in the elementary school years and beyond.

NOTE

Preparation of this chapter and some of the research described in it was supported in part by the National Reading Research Center of the Universities of Georgia and Maryland and by the National Institute of Child Health and Human Development (principal investigators Linda Baker, Susan Sonnenschein, and Robert Serpell). I deeply appreciate the contributions of my other colleagues on the Early Childhood Project: Robert Serpell, Susan Sonnenschein, Hibist Astatke, Evangeline Danseco, Marie Dorsey, Sylvia Fernandez-Fein, Victoria Goddard-Truitt, Linda Gorham, Susan Hill, Kirsten Mackler, Tunde Morakinyo, Kim Munsterman, Deborah Scher, Diane Schmidt, Dewi Smith, Sharon Teuben-Rowe, and Helen Williams. Any opinions, findings, conclusions, or recommendations expressed in this chapter are those of the author and do not necessarily reflect the views of the National Reading Research Center, the Office of Educational Research and Improvement, or the National Institute of Child Health and Human Development.

REFERENCES

Afflerbach, P. (1996). Engaged assessment of engaged reading. In L. Baker, P. Afflerbach, & D. Reinking (Eds.), *Developing engaged readers in school and home communities* (pp. 191–214). Mahwah, NJ: Erlbaum.

Alvermann, D. E., & Guthrie, J. T. (1993). The National Reading Research Center. In A. P. Sweet & J. I. Anderson (Eds.), *Reading research into the year 2000* (pp. 129–150). Hillsdale, NJ: Erlbaum.

Alvermann, D. E., Young, J. P., & Green, C. (1997). *Adolescents' negotiations of voluntary out-of-school reading discussions* (Reading Research Report No. 71). Athens, GA: Universities of Georgia and Maryland, National Reading Research Center.

Anderson, R. C., Hiebert, E. H., Scott, J. A., & Wilkinson, I. A. (1985). *Becoming a nation of readers: The report of the Commission of Reading*. Washington, DC: National Institute of Education.

Anderson, R. C., Wilson, P. T., & Fielding, L. G. (1988). Growth in reading and how children spend their time outside of school. *Reading Research Quarterly, 23*, 285–303.

Au, K. H. (1993). *Literacy instruction in multicultural settings*. Fort Worth, TX: Harcourt, Brace, Jovanovich.

Baker, L., Afflerbach, P., & Reinking, D. (1996). Developing engaged readers in school and home communities: An overview. In L. Baker, P. Afflerbach, & D. Reinking (Eds.), *Developing engaged readers in school and home communities* (pp. xii–xxvii). Mahwah, NJ: Erlbaum.

Baker, L., Allen, J. B., Shockley, B., Pellegrini, A. D., Galda, L., & Stahl, S. (1996). Connecting school and home: Constructing partnerships to foster reading development. In L. Baker, P. Afflerbach, & D. Reinking (Eds.), *Developing engaged readers in school and home communities* (pp. 21–41). Mahwah, NJ: Erlbaum.

Baker, L., Fernandez-Fein, S., Scher, D., & Williams, H. (1998). Home experiences related to the development of word recognition. In J. L. Metsala & L. C. Ehri (Eds.), *Word recognition in beginning literacy* (pp. 263–287). Mahwah, NJ: Erlbaum.

Baker, L., & Mackler, K. (1997, April). Contributions of children's emergent literacy skills and home experiences to grade 2 word recognition. In R. Serpell, S. Sonnenschein, & L. Baker (Chairs), *Patterns of emerging competence and sociocultural context in the early appropriation of literacy*. Symposium presented at the meeting of the Society for Research in Child Development, Washington, DC.

Baker, L., Scher, D., & Mackler, K. (1997). Home and family influences on motivations for literacy. *Educational Psychologist, 32*, 69–82.

Baker, L., Serpell, R., & Sonnenschein, S. (1995). Opportunities for literacy learning in the homes of urban preschoolers. In L. M. Morrow (Ed.), *Family literacy: Connections in schools and communities* (pp. 236–252). Newark, DE: International Reading Association.

Baker, L., Sonnenschein, S., & Cerro, L. C. (1997). *Mothers' reports of their homework practices with their elementary school children and a comparison with teachers' views*. Unpublished manuscript, University of Maryland, Baltimore County.

Baker, L., Sonnenschein, S., Serpell, R., Fernandez-Fein, S., & Scher, E. (1994). *Contexts of emergent literacy: Everyday home experiences of urban pre-kindergarten children* (Reading Research Report No. 24). Athens, GA: Universities of Georgia and Maryland, National Reading Research Center.

Baker, L., Sonnenschein, S., Serpell, R., Scher, D., Fernandez-Fein, S., Munsterman, K., Hill, S., Goddard-Truitt, V., & Danseco, E. (1996). Early literacy at home: Children's experiences and parents' perspectives. *The Reading Teacher, 50*, 70–72.

Blum, I. H., Koskinen, P. S., Tennant, N., Parker, E. M., Straub, M., & Curry, C. (1995). Using audiotaped books to extend classroom literacy instruction into the homes of second-language learners. *Journal of Reading Behavior, 27*, 535–563.

Britt, G., & Baker, L. (1997). *Engaging parents and kindergartners in reading through class lending library* (Instructional Resource No. 41). Athens, GA: Universities of Georgia and Maryland, National Reading Research Center.

Brody, G. H., Stoneman, Z., Flor, D., McCrary, C., Hastings, L., & Conyers, O. (1994). *Financial resources, parent psychological functioning, parent co-caregiving, and early adolescent reading competence in rural two-parent African American families* (Reading Research Report No. 20). Athens, GA: Universities of Georgia and Maryland, National Reading Research Center.

Bronfenbrenner, U. (1979). *The ecology of human development.* Cambridge, MA: Harvard University Press.

Bus, A. G., van Ijzendoorn, M. H., & Pellegrini, A. D. (1995). Joint book reading makes for success in learning to read: A meta-analysis on intergenerational transmission of literacy. *Review of Educational Research, 65*, 1–21.

Chaney, C. (1994). Language development, metalinguistic awareness, and emergent literacy skills of 3-year-old children in relation to social class. *Applied Psycholinguistics, 15*, 371–394.

Crain-Thoreson, C., & Dale, P. S. (1992). Do early talkers become early readers? Linguistic precocity, preschool language, and emergent literacy. *Developmental Psychology, 28*, 421–429.

Cunningham, A. E., & Stanovich, K. E. (1993). Children's literacy environments and early word recognition subskills. *Reading and Writing: An Interdisciplinary Journal, 5*, 193–204.

DeBaryshe, B. D. (1995). Maternal belief systems: Linchpin in the home reading process. *Journal of Applied Developmental Psychology, 16*, 1–20.

Doiron, R., & Shapiro, J. (1988). Home literacy environment and children's sense of story. *Reading Psychology, 9*, 187–201.

Durkin, D. (1966). *Children who read early.* New York: Teachers College Press.

Edwards, P. A. (1994). Responses of teachers and African American mothers to a book reading intervention program. In D. K. Dickinson (Ed.), *Bridges to literacy: Children, families, and schools* (pp. 175–208). Cambridge, MA: Blackwell.

Ehri, L. C. (1984). How orthography alters spoken language competencies in children learning to read and spell. In J. Downing & R. Valdim (Eds.), *Language awareness and learning to read* (pp. 119–147). New York: Springer-Verlag.

Ehri, L. C. (1991). Development of the ability to read words. In R. Barr, M. L. Kamil, P. B. Mosenthal, & P. D. Pearson (Eds.), *Handbook of reading research* (Vol. 2, pp. 383–417). White Plains, NY: Longman.

Fernandez-Fein, S., & Baker, L. (1997). Rhyme sensitivity and relevant experiences in preschoolers from diverse backgrounds. *Journal of Literacy Research, 29*, 433–459.

Fitzgerald, J. (1995). English-as-a-second-language reading instruction in the United States: A research review. *JRB: A Journal of Literacy, 27*, 115–152.

Fitzgerald, J., Spiegel, D. L., & Cunningham, J. W. (1991). The relationship between parental literacy level and perceptions of emergent literacy. *Journal of Reading Behavior, 23*, 191–219.

Gambrell, L. B., Almasi, J. F., Xie, Q., & Heland, V. J. (1995). Helping first graders get a running start in reading. In L. M. Morrow (Ed.), *Family literacy: Connections in schools and communities* (pp. 143–154). Newark, DE: International Reading Association.

Gambrell, L. B., & Morrow, L. M. (1996). *Elementary students' motivation to read* (Reading Research Report No. 52). Athens, GA: Universities of Georgia and Maryland, National Reading Research Center. (ERIC Document Reproduction Services No. ED 395 279)

Goldenberg, C., Reese, L., & Gallimore, R. (1992). Effects of literacy materials from school on Latino children's home experiences and early reading achievement. *American Journal of Education, 100,* 497–536.

Goodman, Y. (1986). Children coming to know literacy. In W. H. Teale & E. Sulzby (Eds.), *Emergent literacy: Writing and reading* (pp. 1–14). Norwood, NJ: Ablex.

Goodnow, J. J., & Collins, W. A. (1990). *Development according to parents.* Hillsdale, NJ: Erlbaum.

Gough, P. B., Ehri, L. C., & Treiman, R. (Eds.). (1992). *Reading acquisition.* Hillsdale, NJ: Erlbaum.

Guthrie, J. T., & Greaney, V. (1991). Literacy acts. In R. Barr, M. L. Kamil, P. Mosenthal, & P. D. Pearson (Eds.), *Handbook of reading research* (Vol. II, pp. 68–96). New York: Longman.

Guthrie, J. T., Schafer, W. D., Wang, Y. Y., & Afflerbach, P. (1995). Relationships of instruction on reading: An exploration of social, cognitive, and instructional connections. *Reading Research Quarterly, 30*(1), 8–25.

Guthrie, J. T., Van Meter, P., McCann, A. D., Wigfield, A., Bennett, L., Poundstone, C. C., Rice, M. E., Faibisch, F. M., Hunt, B., & Mitchell, A. (1996). Growth of literacy engagement: Changes in motivations and strategies during Concept-Oriented Reading Instruction. *Reading Research Quarterly, 31,* 306–332.

Hannon, P. (1995). *Literacy, home, and school.* Bristol, PA: Falmer.

Harste, J. C., Burke, C. L., & Woodward, V. A. (1982). Children's language and world: Initial encounters with print. In J. A. Langer & M. T. Smith-Burke (Eds.), *Reader meets author/Bridging the gap* (pp. 105–131). Newark, DE: International Reading Association.

Heath, S. B. (1983). *Ways with words: Language, life and work in communities and classrooms.* Cambridge: Cambridge University Press.

Heath, S. B. (1991). The sense of being literate: Historical and cross-cultural features. In R. Barr, M. L. Kamil, P. Mosenthal, & P. D. Pearson (Eds.), *Handbook of reading research* (Vol. II, pp. 3–25). New York: Longman.

Hemphill, L., & Snow, C. (1996). Language and literacy development: Discontinuities and differences. In D. R. Olson & N. Torrance (Eds.), *The handbook of education and human development* (pp. 173–201). Cambridge, MA: Blackwell.

Huey, E. B. (1908). *The psychology and pedagogy of reading.* Cambridge, MA: MIT Press.

Koskinen, P. S., Blum, I. H., Tennant, N., Parker, E. M., Straub, M., & Curry, C. (1995). *Have you heard any good books lately? Encouraging shared reading at home with books and audiotapes* (Instructional Resource No. 15). Athens, GA: Universities of Georgia and Maryland, National Reading Research Center.

Lareau, A. (1989). *Home advantage: Social class and parental intervention in elementary education.* London: Falmer.

Marvin, C., & Mirenda, P. (1993). Home literacy experiences of preschoolers enrolled in Head Start and special education programs. *Journal of Early Intervention, 17*, 351–367.

Mason, J. M., & Allen, J. (1986). A review of emergent literacy with implications for research and practice in reading. In E. Z. Rothkopf (Ed.), *Review of research in education* (Vol. 13, pp. 3–48). Washington, DC: American Educational Research Association.

McCarthey, S. J. (1997). Connecting school literacy practices in classrooms with diverse populations. *Journal of Literacy Research, 29*, 145–182.

McLane, J. B., & McNamee, G. D. (1990). *Early literacy*. Cambridge, MA: Harvard University Press.

Moll, L. C., & Greenberg, J. B. (1990). Creating zones of possibilities: Combining social contexts for instruction. In L. C. Moll (Ed.), *Vygotsky and education* (pp. 319–348). Cambridge: Cambridge University Press.

Morrow, L. M. (1983). Home and school correlates of early interest in literature. *Journal of Educational Research, 76*, 221–230.

Morrow, L. M. (1989). *Literacy development in the early years*. Englewood Cliffs, NJ: Prentice-Hall.

Morrow, L. M., & Young, J. (1996). *Parent, teacher, and child participation in a collaborative family literacy program: The effects on attitude, motivation, and literacy achievement* (Reading Research Report No. 64). Athens, GA: Universities of Georgia and Maryland, National Reading Research Center.

Mullis, I. V. S., Campbell, J. R., & Furstrup, A. E. (1993). *NAEP 1992 reading report card for the nation and the states*. Washington, DC: Educational Testing Service/ Office of Educational Research and Improvement.

Munsterman, K. A., & Sonnenschein, S. (1997, April). Qualities of storybook reading interactions and their relations to emergent literacy. In R. Serpell, S. Sonnenschein, & L. Baker (Chairs), *Patterns of emerging competence and sociocultural context in the early appropriation of literacy*. Symposium presented at the meeting of the Society for Research in Child Development, Washington, DC.

Neuman, S. (1986). The home environment and fifth-grade students' leisure reading. *Elementary School Journal, 86*, 333–343.

Neuman, S. B. (1991). *Literacy in the television age*. Norwood, NJ: Ablex.

Neuman, S., & Roskos, K. (1997). Literacy knowledge in practice: Contexts of participation for young writers and readers. *Reading Research Quarterly, 32*, 10–32.

Oldfather, P., & Wigfield, A. (1996). Children's motivations for literacy learning. In L. Baker, P. Afflerbach, & D. Reinking (Eds.), *Developing engaged readers in school and home communities* (pp. 89–113). Mahwah, NJ: Erlbaum.

Olson, D. R. (1984). "See! Jumping!" Some oral language antecedents of literacy. In H. Goelman, A. A. Oberg, & F. Smith (Eds.), *Awakening to literacy* (pp. 185–192). London: Heinemann.

Pellegrini, A. D., Galda, L., Perlmutter, J., & Jones, I. (1994). *Joint reading between mothers and their Head Start children: Vocabulary development in two text formats* (Reading Research Report No. 13). Athens, GA: Universities of Georgia and Maryland, National Reading Research Center.

Pellegrini, A. D., Galda, L., Shockley, B., & Stahl, S. A. (1994). *The nexus of social and literacy experiences at home and school: Implications for first-grade oral language and literacy* (Reading Research Report No. 21). Athens, GA: Universities of Georgia and Maryland, National Reading Research Center.

Phillips, G., & McNaughton, S. (1990). The practice of storybook reading to preschoolers in mainstream New Zealand families. *Reading Research Quarterly, 25,* 196–212.

Purcell-Gates, V. (1996). Stories, coupons, and the TV Guide: Relationships between home literacy experiences and emergent literacy knowledge. *Reading Research Quarterly, 31,* 406–428.

Raz, I. T., & Bryant, P. (1990). Social background, phonological awareness and children's reading. *British Journal of Developmental Psychology, 8,* 209–225.

Reinking, D., & Watkins, J. (1997). *A formative experiment investigating the use of multimedia book reviews to increase elementary students' independent reading* (Reading Research Report No. 73). Athens, GA: Universities of Georgia and Maryland, National Reading Research Center.

Reinking, D., & Wu, J. H. (1990). Reexamining the research on television and reading. *Reading Research and Instruction, 29,* 30–43.

Rowe, K. J. (1991). The influence of reading activity at home on students' attitudes towards reading, classroom attentiveness and reading achievement: An application of structural equation modelling. *British Journal of Educational Psychology, 61,* 19–35.

Scarborough, H. S., & Dobrich, W. (1994). On the efficacy of reading to preschoolers. *Developmental Review, 14,* 245–302.

Scher, D., & Baker, L. (1996, April). *Attitudes toward reading and children's home literacy environments.* Poster session presented at the meeting of the American Educational Research Association, New York.

Scher, D., & Baker, L. (1997, April). Children's conceptions and motivations regarding reading and their relations to parental ideas and home experiences. In R. Serpell, S. Sonnenschein, & L. Baker (Chairs), *Patterns of emerging competence and sociocultural context in the early appropriation of literacy.* Symposium presented at the meeting of the Society for Research in Child Development, Washington, DC.

Scott-Jones, D. (1991). Black famililes and literacy. In S. B. Silvern (Ed.), *Advances in reading/language research: Vol. 5. Literacy through family, community, and school interaction* (pp. 173–200). Greenwich, CT: JAI Press.

Searls, D. T., Mead, N. A., & Ward, B. (1985). The relationship of students' reading skills to TV watching, leisure time reading, and homework. *Journal of Reading, 29,* 158–162.

Serpell, R., Baker, L., & Sonnenschein, S. (1995). Home and school contexts of emergent literacy (Instructional Resource No. 18). Athens, GA: Universities of Georgia and Maryland, National Reading Research Center.

Serpell, R., Baker, L., Sonnenschein, S., Gorham, L., & Hill, S. (1996). *Cooperative communication among parents and teachers about children's emergent literacy.* Unpublished manuscript.

Serpell, R., Sonnenschein, S., Baker, L., Hill, S., Goddard-Truitt, V., & Danseco, E. (1997). *Parental ideas about development and socialization of children on the threshold of schooling* (Research Report No. 78). Athens, GA: Universities of Georgia and Maryland, National Reading Research Center.

Shockley, B., Michalove, B., & Allen, J. (1995). *Creating parallel practices: A home-to-school and school-to-home partnership* (Instructional Resource No. 13). Athens, GA: Universities of Georgia and Maryland, National Reading Research Center.

Snow, C. E., Barnes, W. S., Chandler, J., Goodman, I. F., & Hemphill, L. (1991). *Unfulfilled expectations: Home and school influences on literacy.* Cambridge, MA: Harvard University Press.

Sonnenschein, S., Baker, L., Serpell, R., Scher, D., Goddard-Truitt, V., & Munsterman, K. (1996, August). *The relation between parental beliefs about reading development and storybook reading practices in different sociocultural groups in Baltimore.* Paper presented at the biennial meeting of the International Society for the Study of Behavioral Development, Quebec City.

Sonnenschein, S., Baker, L., Serpell, R., Scher, D., Goddard-Truitt, V., & Munsterman, K. (1997). Parental beliefs about ways to help children learn to read: The impact of an entertainment or a skills perspective. *Early Child Development and Care, 127–128,* 111–118.

Sonnenschein, S., Baker, L., Serpell, R., & Schmidt, D. (in press). The importance of the home perspective for children's literacy development. In J. Christie & K. Roskos (Eds.), *Play and literacy in the early years: Cognitive, ecological and sociocultural perspectives.* Mahwah, NJ: Erlbaum.

Sonnenschein, S., Brody, G., & Munsterman, K. (1996). The influence of family beliefs and practices on children's early reading development. In L. Baker, P. Afflerbach, & D. Reinking (Eds.), *Developing engaged readers in school and home communities* (pp. 3–20). Mahwah, NJ: Erlbaum.

Stipek, D., Milburn, S., Clements, D., & Daniels, D. H. (1992). Parents' beliefs about appropriate education for young children. *Journal of Applied Developmental Psychology, 13,* 293–310.

Sulzby, E., & Teale, W. (1991). Emergent literacy. In R. Barr, M. L. Kamil, P. Mosenthal, & P. D. Pearson (Eds.), *Handbook of reading research* (Vol. II, pp. 727–758). New York: Longman.

Taylor, D., & Dorsey-Gaines, C. (1988). *Growing up literate: Learning from inner city families.* Portsmouth, NH: Heinemann.

Teale, W. H. (1984). Reading to young children: Its significance for literacy development. In H. Goelman, A. A. Oberg, & F. Smith (Eds.), *Awakening to literacy* (pp. 110–121). London: Heinemann.

Teale, W. H. (1986). Home background and young children's literacy development. In W. H. Teale & E. Sulzby (Eds.), *Emergent literacy: Writing and reading* (pp. 173–205). Norwood, NJ: Ablex.

Thompson, R., & Mixon, G. A. (1997). *The reading engagement of inner-city African-American parents: Implications for middle grade children's reading at home.* Manuscript in preparation.

Thompson, R., Mixon, G., & Serpell, R. (1996). Engaging minority students in reading: Focus on the urban learner. In L. Baker, P. Afflerbach, & D. Reinking (Eds.), *Developing engaged readers in school and home communities* (pp. 43–63). Mahwah, NJ: Erlbaum.

Wells, G. (1986). *The meaning makers: Children learning language and using language to learn.* Portsmouth, NH: Heinemann.

White, K. R. (1982). The relation between socioeconomic status and academic achievement. *Psychological Bulletin, 91,* 461–481.

Whitehurst, G. J., Epstein, J. N., Angell, A. L., Payne, A. C., Crone, D. A., & Fischel, J. E. (1994). Outcomes of an emergent literacy intervention in Head Start. *Journal of Educational Psychology, 86,* 542–555.

Wigfield, A., & Asher, S. R. (1984). Social and motivational influences on reading. In P. D. Pearson, R. Barr, M. Kamil, & P. Mosen (Eds.), *Handbook of reading research* (pp. 423–452). New York: Longman.

Wigfield, A., & Guthrie, J. T. (in press). Relations of children's motivation for reading to the amount and breadth of their reading. *Journal of Educational Psychology.*

Wigfield, A., Wilde, K., Baker, L., Fernandez-Fein, S., & Scher, D. (1996). *The nature of children's motivations for reading, and their relations to reading frequency and reading performance* (Reading Research Report No. 63). Athens, GA: Universities of Georgia and Maryland, National Reading Research Center.

CHAPTER 6

Modes of Inquiry into Studying Engaged Reading

Donna E. Alvermann

T HE CHALLENGE OF DESIGNING, conducting, and interpreting research studies aimed at engaging or drawing children into reading is made more complex by the variety in modes of inquiry currently available to literacy researchers. This is as it should be. Questions dealing with the motivational, cognitive, and social aspects of engaged reading require researchers to have at their disposal a wide array of inquiry modes. Although having such an array handy is advantageous, too often it is easy to overlook the very different assumptions that undergird researchers' beliefs about one mode or another.

In this chapter, I focus on the assumptions underlying several studies of reading engagement. While the studies themselves are important for what they substantively contribute to the engagement perspective, it is the nature of the underlying assumptions that is of primary interest here. In choosing to look more closely at the modes of inquiry that researchers have used to study engaged reading, I faced the dilemma of deciding which to include and how to categorize them for purposes of this chapter. Although each approach is more useful for some purposes (and for some individuals) than for others, in the end I considered which would best accommodate my examination of a variety of studies on engaged reading—although I freely admit that such consideration was not value free.

To begin, I outline what seems to me to lie at the heart of understanding differences in modes of inquiry into studying engaged reading, namely, researchers' competing belief systems. From there I move into examples from the existing literature on reading engagement that illustrate how these belief systems play out in the different approaches researchers use to frame their studies. Finally, I draw from those examples in describing implications for further inquiry into engaged reading, but not before questioning the virtual absence of a critical mode of inquiry in the existing literature on reader engagement.

COMPETING BELIEFS

Dichotomous ways of viewing the world are highly ingrained in the American psyche. Not surprisingly, therefore, many researchers in the United States are prone to view knowledge as being either objectively or subjectively constructed. Those who side with the objectivist viewpoint do so on the grounds that scientific knowledge is value neutral. That is, the people and events studied can be separated from the one doing the research such that both the objects of study and the researcher remain unchanged throughout the investigation. Even if no practicing researcher would subscribe to this idealistic view of objectivity, he or she might design a study to be as free of researcher contamination as possible. At the other extreme, those who lay claim to the subjective view of reality, do so in the belief that historical, social, cultural, linguistic, economic, racial, ethnic, and gender considerations all play a role in how knowledge gets constructed. To their way of thinking, research can never be value neutral (Code, 1991; Lave, 1996).

As one might imagine, it would be rare to find anyone situated purely in the objectivist or subjectivist camp. Instead, the more likely scenario would find researchers taking into account the various trade-offs in viewing knowledge construction from either of the two perspectives. For example, those who design studies of a quasi-experimental nature would know that their findings could never be completely free of researcher bias and so would take steps to interpret their results accordingly. Although less concerned about personal bias, researchers who use ethnographic methods would know to employ certain procedures to protect against their voices overpowering those of their participants.

Just as there is no real dividing line between sea and land, but rather what is known as the coastal zone (Berthoff, 1990),[1] so, too, there is no way to delineate a purely qualitative study from a purely quantitative one. In fact, some researchers deliberately mix elements of one paradigm with another—a practice that is not without its critics, however (Jacob, 1982). Still, proponents of mixing elements from different paradigms view the situation pragmatically: Why not use a medley of approaches to answer questions of a complex nature, they argue.

Those who favor framing their research primarily from one perspective contend that the assumptions driving that perspective are not wholly compatible with those underlying other perspectives. Nor are the data easily (if ever) interpretable across research paradigms. The controversy over mixing paradigms, while far from being resolved, is part of the larger debate over what educational research is and what it ought to be (Donmoyer, 1993, 1996). And that issue—what counts as research—is tied directly to the competing belief systems that guide researchers' work.

TEACHER RESEARCH AS A MODE OF INQUIRY

If research on engaged reading is to be useful to teachers and others who work with children and adolescents on a daily basis, it must link theory and practice. Whether conducting inquiry in their own classrooms (e.g., Atwell, 1991; Fecho, 1998) or as members of collaborative arrangements with university-based research-ers (Allen, Cary, & Delgado, 1995; Commeyras & Sumner, in press), teacher researchers bridge the so-called theory–practice divide in two important ways: (1) They ensure that the research questions guiding a study are relevant and prac-tical, and (2) they create a sense of ownership in implementing the findings (Baumann, Shockley, & Allen, 1997).

Teacher researchers do not necessarily agree among themselves as to what counts as inquiry and how such inquiry should be conducted (Gitlin et al., 1992; Sagor, 1992). Some, for example, contend that teacher research as a mode of in-quiry is unique and should not be considered a hybrid of other inquiry modes, such as case studies, ethnographies, and the like (Atwell, 1991; Bissex & Bullock, 1987; Cochran-Smith & Lytle, 1993). Others (e.g., Baumann et al., 1997) subscribe to a more inclusive view of inquiry—one that deems reflection and action based on systematic observations of classroom life as the essential qualities of teacher research.

Roughly 3 decades ago, Jackson (1968) put out a call for researchers to "move up close to the phenomena of the teacher's world" (p. 159). Although the research on teaching reading and reading teacher education has expanded greatly since Jackson petitioned those in the academy to leave their ivory tower for a view of the classroom as teachers see it, the gap between theory and practice still exists. Why? To some in the academy, the gap appears to have widened as a result of their not keeping up with the changes that have occurred in classrooms poised to enter the new millennium. For others, there is a sense that classroom teachers mistrust outsiders' expertise, particularly when that expertise is bound up in re-search or theory that has failed in the past to make a difference in students' lives over a sustained period of time (Hatch, 1993).[2] To still others, most notably teacher researchers, the problem lies in what they perceive to be university-based research-ers' inattention to teachers' personal practical knowledge. The assumption under-lying each of these explanations is that unless university-based researchers attend to how knowledge is shaped by the contexts in which teachers and students work, there is little hope of bridging the gap between theory and practice (Clandinin & Connelly, 1996). This assumption has its roots in what some cognitivists (e.g., Brown, Collins, & Duguid, 1989) and anthropologists (e.g., Lave, 1996; Lave & Wenger, 1991) have referred to as a situated approach to learning.

Situated Learning

Such an approach seems to resonate with the goals of teacher research as a mode of inquiry into engaged reading, for several reasons. First, it speaks to how knowledge about engaged reading practices is shaped by the contexts in which teachers and students work. In Lave's (1988) words, situated learning is "a theory of active social actors, located in time and space, reflexively and recursively acting upon the world in which they live and which they fashion at the same time" (p. 8). This active learner element is part and parcel of engaged reading, especially given its emphasis on drawing children into literacy in ways that will sustain their interest in reading over a lifetime.

Second, situated learning as conceived by Lave (1996) takes into account the need for teachers to "address questions about teaching through research focused on learners learning" (p. 158). Analogously, what better way to study engaged readers reading than to observe them for the purpose of answering questions that arise from teachers' concerns? That this can be accomplished through an apprenticeship model is even more interesting, for it suggests that engaged readers are never passive learners but rather are always directing their own actions in a literate environment that they co-construct with others.

Finally, situated learning as viewed through the apprenticeship metaphor links to teacher research by virtue of its insistence on reflexivity as a way of being and knowing in classrooms. This point is made clear by Lave (1996) in her agenda for research on teaching:

> If teachers teach in order to affect learning, the only way to discover whether they are having effects and if so what those are, is to explore whether, and if so how, there are changes in the participation of learners learning in their various communities of practice. If we intend to be thorough, and we presume teaching has some impact on learners, then such research would include the effects of teaching on teachers as learners as well. Together these comprise a short agenda for research on teaching. (p. 158)

In classrooms where engaged reading is evident, teachers are learning right along with their students. The old and tired binary that separates teachers from students along traditional hierarchies of power and expertise breaks down when an apprenticeship model is in operation. This model, like the context-shaping assumption that underlies much of teacher research, suggests that those who instruct engaged readers are themselves engaged in the process of learning about their own teaching.

Examples from the Literature on Teacher Research

Studies in which teachers have participated as inquirers into their own practices and beliefs about engaged reading have generated new findings and insights that would have been difficult, if not impossible, to achieve under more traditional methods. For example, one teacher who was a member of the National Reading Research Center's School Research Consortium (Baumann, Shockley, & Allen, 1996) reflected on her role as teacher researcher in light of what it meant to be a learner:

> I have to be a learner in and out of my classroom so I won't lose sight of what it's like for my students—so I will continue to hear their voices. I don't ever want to see myself up in the front of that classroom again sitting on a stool with all the answers. (p. 31)

Other teachers, who were also members of the NRRC's School Research Consortium, experienced firsthand what it meant to bridge the theory–practice divide. They were teacher researchers in a project known as the Kingsbridge Road Collaborative (Allen et al., 1995), an inquiry group formed when faculty from two rural elementary schools that previously had worked in isolation from each other elected to join in creating a teacher learning community to study engaged reading. This group documented how ownership of the inquiry process developed over the course of a year as members in the learning community grew to appreciate the value of finding answers to questions that they generated from their own practices.

Another example from the literature that documents how a teacher's practice became the source of a year-long inquiry is Fecho's (1998) account of what transpired one afternoon as he attempted to engage his students in reading a poem written by a well-known, African American author:

> It was my eighth period English class that led me to reconsider the way in which language was taught and learned in my classroom. We were reading "Beautiful Black Men," a poem by Nikki Giovanni. Although its lines contain such dated terms as "outasite Afros" and "driving their hogs," the poem is a celebration of African American identity in straight forward street language and dialect. It was, I thought, safe—meaning that it seemed to have no political edge relative to other poems by the author and her contemporaries—and would stir no controversy in my class. While I often pick provocative texts, the purpose for studying this poem was to examine the vivid and colloquial use of language by Giovanni.
>
> Yet, as my students finished the read-aloud, I could see that they were unsettled. There was a terseness about their responses to my questions that was quite unlike the usual affability of this group. Through the year they had challenged me, kidded me, and questioned me, but had rarely shut me out. However, this poem that I thought would set them talking about life "back in the day" and the positive African American images inherent within the verses, instead had made them tight-lipped and seemingly disgruntled. Moreover, when I mentioned their disquietude, their response was that it was really nothing and I shouldn't worry.
>
> I could have let it drop, ignored the awkwardness as I have done in the past, and gone on to the next poem. But I didn't—couldn't—and I pressed the issue. Finally,

Latonya, who was always upfront about her opinions, blurted, "She making fun of the way Black people talk."

There it was. I thought the poem to be a celebration. I believe Nikki Giovanni intended it as such. But my students saw it as a put down, a parody. My "safe" poem had heated up in ways that were both political and personal. And life in my classroom would never be the same. (p. 75)

So began a year-long class project in which Fecho engaged his students as co-inquirers into the political nature of language. His goal was to develop an increased understanding of the role language played in their lives, individually and collectively as members of the class.

In each of the examples above, teachers' belief systems had an impact on how they framed their inquiries. Whether through self-reflection or through acting reflexively and recursively in contexts that shaped (and were shaped by) them, these teachers demonstrate that there is little reason to doubt that the theory–practice divide can be crossed in studying engagement in reading when the mode of inquiry is teacher research.

INTERPRETIVE MODES OF INQUIRY

The goal of the interpretive researcher is to understand from the point of view of the researched what (and how) meaning is attached to specific phenomena, such as engaged reading. Although disagreements exist as to the extent of interaction that is permissible between the knower (the researcher) and the known (the researched) before a study's validity is questioned, generally speaking the researcher is cautioned about the need to keep his or her subjectivity somewhat in check (Hammersley & Atkinson, 1986). Procedures for assisting the researcher to do this include bracketing (i.e., putting a hold on his or her own experiences, expectations, and values while observing and interpreting the same in others) and member checking (e.g., asking the researched to read the researcher's field notes and verify their accuracy). As Hammersley and Atkinson warn, "there can be no question of total commitment, surrender, or becoming. There must always remain some part held back, some social and intellectual distance" (p. 102).

This warning against what some methodologists have labeled *going native* sets interpretive research apart from the teacher research discussed previously. It bears mentioning here, however, because the assumption is that in studies of engaged reading that use the interpretive mode of inquiry, the researcher is the instrument through which the data are first processed and then represented. This being the case, differences in the degree to which a researcher's experiences and values enter into the interpretation of the data will affect what can be learned from the participants in a study. For example, in writing about how we can imagine the life worlds of our participants when they differ from our own, Finders (1992) wrote:

> How can we imagine worlds that are often very far from our own? How can we un-
> tangle our own deeply entrenched assumptions? Perhaps before we can look in, we
> must look out. Our understanding of what it means to be part of a family, part of a
> community, part of a classroom, is socially defined. As an Anglo teacher, I struggle
> to quiet voices from my own farm family, echoing as always some unstated stan-
> dard. While events in our own classrooms, in our own lives, may be at first too close
> to see, ethnographies can provide . . . lenses that allow us to uncover the assump-
> tions that drive decisions about policies and practices in our curriculums and class-
> rooms. (p. 60)

A few years later, Finders would write her own ethnography in the form of a dissertation while a doctoral student at the University of Iowa. That study, which is described next, took place in a setting not unlike that where she once taught. Whereas events in her own classroom may have been, as she noted above, "too close to see," an ethnographic study of a different classroom provided the lens she needed to understand how a junior high school's curriculum for engaging students in schooled literacy tasks could be subverted.

Ethnographies of Reader Engagement

From Finders's (1997) year-long ethnography, we learn how two groups of ado-lescent girls, whom she came to call the Social Queens and the Tough Cookies, managed to undermine their school's sanctioned literacy practices by developing a "literate underlife" (p. 1)—a special type of nonacademic literacy that enabled them to maintain certain social roles and allegiances. For the Social Queens, this literate underlife consisted of surreptitiously passing notes, writing graffiti, and reading teen magazines—all activities that these teenagers perceived as document-ing their resistance to the school's authority to name what was engaging for them.

For the Tough Cookies, literate underlife consisted of resisting attempts by the teachers to engage them in shared reading and writing activities, especially with members of the class who were from families of a higher socioeconomic level. In these girls' eyes, such activities posed a threat to their personal chances of making it in the world. For as we learn through Finders's interpretations of her interviews with the Tough Cookies, these teenagers viewed reading as a solitary act—one that needed guarding if they were to achieve independence and success in life.

Because this ethnography, like others, is by its very nature culturally and contextually bound, we cannot assume that similar forms of literate underlife would be found in other junior high schools. To compensate for the limited transferability of findings from ethnographic studies, some methodologists recommend looking for patterns in the research literature that support a common theme (Lincoln & Guba, 1985). In the literature on reading engagement among young adolescents, for example, an ethnography by Wells (1996) comes readily to mind. In that study of rising eighth graders, Wells, like Finders (1997), found a resistance to literacy tasks that school authorities viewed as engaging but students considered boring and irrelevant. The net effect was an underground literacy created by students in which the amount of writing they produced through clandestine letter-writing activities far outweighed what they wrote for their classes. Like the Social Queens in Finders's (1997) study, the students who participated in Wells's ethnography demonstrated they were quite adept at transforming schooled literacy tasks into practices that fit more comfortably with their teenage identities.

Sociolinguistic Studies of Engaged Readers

Another form of interpretive inquiry is a sociolinguistic analysis of the influence of social and cultural factors within a speech community on its language patterns. Researchers interested in learning from groups of engaged readers how certain material conditions affect classroom talk about texts sometimes choose to frame their work within a sociolinguistic perspective because it provides them with a means of analyzing the language patterns of such groups. For example, some researchers (Almasi, 1995; Green, Kantor, & Rogers, 1991) have analyzed student talk for the clues it can provide in helping them better understand how different contexts shape (and are shaped by) a speech community's rules for who can say what to whom, when, and under which conditions. A key assumption underlying this mode of inquiry is that by listening to the voices of students, it is possible to draw inferences about the contextual factors affecting a reader's engagement (or lack thereof). A corollary to that assumption is that students who are motivated to read are more likely to view themselves as competent learners (McCombs, 1995).

Interpreting how engaged readers understand their world by analyzing their verbal give-and-take is a defining characteristic of studies framed within a sociolinguistic perspective. This characteristic makes a sociolinguistic perspective particularly well suited for research on reader engagement for a number of reasons, not the least of which has to do with researchers' interest in documenting engaged readers' knowledge of self and others. Because classrooms are social systems complete with norms and expectations, rights and responsibilities, and role relationships that teachers and students construct over time (Green et al., 1991; Gumperz, 1981), researchers need a mode of inquiry that enables them to identify patterns of talk from which they can trace the social and cultural conditions that produced the patterns. These tracings, in turn, can be used to make inferences about engaged readers' knowledge of themselves as well as their peers in terms of how classroom talk facilitates learning.

Studies conducted within a sociolinguistic perspective have shown that students' engagement in classroom talk about texts can contribute to students' knowledge growth in at least four important ways. First, their participation in peer-group discussions can lead to an awareness of the need to consider multiple points of view as well as an understanding of how different viewpoints can contribute to their own comprehension (Almasi, McKeown, & Beck, 1996; Alvermann et al., 1996; Eeds & Wells, 1989). Second, their interactions with others also can lead to an increased awareness of self in relation to others (Cazden, 1988; Green et al., 1991). Third, their active involvement in producing classroom discourse can serve as a catalyst for acquiring knowledge about reading processes and written language conventions (Kantor, Miller, & Fernie, 1992; Neuman & Roskos, 1992). Fourth, their interactions with others more knowledgeable than themselves (whether teachers or their peers) can provide a forum for sharing knowledge about literary and narrative elements that are essential for developing a critical stance toward literature (Rogers, 1987, 1991).

In analyzing data on reader engagement from a sociolinguistic perspective, a researcher needs to keep in mind that this mode of inquiry positions individual learners in the context of evolving social activities, some of which themselves may offer positions that learners are theoretically free to take up or resist. Obidah (1998), for example, was well aware of this fact and made use of it when analyzing the data from her study of two African American girls, LaTasha and Natalia, who resisted taking up the positions offered them in their assigned textbook readings on the ancient African empires of Ghana, Mali, and Songhay. Sensing the girls' frustration with their white teacher's attempt to engage them in a study of their cultural heritage, Obidah was able to show through her analysis of their language patterns (e.g., "Never mind!" spoken emphatically several times in response to their teacher's well-intentioned but misguided questioning) that LaTasha and Natalia had sensed that their own questions dealing with self-identity and the Black presence in American history were not going to be addressed.

In summary, both ethnographic and sociolinguistic approaches to interpretive inquiry appear to have served some specific needs of researchers whose interests lie in studying the nature of engaged reading. In particular, these approaches have lent themselves to the examination of influences on engaged reading such as gender (e.g., Finders, 1997) and race (e.g., Obidah, 1998). That more researchers have not considered such influences may be due in part to the fact that critical modes of inquiry are largely missing in the literature on engaged reading.

PREDICTIVE MODES OF INQUIRY

Unlike teacher research, with its goal of bridging the theory–practice gap, and interpretive perspectives that seek understanding from the participant's point of view, predictive modes of inquiry aspire to bring order to domains of knowledge, such as reader engagement, by reducing the ambiguities and complexities that constitute these domains. Experimental, quasi-experimental, correlational, and factor analytical approaches (among others) make up what generally are referred to as the predictive modes of inquiry.

A common assumption underlying each of these approaches is that it is possible to isolate (or at least control for) the messy "real-world" variables in the phenomenon of interest—in this case, engaged reading. Unlike teacher researchers and interpretivist researchers who include these real-world factors (e.g., emotions, desires, and feelings) because they believe doing so validates their work and increases their ability to understand a phenomenon, researchers working within various predictive modes of inquiry believe that the more they distance themselves from things that exist only in the mind, the more valid and objective their findings will be. Of course, as noted earlier, there is no such thing as purely objective or subjective research; rather, there is research that attempts to single out causes and effects rather than deal globally with the ambiguities and complexities surrounding a phenomenon like engaged reading.

To "predict," a word derived from two Latin terms that together mean "telling before," means to "say in advance what one believes will happen" (*Webster's New World Dictionary*, 3rd ed.). Researchers typically predict what they believe will occur when they manipulate two or more variables according to a set of stated principles operating within a theory that is either well developed or in an emerging stage of development. Because the engagement perspective in reading is not a theory in itself, researchers working within this perspective who want to hypothesize relations among variables have had to turn to theories that are amenable to explaining what engaged readers do. Generally, they have turned to theories of motivation (e.g., Deci, Vallerand, Pelletier, & Ryan, 1991; Maehr & Pintrich, 1993) and strategic reading (e.g., Paris, Wasik, & Turner, 1991; Pressley et al., 1994). Examples of studies from each of these areas are included next for the purpose of showing how predictive modes of inquiry, used within established theoretical frameworks, have supported investigations into the engagement perspective on reading.

STUDIES OF MOTIVATED READER ENGAGEMENT

In an effort to measure changes in elementary students' motivations for reading and their relations to reading frequency and reading performance, Guthrie and his colleagues (1996) designed a multifaceted research project that included both a year-long classroom intervention study and the administering of the Motivations for Reading Questionnaire (MRQ) to approximately 600 fifth- and sixth-grade children (Wigfield, Baker, Fernandez-Fein, Scher, & Wilde, 1996). The intervention portion of the project involved 2 third-grade and 2 fifth-grade classes in a new approach to engaging students in literacy activities that featured an integrated reading/language arts and science program. This program, Concept-Oriented Reading Instruction, had been developed earlier by Guthrie, McGough, Bennett, and Rice (1996) using principles of motivation theory that support the use of curiosity, aesthetic enjoyment, and challenge in developing intrinsic motivations. There was also a strategies component to the intervention that involved students in searching for information and communicating with others through writing. The MRQ assessed 11 dimensions of children's reading motivations.

Although substantively of interest because the students' intrinsic motivations for reading correlated highly with their use of higher-order reading strategies, what is of primary interest here is that these studies provided a type of information that was unavailable from the other modes of inquiry discussed earlier. What these two studies contribute to future research on the engagement perspective in reading is a validated reading program and an instrument that has been shown to reliably measure several dimensions of children's motivations for reading.

STUDIES OF STRATEGICALLY ENGAGED READERS

Reading strategically is thought to be a distinguishing mark of engaged learners. Some researchers interested in finding empirical support for this hypothesis have asked questions of an "if–then" nature—that is, questions that seek answers to whether introducing a certain intervention, such as transactional instruction of reading comprehension strategies (Pressley et al., 1994), will improve students' performance when they engage in demanding tasks that require them to read for the purpose of learning and remembering specific information. Other researchers working in fields related to literacy education—for example, in the area of cognitive engagement—have asked questions about students' ability to use self-regulating strategies when it comes to comprehending their assigned texts (Pintrich & DeGroot, 1990). Studies of this nature generally have found that students who engage in self-regulating behaviors are more apt to engage willingly in difficult academic tasks.

Studies conducted using predictive modes of inquiry figure prominently in the growing body of literature on engaged reading, particularly those that examine students' motivations for reading and the strategies they use in accomplishing demanding literacy tasks. However, obtaining permission to conduct long-term studies of this nature in regular classroom settings can be difficult. At most schools and universities, the boards that review proposed research projects frown on studies that disrupt normal classroom procedures. Researchers interested in conducting experimental or even quasi-experimental studies often find themselves making adjustments in their designs to accommodate the concerns of the various institutions that control entry to the sites. When this is the case, it is even more important that researchers consider what can be gained from using information available from studies conducted within other, less intrusive modes of inquiry. By looking for convergences across paradigms, it is possible to overcome the limitations of any one approach.

IMPLICATIONS FOR FURTHER INQUIRY
INTO ENGAGED READING

As noted earlier, complementary findings that converge across approaches within different modes of inquiry are helpful in fleshing out what is entailed in engaged reading. An approach that is largely missing from the existing literature, however, is one that theorists refer to as critical in nature (Denzin & Lincoln, 1995; Lather, 1991). Critical approaches typically are associated with modes of inquiry based on feminist, Marxist, and Freirian theories.

The fact that critical modes of inquiry currently are underrepresented in the literature on engaged reading is troublesome. Without a deeper understanding than we now have of the engaged reader, we cannot hope to predict with accuracy how students' social class, race, ethnicity, gender, age (or any number of other identity factors) will mediate their engagement with texts. Nor can we predict at this point what it is that will engage students who do not know or seldom use English as their language of choice. A continued lack of knowledge of these factors for any substantial time is likely to result in practitioners viewing the engagement perspective on reading as less and less useful to them because of the growing diversity in school populations.

As the previous sections of this chapter illustrate, different ways of thinking about research influence differentially what we can "know" about engaged reading. In part, at least, our ideas about the engaged reader are a consequence of the mode of inquiry we used to generate them. Fortunately, researchers interested in reader engagement have drawn from a variety of inquiry modes to frame their studies. Doing so has opened the field to a number of different and enriching perspectives on the construct of engaged reading. For example, the interpretive work of Finders (1997) and Wells (1996), plus Oldfather's (1994) interpretive approach to student engagement through a construct she called "honored voice," have all contributed to the engagement perspective on reading in a way that no amount of hypothesis testing within traditional motivation theory could have accomplished. At the same time, however, we needed the quantitative approach that Wigfield and colleagues (1996) took, to demonstrate the several dimensions of children's motivations for reading that were present in a large sample of children representing a number of different types of readers.

Finally, it is worth considering what we have learned from using different modes of inquiry to study engaged reading. As a practice, it has been beneficial for several reasons. First, it has created opportunities to pose different kinds of questions—questions that otherwise might have gone unasked. Second, it has enabled comparisons of findings between studies that control for confounding variables and those that do not attempt any such control. Third, it has resulted in increased reporting of convergent findings across different modes of inquiry— all of which permit researchers to say with greater confidence what it is that is "known" (and unknown) about the engagement perspective on reading.

NOTES

1. According to Berthoff (1990), "dichotomizing is an act of mind, not of Nature" (pp. 13–14).
2. Hatch (1993) counters this claim with a reminder that the fault does not lie entirely with researchers; it must be shared at least partially with the schools, which frequently do not sustain educational reforms.

REFERENCES

Allen, J., Cary, M., & Delgado, L. (Coordinators for the Kingsbridge Road Research Team). (1995). *Exploring blue highways: Literacy reform, school change, and the creation of learning communities*. New York: Teachers College Press.

Almasi, J. F. (1995). The nature of fourth graders' sociocognitive conflicts in peer-led and teacher-led discussions of literature. *Reading Research Quarterly, 30*, 314–351.

Almasi, J. F., McKeown, M. G., & Beck, I. L. (1996). The nature of engaged reading in classroom discussions of literature. *Journal of Literacy Research, 28*, 107–146.

Alvermann, D. E., Young, J. P., Weaver, D., Hinchman, K. A., Moore, D. W., Phelps, S. F., Thrash, E. C., & Zalewski, P. (1996). Middle- and high-school students' perceptions of how they experience text-based discussions: A multicase study. *Reading Research Quarterly, 31*, 244–267.

Atwell, N. (1991). *Side by side: Essays on teaching to learn*. Portsmouth, NH: Heinemann.

Baumann, J. F., Shockley, B., & Allen, J. (1996). *Methodology in teacher research* (Perspective No. 10). Athens, GA: Universities of Georgia and Maryland, National Reading Research Center.

Baumann, J. F., Shockley, B., & Allen, J. (1997). Methodology in teacher research: Three cases. In J. Flood, S. B. Heath, & D. Lapp (Eds.), *A handbook for literacy educators: Research on teaching the communicative and visual arts* (pp. 121–143). New York: Macmillan.

Berthoff, A. E. (1990). Killer dichotomies: Reading in/reading out. In K. Ronald & H. Roskelly (Eds.), *Farther along* (pp. 12–24). Portsmouth, NH: Boynton/Cook.

Bissex, G. L., & Bullock, R. H. (Eds.). (1987). *Seeing for ourselves: Case-study research by teachers of writing*. Portsmouth, NH: Heinemann.

Brown, J. S., Collins, A., & Duguid, P. (1989). Situated cognition and the culture of learning. *Educational Researcher, 18*(1), 32–42.

Cazden, C. (1988). *Classroom discourse: The language of teaching and learning.* Portsmouth, NH: Heinemann.

Clandinin, D. J., & Connelly, F. M. (1996). Teachers' professional knowledge landscapes: Teacher stories—stories of teachers—school stories—stories of schools. *Educational Researcher, 25*(3), 24–30.

Cochran-Smith, M., & Lytle, S. (1993). *Inside/outside: Teacher research and knowledge.* New York: Teachers College Press.

Code, L. (1991). *What can she know? Feminist theory and construction of knowledge.* Ithaca, NY: Cornell University Press.

Commeyras, M., & Sumner, G. (in press). Questions children want to discuss about literature: What teachers and students learned in a second-grade classroom. *Elementary School Journal.*

Deci, E. L., Vallerand, R. J., Pelletier, L. G., & Ryan, R. M. (1991). Motivation and education: The self-determination perspective. *Educational Psychologist, 26,* 325–346.

Denzin, N., & Lincoln, Y. (1995). *Handbook of qualitative research.* Thousand Oaks, CA: Sage.

Donmoyer, R. (1993). Yes, but is it research? *Educational Researcher, 22*(3), 41.

Donmoyer, R. (1996, April). *The very idea of a knowledge base.* Paper presented at the meeting of the American Educational Research Association, San Francisco.

Eeds, M., & Wells, D. (1989). Grand conversations: An exploration of meaning construction in literature study groups. *Research in the Teaching of English, 23,* 4–29.

Fecho, B. (1998). Race, literacy, and the critical inquiry classroom. In D. E. Alvermann, K. A. Hinchman, D. W. Moore, S. F. Phelps, & D. R. Waff (Eds.), *Reconceptualizing the literacies in adolescents' lives* (pp. 75–102). Mahwah, NJ: Erlbaum.

Finders, M. (1992). Looking at lives through ethnography. *Educational Leadership, 50,* 60–65.

Finders, M. J. (1997). *Just girls.* New York: Teachers College Press.

Gitlin, A., Bringhurst, K., Burns, M., Cooley, V., Myers, B., Price, K., Russell, R., & Tiess, P. (1992). *Teachers' voices for school change: An introduction to educative research.* New York: Teachers College Press.

Green, J. L., Kantor, R. M., & Rogers, T. (1991). Exploring the complexity of language and learning in classroom contexts. In L. Idol & B. F. Jones (Eds.), *Educational values and cognitive instruction: Implications for reform* (pp. 333–364). Hillsdale, NJ: Erlbaum.

Gumperz, J. (1981). Conversational inference and classroom learning. In J. Green & C. Wallat (Eds.), *Ethnography and language in educational settings* (pp. 3–24). Norwood, NJ: Ablex.

Guthrie, J. T., McGough, K., Bennett, L., & Rice, M. E. (1996). Concept-Oriented Reading Instruction: An integrated curriculum to develop motivations and strategies for reading. In L. Baker, P. Afflerbach, & D. Reinking (Eds.), *Developing engaged readers in school and home communities* (pp. 165–190). Mahwah, NJ: Erlbaum.

Guthrie, J. T., Van Meter, P., McCann, A. D., Wigfield, A., Bennett, L., Poundstone, C. C., Rice, M. E., Faibisch, F. M., Hunt, B., & Mitchell, A. (1996). Growth of literacy engagement: Changes in motivations and strategies during Concept-Oriented Reading Instruction. *Reading Research Quarterly, 31,* 306–332.

Hammersley, M., & Atkinson, P. (1986). *Ethnography: Principles in practice*. New York: Tavistock.

Hatch, T. (1993). From research to reform: Finding better ways to put theory into practice. *Educational Horizons, 71*, 197–202.

Jackson, P. W. (1968). *Life in classrooms*. New York: Holt, Rinehart & Winston.

Jacob, E. (1982). Combining ethnographic and quantitative approaches. In P. Gilmore & A. A. Glatthorn (Eds.), *Children in and out of school: Ethnography and education* (pp. 124–147). Washington, DC: Center for Applied Linguistics.

Kantor, R., Miller, S. M., & Fernie, D. E. (1992). Diverse paths to literacy in a preschool classroom: A sociocultural perspective. *Reading Research Quarterly, 27*, 184–201.

Lather, P. (1991). *Getting smart*. New York: Routledge.

Lave, J. (1988). *Cognition in practice: Mind, mathematics, and culture in everyday life*. Cambridge: Cambridge University Press.

Lave, J. (1996). Teaching, as learning, in practice. *Mind, Culture, and Activity, 3*, 149–164.

Lave, J., & Wenger, E. (1991). *Situated learning: Legitimate peripheral participation*. New York: Cambridge University Press.

Lincoln, Y., & Guba, E. (1985). *Naturalistic inquiry*. Beverly Hills, CA: Sage.

Maehr, M. L., & Pintrich, P. R. (Eds.). (1993). *Advances in motivation and achievement* (Vol. 8). Greenwich, CT: JAI Press.

McCombs, B. L. (1995, Winter). Understanding the keys to motivation to learn. *What's noteworthy on learners, learning, schooling* [Brochure] (pp. 5–12). Aurora, CO: Mid-Continent Regional Educational Laboratory.

Neuman, S. B., & Roskos, K. (1992). Literacy objects as cultural tools: Effects on children's literacy behaviors in play. *Reading Research Quarterly, 27*, 202–225.

Obidah, J. (1998). Black: My-story. In D. E. Alvermann, K. A. Hinchman, D. W. Moore, S. F. Phelps, & D. R. Waff (Eds.), *Reconceptualizing the literacies in adolescents' lives* (pp. 51–72). Mahwah, NJ: Erlbaum.

Oldfather, P. (1994). *When students do not feel motivated for literacy learning: How a responsive classroom culture helps* (Reading Research Report No. 8). Athens, GA: Universities of Georgia and Maryland, National Reading Research Center.

Paris, S. G., Wasik, B. A., & Turner, J. C. (1991). The development of strategic readers. In R. Barr, M. L. Kamil, P. Mosenthal, & P. D. Pearson (Eds.), *Handbook of reading research* (Vol. II, pp. 609–640). New York: Longman.

Pintrich, P. R., & DeGroot, E. V. (1990). Motivational and self-regulated learning components of classroom academic performance. *Journal of Educational Psychology, 82*(1), 33–40.

Pressley, M., El-Dinary, P. B., Brown, R., Schuder, T. L., Pioli, M., Green, K., & Gaskins, I. (1994). Transactional instruction of reading comprehension strategies. *Reading and Writing Quarterly, 10*, 5–19.

Rogers, T. (1987). Exploring a socio-cognitive perspective on the interpretive processes of junior high school students. *English Quarterly, 20*, 218–230.

Rogers, T. (1991). Students as literary critics: The interpretive experiences, beliefs, and processes of ninth-grade students. *Journal of Reading Behavior, 23*, 391–423.

Sagor, R. (1992). *How to conduct collaborative action research*. Alexandria, VA: Association for Supervision and Curriculum Development.

Wells, M. C. (1996). *Literacies lost: When students move from a progressive middle school to a traditional high school.* New York: Teachers College Press.

Wigfield, A., Baker, L., Fernandez-Fein, S., Scher, D., & Wilde, K. (1996). *The nature of children's motivations for reading, and their relations to reading frequency and reading performance* (Reading Research Report No. 63). Athens, GA: Universities of Georgia and Maryland, National Reading Research Center.

CHAPTER 7

Reading Engagement and School Reform: Challenges for Leadership in Literacy Education

Louise Cherry Wilkinson

THE LACK OF UNIVERSAL LITERACY is a central problem in American society. Eminent national organizations, such as the International Reading Association and the U.S. Department of Education, have studied the prevalence of literacy in America and have concluded that we have failed to attain the national goal that every adult will be literate and have the skills needed to compete in the global economy. In 1989, at the first U.S. national education summit, the governors met to set national educational goals to be achieved by 2000. They specifically linked America's achievement of universal literacy to the future success of the American economy.

The NRRC was established by John Guthrie and Donna Alvermann in 1992 with funding from the federal government, with the goal of improving and informing educational practice in reading. From its inception, the NRRC was a highly innovative endeavor, departing from traditional federally funded educational research and development centers in two significant ways. First, the NRRC was defined by a clear conceptual focus: the *engagement perspective on reading*, which, as John Guthrie and Emily Anderson state in Chapter 2, is distinctly different from the standard and widely accepted view of what is important in learning to read:

> In our view, reading should be conceptualized as an engagement. Engaged readers not only have acquired reading skills, but use them for their own purposes in many contexts. They possess beliefs, desires, and interests that energize the hard work of

becoming literate. From this perspective, motivations and social interactions are equal to cognitions as foundations for reading. . . . *Our view is that engagement in reading is a motivated mental activity with vital consequences for world knowledge and social participation.*

In Chapter 6, Donna Alvermann states that the engagement perspective on reading has focused researchers' attention on understanding *why* children from prekindergarten through senior high school choose to read. She notes that questions dealing with social and motivational factors for why individuals read require a complex array of inquiry modes. For instance, qualitative approaches are specifically compatible with highly contextualized studies of classroom practice, but these approaches alone cannot do justice to the magnitude of questions surrounding the engagement perspective. Quantitative approaches also are necessary if academics and practitioners are to find answers of a more generalized nature.

The second defining principle of the NRRC is a fundamental commitment directly toward improving the educational practices of teaching and learning to read. Donna Alvermann has noted that finding better ways to put ideas gleaned through reading research into classroom practice is a goal the NRRC has explored with vigor. In Chapter 6, she articulates the strong link between research and practice:

> If research on engaged reading is to be useful to teachers and others who work with children and adolescents on a daily basis, it must link theory and practice. . . . [T]eacher researchers bridge the so-called theory–practice divide in two important ways: (1) They ensure that the research questions guiding a study are relevant and practical, and (2) they create a sense of ownership in implementing the findings.

Donna Alvermann, at the University of Georgia, and John Guthrie, at the University of Maryland, assembled a strong team of experts on all aspects of reading research and effective reading practices. Their work between 1990 and 1997 is the subject of this volume; this chapter includes a consideration of the implications of that corpus of new work for educational policies in the United States.

I begin with a summary of the key issues in the current U. S. policy environment. The discussion highlights the substance and significance of the recent Goals 2000: Educate America Act of 1994 and its predecessor, Improving America's Schools: Goals 2000 Act of 1993, as well as the general policy direction from 1992 to 1997 with emphasis on standards-based educational reform and objective assessment of students' learning in core curricular areas, including the language arts.

Next, I examine the significance of the NRRC accomplishments within the context of current educational policy reform. The chapter concludes with suggestions for improving literacy learning in the future, and for how to relate educational reforms, research, and practices to maximize the chances that America truly can become a nation of readers by the turn of the twenty-first century.

THE CURRENT ENVIRONMENT FOR POLICY REFORM
IN THE UNITED STATES

The concept of Systemic School Reform (SSR) was introduced into the public debate about education in the United States as a way to improve schooling nationwide. SSR was formulated to change American classrooms and has had significant consequences for the ways language and literacy are taught, learned, and assessed today.

The importance of Systemic School Reform was exemplified by the Clinton administration's first major school reform bill, Improving America's Schools: Goals 2000 Act of 1993. Systemic School Reform was the foundation for the legislation.

Systemic School Reform referred to the process of making and implementing educational policy; the notion was to make policy more effective by making it less like a top-down "teaching is telling" mandate from high-level administrators and legislators (Elmore, 1993). SSR emphasized the need for communicating effectively, so that making educational policy would be seen as a positive process for all involved.

The concept incorporated a design for a systemic state structure that would support school-site efforts to improve classroom learning and instruction. The original idea was that the structure should be based on clear and challenging standards for students' learning. Policy components would be tied directly to standards that would support each other and guide classroom teachers and school administrators about how to optimize instruction. The states were seen as the critical providers of two fundamental aspects for universal educational excellence: (1) a unifying vision and set of goals, and (2) a coherent system of instructional guidance.

Regarding "the vision thing," each state was mandated to provide coherent direction for educational reform throughout the state and was to develop a common vision of what schools should be like. The value of providing an intellectually stimulating and engaging education for all students was the central concern. Both coherence and a point of view had to be accommodated.

Key Policy Elements of Educational Reform

Regarding the second aspect, the essential components of Systemic School Reform, educational policy makers devised a set of key policy elements that would be necessary to provide a coherent system of instructional guidance. These elements included the following:

- *Curriculum frameworks and materials.* Curriculum frameworks set out the best consensus of thinking in the field about the knowledge, processes, and skills that students needed to know in each core curriculum area. The emphasis was on in-depth understanding, higher-order thinking, problem solving, hands-on experiences, and the integration of content and pedagogy. One often cited successful example of a curricular framework is the National Council of Teachers of Mathematics (NCTM) 1989 mathematics standards. Schools were to select specific curriculum materials that would support the instruction guided by the frameworks.

- *Teacher education and professional development.* States had to ensure that both new and continuing teachers would have the knowledge of subject matter, pedagogy, and instructional skills so that they could teach the content specified by the frameworks. States were to support excellence programs to prepare teachers and exhibit a commitment to the continuing professional development of teachers.
- *Accountability assessment.* States had to develop a system to measure and report what students knew, which would be tied to what the curriculum frameworks specified. Assessment instruments required attention and support commensurate with their significant role in the system. Instruments were to be developed that would reveal the knowledge assumed to have been learned; relying exclusively on paper-and-pencil multiple choice tests would not address this need.
- *Governance.* For SSR to work, the responsibilities and accountability had to be clearly specified. The research literature suggests that three elements are critical for instructional success: (1) a staff of well-trained professionals who use their knowledge with their students to meet goals; (2) an internal governance structure that allows teachers to be decision makers; and (3) a well-supported and flexible infrastructure that supports teachers in this work.
- *Finance.* States were to ensure that schools had sufficient resources to implement the other elements in a high-quality way.

Thus, SSR dictated a focus on outcomes, where students' performance on learning tasks is the product to be measured (not processes such as thinking and talking). The focus was on teaching and learning subject matter (not affective development, emotional well-being, or social adjustment).

Blueprint for Action for SSR

At the beginning of the 1990s, the ideas for SSR were translated into an action plan to be implemented across America. In 1993, Richard Elmore argued that for SSR to succeed, the action focus had to be on deploying resources against students' performance; that is, to achieve the greatest percentage of children performing at the highest possible levels. To do this, educational administrators needed to act as managers of performance, and not in the role of power brokers whose main aim was to protect their turf and their budget. In terms of policy, the philosophy of "less is more" reigned; that is, less bureaucratization and rigid rules would allow more flexible and creative problem solving by teachers and administrators to attain the goal of maximizing students' learning. Teachers had to be seen by themselves and others as the individuals mainly responsible for problem solving and were to be given maximum autonomy to achieve their goals. Schools, in turn, had to be seen as performance centers, where the most important task was to achieve increased student learning and performance. The notion of the school as a cog in the wheel or unit in a big bureaucracy was to be abandoned. Finally, there had to be an emphasis on the professionalization of teachers, as exemplified in the NCTM frameworks, where the concept is of the teacher on the leading edge of problem solving. The focus was on developing the knowledge of the student and on consistent improvement in the student's demonstration of that growing knowledge as revealed by performance on assessment instruments.

Unanswered Questions of SSR

Even before SSR action plans got started, educators raised significant concerns (e.g., Silliman, Wilkinson, Mortinsen-Reed, & Scheer, in press). For example, SSR emphasized a focus on teaching and learning content matter as demonstrated in performance assessments, which are often synonymous with the notorious "high-stakes" exams. The focus was on outcomes, not processes. SSR took the point of view that all American children were to be included in this new plan; yet, little was said about individual differences and diversity among children. The emphasis was on empowering teachers, which typically was interpreted as "regular education" teachers. Other educational professionals were not mentioned.

At the time of SSR's introduction, certain questions were raised about the utility of the SSR approach: What do the curriculum frameworks really mean? How can they be adapted to address diverse populations of children? How could teachers be equipped to do this well and to be fair to each child? The SSR approach also naively assumed that educators could focus just on learning content, and ignore all the distractions—such as affective, emotional, and social factors. If learning were that simple, then we would have approached it without needless interference from these other psychological factors. Children differ significantly in their readiness to learn, their motivation to learn, their ability to focus and sustain learning in classrooms—and in countless other ways. Do we just assume that the same presentation of materials, stage-managed by one regular education teacher, will be sufficient for all children in her classroom? Further, is school just about learning content matter—or should it include learning about how to get along with each other, citizenship, sharing, and other values that undergird our democracy?

The SSR concern about professional development of teachers was laudable and essential. However, the implication from the SSR discussions was that this constitutes professional development only for regular education teachers. Where do special educators, school psychologists, speech/language pathologists, school counselors, among other specialists, fit in? How will their expertise with special populations of children best be used—if at all? How can regular education teachers optimally deal with the increased student body diversity in their classes without assistance from these experts? Doesn't professional development include paths for all educational professionals to find ways to work together for the benefit of children?

Finally, the concern of assessment, the critiques of "high-stakes" standard examinations, has permeated recent debates on American education. ssr did not address the important issue of alternative assessment.

Progress Report on Standards-Based Educational Reform

In March 1996, at the National Education Summit, the U.S. governors and other leaders reaffirmed their original commitment to the national goals adopted by the governors attending the Education Summit in 1989. The emphasis was less on the federal role in the improvement of education, and more on a greater recognition that schools must adopt rigorous standards shared either statewide and/or locally as the key to success. Later in 1996, the results of the first nationwide study of the status of Systemic School Reform were released by Margaret Goertz, Robert Floden, and Jennifer O'Day (1996). The authors summarized their findings of a 3-year study of the standards-based reform conducted by research teams in California, Michigan, and Vermont. In each state, case studies of four schools in two districts designated to be active and capable in education reform were conducted. The gist of their study is as follows: "Overall we conclude that while states and local school districts have taken major steps to reform the ways they teach and assess their students, the road to reform is arduous, full of bumps and still under construction" (p. 1).

Goertz and colleagues (1996) came to five conclusions about the status of educational reform, which address the following aspects: (1) instructional practices, (2) professional development of educators, (3) coordination of the various levels of educational policies affecting schools, (4) issues of educational equity and student diversity, and (5) the stability of the political environment affecting school reform across the nation. In an effort to provide a snapshot of the status of educational reform in the United States at this time, each of these aspects will be discussed briefly. This discussion should provide a context for the interpretation of the impact of the NRRC.

Balancing Old and New Instructional Practices

The two fundamental principles of ssr and standards-based reform are that states must provide a unifying vision of what students should know, and they must provide a coherent system of instructional practices and assessments. The findings of Goertz and colleagues show that some states took inspiration for constructing their own standards from well-regarded national standards-setting projects, such as that of the NCTM. The recently released national *Standards for the English Language Arts* of the IRA and the NCTE also exemplify such benchmark content standards:

> The vision guiding these standards is that all students must have the opportunities and resources to develop the language skills they need to pursue life's goals and to participate fully as informed, productive members of society. These standards assume that literacy growth begins before children enter school as they experience and experiment with literacy activities—reading and writing, and associating spoken words with their graphic representations. Recognizing this fact, these standards encourage the development of curriculum and instruction that make productive use of the emerging literacy abilities that children bring to school. Furthermore, the standards provide ample room for the innovation and creativity essential to teaching, and learning. They are not prescriptions for particular curriculum or instruction.
>
> Although we present these standards as a list, we want to emphasize that they are not distinct and separable; they are, in fact, interrelated and should be considered as a whole.

1. Students read a wide range of print and nonprint texts to build an understanding of texts, of themselves, and of the cultures of the United States and the world; to acquire new information; to respond to the needs and demands of society and the workplace; and for personal fulfillment. Among these texts are fiction and nonfiction, classic and contemporary works.
2. Students read a wide range of literature from many periods in many genres to build an understanding of the many dimensions (e.g., philosophical, ethical, aesthetic) of human experience.
3. Students apply a wide range of strategies to comprehend, interpret, evaluate, and appreciate texts. They draw on their prior experience, their interactions with other readers and writers, their knowledge of word meaning and of other texts, their word identification strategies, and their understanding of textual features (e.g., sound–letter correspondence, sentence structure, context, graphics).
4. Students adjust their use of spoken, written, and visual language (e.g., conventions, style, vocabulary) to communicate effectively with a variety of audiences and for different purposes.
5. Students employ a wide range of strategies as they write and use different writing process elements appropriately to communicate with different audiences for a variety of purposes.
6. Students apply knowledge of language structure, language conventions (e.g., spelling and punctuation), media techniques, figurative language, and genre to create, critique, and discuss print and nonprint texts.
7. Students conduct research on issues and interests by generating ideas and questions, and by posing problems. They gather, evaluate, and synthesize data from

a variety of sources (e.g., print and non-print texts, artifacts, people) to communicate their discoveries in ways that suit their purpose and audience.

8. Students use a variety of technological and informational resources (e.g., libraries, databases, computer networks, video) to gather and synthesize information and to create and communicate knowledge.

9. Students develop an understanding of and respect for diversity in language use, patterns, and dialects across cultures, ethnic groups, geographic regions, and social roles.

10. Students whose first language is not English make use of their first language to develop competency in the English language arts and to develop understanding of content across the curriculum.

11. Students participate as knowledgeable, reflective, reactive, and critical members of a variety of literacy communities.

12. Students use spoken, written, and visual language to accomplish their own purposes (e.g., for learning, enjoyment, persuasion, and the exchange of information). (International Reading Association, 1996)

While there is some controversy with respect to these standards, much more difficulty arises when attempts have been made to translate the standards into specific curricula (e.g., texts), instructional practices, and assessment instruments. The research of Immerwahr and Johnson (1996), cited in Goertz and colleagues (1996), shows strong public support for the concept of higher academic standards: Most people want students to master the "basics" before they attempt "higher-order" skills. Immerwahr and Johnson's survey showed that many respondents were not supportive of students using calculators for problem solving involving computation, or of teaching composition without first teaching grammar. The same researchers (Johnson & Immerwahr, 1994) found in a previous study that only a slim majority of Americans agreed with professional educators that multiple choice tests should be replaced with essay examinations. This sentiment was reflected in a feature article by Sara Mosle that appeared on October 27, 1996 in the *New York Times Magazine*, in which she stated:

In recent years, many educators have advocated replacing standardized tests with "portfolios" of students' work—essays, short stories, videos, plays—in an attempt to measure hard-to-quantify abilities. Though as a means of learning, portfolios are wonderful, as a means of testing they are too subjective, too labor-intensive and consequently too costly to implement on a national scale. (p. 68)

In another feature article in the same magazine a month earlier (September 8, 1996), Michale Johnson, a school principal, expressed significant skepticism about the use of portfolios as an alternative form of assessment:

We can develop a bunch of internal criteria for what we think a high-school student should be able to know, and that might mean repeating the ABC's. My definition of

portfolios, I can promise you, is not the same as other people's. Their definition might
be to get a little display board and slap some things up there. Schools need to be held
to some minimum levels of conceptual and behavioral objects that they can demonstrate. (p. 42)

This discussion, appearing in one of the nation's most significant news
publications, stands in sharp contrast to the extensive and careful discussion by
McCarthey, Hoffman, and Galda in Chapter 3. They argue convincingly that portfolio assessment can be used successfully to understand students' learning; this
technique has been applied widely, with positive results.

Even in the three states studied by Goertz and colleagues (1996) that have
taken on reform seriously, a consensus about how content standards in core areas
(e.g., mathematics, science, language arts, social studies) are to be translated into
the curriculum, pedagogy, and assessments has not been achieved.

Enhancing the Capacity of School-Based Educators

Standards-based reform requires ongoing strengthening of the educational system by continuous capacity building. Goertz and colleagues (1996) talk mostly
about enhancing teachers' capacities, which is achieved by professional development. Their findings show that teachers' abilities to support the new vision offered by the standards are affected by multiple factors. These factors include teachers' exposure to new ideas, the networks to which they belong, the school culture,
as well as practical matters such as how much time teachers had to learn new content and approaches to teaching, and their access to materials that were essential
to successfully implementing a curriculum most supportive of the standards.

As noted earlier, this formulation of the issue is limited. Where do special
educators, school psychologists, speech/language pathologists, school counselors,
principals, and other educational professionals who help students learn fit in?
Teachers and other professional educators need opportunities to grow and expand
their expertise; as the knowledge base increases in all the core areas, educators
need to learn how best to teach and assess core curricular areas, and to develop
their approaches to doing this.

Finally, the Goertz and colleagues study raises the issue of public support
for what it really takes to implement new standards across all core curricular areas.
It is not clear that the elected representatives who make the laws and allocate the
tax dollars fully appreciate that professional educators are a resource that must be
continuously enhanced, through professional development, teacher networks, and
interdisciplinary team building, among other activities. As Goertz and colleagues
conclude: "It is also quite possible, however, that helping all children reach more
challenging standards may require greater overall financial investment in education and thus greater public commitment to the future" (p. 6).

Coordinating National, State, and Local Policies
with School-Based Reform

One of the two key SSR principles is coherence within the political system, namely, that the entire educational structure be based on clear and challenging standards for students' learning. Policy components would be tied directly to those standards that support each other and guide classroom teachers and school administrators to optimize instruction. The Goertz and colleagues data do not offer much encouragement that this original vision of SSR has become a reality in the three states studied. While all three states have made significant progress in developing a more coherent policy structure, none can be called successful in the areas of linking curricula within and across grades, aligning curricula and methods of assessment, and linking the professional development of teachers to the standards-based reform.

First, their data show that although content area reforms and new standards do apply across grades K–12 and aim to create smooth transitions between grades, successful articulation has been difficult to achieve in schools, particularly in high schools. They cite as an example that many English language arts reform efforts have been aimed at the lower grades. However, the content and instructional practices used in high school have not changed much and, therefore, are discrepant from the approaches used in elementary and middle schools.

The second area of failure appears to be aligning curricula with methods of assessment. The problem seems to be that districts want to use the same methods of assessment for both student learning and accountability. Goals for each of these activities differ in many significant ways. Public accountability requires a high degree of reliability for the assessment instrument, so that comparisons across groups may be made—national averages, state averages, district by district comparisons, and so on. Standardized tests, by definition, meet that single criterion. However, questions about validity arise. Multiple choice tests do not reveal the student's processes of problem solving or of original composition. While portfolio assessment is seen by many educators as an innovative method of revealing students' capabilities to solve problems and develop writing abilities, it has been criticized simply because it cannot be nationally normed. The criticisms of portfolio assessment are referred to in the prior discussion; namely, that it is capricious and not reliable, and therefore the results cannot be interpreted.

Finally, Goertz and colleagues have found that while the standards-based educational reform movement requires that all participants—students, teachers, parents, among others—change what they learn and how they go about teaching/learning, in fact, the education system has been reluctant to support the necessary level of professional development. In most districts studied, professional development activities were short-term, broad-based, and lacked the kind of follow-through that is necessary for real change. For example, Michigan and Vermont chose to outsource their professional development. Goertz and colleagues point out that this introduces the possibility that the professional development activities themselves are disconnected from the state's own vision and structure. They did find evidence that Michigan's professional development programs varied widely in both scope and quality across districts and did not significantly strengthen the teachers' knowledge of the core curricular areas, or even develop the teachers' capacities to improve their instructional practices to teach that new knowledge.

Ensuring Equal Access to High-Quality Education for All Americans

Although one goal of the standards-based reform movement is to improve education for all American students, achieving this goal, too, has proved elusive for the districts studied. The assumption that educators simply can focus on the learning of content and ignore all the distractions, such as affective, emotional, cultural, and ethnic differences among students, was naive. Goertz and colleagues' findings are not surprising in view of the deep-seated problems described by other investigators. Koretz, Mitchell, Barron, and Keith (1996), for example, have pointed out that

> while many states specifically mention that their content standards and curriculum frameworks are to apply to all students, they do not uniformly define who "all" students are, leaving to interpretation who should and should not be included within the reform. And an emphasis on higher standards has led some teachers to set higher expectations for high-achieving students than for low-achieving students, potentially *increasing* achievement disparities among students. (p. 5).

None of the data cited by Goertz and colleagues are especially encouraging. The problem seems to be that optimizing the learning experiences for *all* American children has not been taken seriously by the standards-based educational reform movement from its inception as Systemic School Reform.

Maintaining a Stable Political Environment to Support Standards-Based Reform

Education has been referred to as faddish; it is not clear whether the assertion, if true, is a cause or an effect of the American political system. We need only to look at the recent complete reversal of the California state curriculum for reading to understand that sustained commitment to a vision that has been validly translated into a coherent framework of a core curriculum, instructional practices, and an adequate assessment program remains an elusive goal. It takes time for educators to learn new content, new curricula, and different assessments and how to interpret them. Unfortunately, the Goertz data do not support the conclusion that the public and its elected representatives are prepared to make that commitment and invest sufficient resources over a sustained time to achieve the results we all want: that all students will learn and be able to demonstrate the appropriate knowledge needed for a fully productive American citizenry. Goertz and colleagues provide evidence of some efforts made to educate politicians about the importance of a sustained commitment. The Michigan legislature appropriated funds to expand the number and scope of that state's Mathematics and Science Centers, which are major sources of professional development, even though at the same time the state's department of education budget was reduced.

The picture is not rosy despite some gains in some states to try to bring stability and commitment to the standards-based reform movement. The policy context is full of contradictions, complexities, and mixed messages. We now turn to a consideration of the impact of the NRRC legacy to American education, in light of the current educational policy context.

RELATING NRRC RESEARCH TO THE CURRENT EDUCATIONAL REFORM POLICIES IN THE UNITED STATES

The most significant policy implication of the NRRC is that it offers an alternative conceptualization of reading competence. As John Guthrie and Emily Anderson sum it up in Chapter 2, "If the engagement perspective is adopted widely throughout the nation, including the policy community, then the discussion of standards will change so that a richer, more comprehensive system for promoting reading can be implemented."

Guthrie and Anderson see the IRA/NCTE *Standards for the English Language Arts* as consistent with the engagement perspective; however, these standards have not been adopted universally. States could base standards on the assumption that reading is only a collection of cognitive strategies for reading and writing. Substituting the engagement perspective for the view of readers as those who master cognitive skills, may be difficult, since the original formulation of SSR emphasizes measurable standard outcomes, *not processes* such as motivation to read. Furthermore, the Goertz data suggest that the public believes that lower-order skills should be mastered first by students. This view of reading as consisting of skills to be learned part by part may be difficult to change. Most Americans seem more comfortable with the more narrow view of reading as a limited cognitive skill and the application of a fragmented approach to the teaching of reading, as exemplified by the phonics approach. The study also suggests that changing instructional and assessment practices is difficult and costly. The status quo may change once the NRRC work is disseminated successfully. Perhaps the most important contribution of the NRRC is that a new, more enriched view of reading has been constructed. Reform must begin with a new idea, but the struggle to implement that vision and coordinate all levels of the educational system to support that vision will be difficult.

A Broader, More Inclusive, More Comprehensive View of Reading

A significant problem for SSR and standards-based reform is the lack of a clear focus on how to ensure that all students master the high standards of the core curriculum. The engagement perspective offers a solution for the core area of literacy. Because the engagement perspective focuses on the motivations for reading, by definition a successful reading program enables all students to become motivated, strategic, and competent readers.

Increasing achievement begins at home, according to Linda Baker (Chapter 5). She focuses on the connections among home, school, and community in fostering the development of reading from an engagement perspective. Her research shows that students are more likely to become engaged readers when they are raised in homes enriched with print, oral language, and opportunities to engage in social interaction about books and the acquisition of knowledge. Her work introduces the dimension of parents as teachers. The discussion of SSR and standards-based reform identifies solely the professional development of teachers, and to some extent educational administrators. The implication from Baker's review is that we need opportunities for parents to learn how to foster the development of reading in their children, if children are to succeed in school. Additionally, teachers and parents need to coordinate their work with literacy instruction in home and school. This will not happen automatically. Programs must be developed around the concept of the engaged reader, bridging the transition between home and school for students.

Instructional Practices, Curricula, Assessments, and Professional Development

Just as the vision of reading differs significantly between the engagement perspective and the old view of reading as a collection of skills, so do the kinds of instructional practices, curricula, and assessments identified by the NRRC as key to reading mastery. The policy implications from this work are clear: If one adopts an engagement perspective as the educational vision for reading competence, then certain instructional practices must be implemented in the classroom. Furthermore, the curriculum should be able to support these pedagogical practices optimally, and the use of portfolio assessment is a necessity, since the mastery of certain aspects of reading can be revealed only by rich qualitative data.

The engagement perspective requires educators to change their instructional practices significantly, adopting a student-centered classroom and implementing the instructional principles that Sarah McCarthey and colleagues and Cynthia Hynd describe in Chapters 3 and 4, respectively. John Guthrie and Emily Anderson note that reading lessons are designed to motivate students to want to read, as well as to provide opportunities to develop skills, knowledge, and social competencies.

Activities such as debating and discussion, having students serve as teachers, and using portfolios as the primary method of assessment are typical for engaged classrooms. McCarthey, Hoffman, and Galda presented eight goals for elementary reading and derived the following instructional practices that should characterize teaching from an engagement perspective: (1) nurturing learning about the alphabet, (2) nurturing the development of fluency, (3) nurturing the development of flexibility, (4) facilitating student responding, (5) connecting knowledge and inquiry, (6) linking personal interests and motivations, (7) supporting reflection on reading processes, and (8) encouraging reflection on goals and progress. Their discussion of portfolio assessment is comprehensive and compelling, reflecting an enlightened view of the benefits. Hynd's discussion of the instructional requirements for implementing an engagement perspective fully in middle and high school is compelling. She offers specific instructional guidelines for teachers, including teaching with analogies, using information about the way texts should be written, effectively using the social system of classrooms to support learning, and using computerized texts to motivate students.

Linda Baker also raises the issue of how best to measure reading competence. The Goertz data suggest that the majority of Americans want to rely on standardized tests as the measure of what their children know. Educators must become more effective in explaining the advantages of qualitative and nonformal assessments to the American public, if these instruments are to be implemented in classrooms.

IMPROVING LITERACY LEARNING: RELATING EDUCATIONAL REFORM, RESEARCH, AND PRACTICE

Adopting the engagement perspective on reading requires a fundamental shift in thinking about literacy and its acquisition. As Guthrie and Anderson note in Chapter 2:

> Reading is not merely a skill. It is not limited to an achievement in the cognitive domain. Reading is better understood as an engagement of the person in a conceptual and social world. This view of reading has profound implications for education and people who have a stake in education. Taken seriously, the engagement perspective on reading changes the landscape. It alters the classroom for teachers, the home for parents, the problem-space for researchers and the challenges for policy makers.

This perspective challenges popular beliefs about reading—what it is, how to teach it, and how to measure it. The chapters in this volume present a compelling case of precisely what we need to do: fundamentally alter the ways we think about reading and schooling in America. The discussion of the present educational policy context, standards-based reform, may appear to be somewhat discouraging. It is, however, only a snapshot of the present. The future is seen in the engagement perspective on reading and the corpus of research resulting from the NRRC.

To examine the policy implications of the reading engagement perspective, several aspects of systemic reform must be considered. These include goals, assessments, instruction, and professional development. First, what does it mean to suggest that the engaged reader should be a goal of schooling? We conclude that producing engaged readers is an aim of schooling. In addition to competence in the skills of word recognition and comprehension, schools should attempt to promote engaged readers. Traditionally, the skill and the use of that skill have been separated. In the past, the obligation of schools has been to confer a skill and let the person decide whether and how to use that skill. This book argues, however, that the skill and its utilization are not easily divorced. Like fluency in a foreign language, ability and use are connected. Without frequent use, people lose their ability to speak a foreign language. Both ability and use are necessary to continued fluency in reading as in language.

Many challenges surround the notion of designating the engaged reader as an aim of education. This goal must be explicated within levels of the different grades. How much reading and what kind of books should be read at grades 3, 5, 8, and 11? What kinds of conditions should be placed on the reading activities? Are home and school reading treated equally? Does reading information for reference on the Web count the same as reading classic literature?

Assessment in education traditionally has not incorporated the engaged reader as a formal dimension. However, to implement this aim, we will need policy-relevant indicators of success and failure. Assessment of the engaged reader requires a reading activity record. The state of being a reader is a set of practices for which we need an account of previous history. Using such historical records is not an unknown practice for evaluating accountability in our society. For example, in driving an automobile one's competence is judged on the basis of the individual's safe driving history. Successful performances of medical students are judged partly on the basis of their effective practice over time in a medical hospital internship, as evaluated by an attending physician. Thus far assessment of historical records has not been used for accountability in education. However, it is possible to do so.

In schools, the performance of students as engaged readers can be judged from portfolios of their work. Researcher Kathryn Au (1997) has done just this. Collecting children's reading activity logs, responses to stories, and other artifacts, teachers made ratings about children's ownership of literacy. These ratings were placed on a scale from low to high, much like the rubrics for evaluating writing. Children's book logs could be designed to represent number of books read per year or number of hours spent reading in a year. Student writing logs could display the quantity and quality of their responses to literature. Products and artifacts from projects in school (e.g., reports) could be judged by teachers or outside experts for the extensiveness of the evidence for the engaged reader that they displayed. Many forms of performance assessments are now entering the picture of accountability in education.

Promoting engaged readers in the classroom as a part of mainstream instruction is perhaps the most challenging issue of policy. We do have resources. Principles and professional practices for promoting engaged readers and motivation in the classroom are gaining recognition. Literature reviews are available for researchers (Guthrie & Alao, 1997; Stipek, 1996); practical interpretations of engagement in the classroom are being published in journals for teachers (Cambourne, 1988); and a recent book on the topic has been published for teachers. As several chapters in this book suggest, teaching that emphasizes supporting the engaged reader will look different from traditional instruction. This teaching will emphasize following children's interests; teachers will focus on children's questions as cornerstones of instructional decision making. Children's personal goals for learning will guide the reading and writing activities that teachers set up, and children's development of long-term motivation will guide the teacher's sense of success and failure.

Infusing engaged readers into instruction complicates the picture. The tradition of teaching skills in a widely recognized "scope and sequence" cannot be abandoned. Children still need reading skills. The concept of the engaged reader cannot exist devoid of competencies. Yet, these skills should be tailored to the needs of students and the priority students place on becoming interested readers. Skills will stand in the service of engagement. This blend of reader ability and readership in the classroom will be an unprecedented challenge to teachers.

Significant extensions of professional involvement will be required to implement our model of the engaged reader. How can teachers and schools implement an emphasis on engagement in reading and language arts curriculum? It appears that significant increases in teacher knowledge will be needed. Teachers will need to understand what reading engagement is, what it looks like, how it develops, and what interferes with it. Although teachers have good instincts for motivation, their academic training does not include theories of motivation, affective development, or the psychology of interest. However, to provide a child-centered, interest-driven curriculum, this is just the knowledge that teachers will need.

In addition to a deeper understanding of child development, teachers will need to learn about a wide variety of children's books. To provide books and materials on appropriate grade levels for diverse children in a classroom relies on a knowledge base now limited to media specialists. Perhaps high technology can enable teachers to work from computer-based menus to locate materials according to grade, topic, and difficulty level.

Is it feasible to expect teachers to assume yet another responsibility? On the one hand, yes, it is feasible because the best teachers are doing it now. Outstanding teachers in many classrooms are promoting engagement. On the other hand, such an endeavor would depend on widespread increases in teacher knowledge, which is expensive. The funds would have to be allocated from the public coffers, which have never been as full as they should be. Until education is commensurate with the professions of law and medicine, it is unlikely it will be funded as fully as it should be. However, the chances that the goal of developing engaged readers will grow in popularity and practice are good. The notion of reading engagement is spreading among researchers and professional educators. It is likely to catch hold in at least some policy centers. How quickly and how permanently this perspective on reading will be established, however, is no more predictable than other swings of fortune in education.

Finally, the issue of public support of the engagement perspective must be considered. Donna Alvermann, in Chapter 6, highlights the contributions that research can make to the improvement of educational practice, and the role that practice has in guiding research programs. The broad, inclusive vision of reading, and the collective work of the NRRC, provide ample evidence that investing in the creation and discovery of new knowledge in the field of reading is beneficial for America. The capacity of our educational system can be enhanced only if there is a solid, relevant knowledge base. The use of multiple perspectives and modes of inquiry, and the partnership between researchers and practitioners, are essential to the creation of this knowledge base.

REFERENCES

Au, K. (1997). Ownership, literacy achievement, and students of diverse cultural backgrounds. In J. T. Guthrie & A. Wigfield (Eds.), *Reading engagement: Motivating readers through integrated instruction.* Newark, DE: International Reading Association.

Cambourne, B. (1988). *The whole story: Natural learning and the acquisition of literacy in the classroom.* Auckland, New Zealand: Ashton Scholastic.

Elmore, R. (1993, November). Systemic reform coming together for change. *Center for Educational Policy Analysis Newsletter*, Rutgers, State University of New Jersey, pp. 1–4.

Goertz, M., Floden, R., & O'Day, J. (1996, June). The bumpy road to education reform. *Consortium for Policy Research in Education Policy*, RB-20, pp. 1–7. University of Pennsylvania.

Guthrie, J. T., & Alao, S. (1997). Designing contexts to increase motivations for reading. *Educational Psychologist, 32*(2), 95–105.

Immerwahr, J., & Johnson, J. (1996). *Americans' views on standards: An assessment by public agenda* (Prepared for the Education Summit of the Nation's Governors and Corporate Executives). New York: Public Agenda Foundation.

International Reading Association. (1996). *Standards for the English language arts.* Newark, DE: International Reading Association.

Johnson, J., & Immerwahr, J. (1994). *First things first: What Americans expect from the public schools*. New York: Public Agenda Foundation.

Johnson, M. (1996, September 8). Scores count. *New York Times Magazine*, pp. 41–45.

Koretz, D., Mitchell, K., Barron, S., & Keith, S. (1996). *Final report: Perceived effects of the Maryland School Performance Assessment Program*. Los Angeles: UCLA, National Center for Research on Evaluation, Standards and Student Testing.

Mosle, S. (1996, October 27). The answer is national standards. *New York Times Magazine*, pp. 48, 68.

Silliman, E., Wilkinson, L. C., Mortinsen-Reed, B., & Scheer, K. (in press). Authentic assessment of writing over time: Interaction of literacy context and genre on syntactic complexity in a student with language learning disabilities. In R. Horowitz (Ed.), *Talk about text: Developing understanding of the world through talk and text*. Newark, DE: International Reading Association.

Stipek, D. (1996). Motivation and instruction. In D. C. Berliner & R. C. Calfee (Eds.), *Handbook of educational psychology* (pp. 85–113). New York: Macmillan.

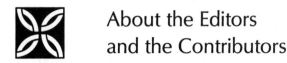

About the Editors
and the Contributors

Donna E. Alvermann (Editor) is Research Professor of Reading Education at the University of Georgia, where she teaches courses in content literacy. Her research focuses on the role of classroom discussion in content literacy instruction. Recently, she has begun to explore the potential of feminist pedagogy and poststructural theory for interpreting literacy practices in middle and high school classrooms. She is a co-chair of IRA's Adolescent Literacy Commission, and is associate editor for the *Journal of Literacy Research*. Also, Dr. Alvermann serves as a member of the Board of Directors for both the College Reading Association and the American Reading Forum. Her recent books include the co-edited volume *Reconceptualizing the Literacies in Adolescents' Lives* and the co-authored (with Stephen F. Phelps) second edition of *Content Reading and Literacy: Succeeding in Today's Diverse Classrooms*. Dr. Alvermann is a recipient of the Oscar S. Causey Award for Outstanding Contributions to Reading Research and the Albert J. Kingston Award for Distinguished Service to the National Reading Conference.

Emily Anderson received her Ph.D. from the University of Maryland, College Park in 1998. Working as a research assistant with John Guthrie at the National Reading Research Center, she conducted research on reading motivation and contexts for learning. Her interests include literacy, motivation, contexts for teaching and learning, and curriculum integration. She has been an elementary classroom teacher and is committed to developing and promoting exemplary literacy programs for children. Her work has been published in *Educational Psychology Review* and *Elementary School Journal*.

Linda Baker is a professor of psychology at the University of Maryland, Baltimore County, and was also a principal investigator at the National Reading Research Center from 1992 to 1997. She received her Ph.D. from Rutgers University in cognitive psychology. Currently her research focus is on longitudinal analysis of children's early reading development from ages 4 to 9 and the contexts at home and school that facilitate it. Recent reports of this research appear in *Educational Psychologist*, the *Journal of Literacy Research*, *The Reading Teacher*, and several edited books. She is also studying children's motivations for reading and how they relate to reading activity and achievement. In addition, she has had a long-term interest in metacognition and comprehension monitoring and continues to publish on those topics. She was co-editor (with Peter Afflerbach and David Reinking) of *Developing Engaged Readers in School and Home Communities*, published in 1996.

Lee Galda is a professor of children's literature at the University of Minnesota. She is the co-author of (with Bernice E. Cullinan) *Literature and the Child* (4th ed.) and (with Bernice E. Cullinan and Dorothy S. Strickland) *Language, Literacy, and the Child* (2nd ed.), as well as numerous articles on children's literature and literacy teaching and learning. She has served as a former children's books department editor for *The Reading Teacher* and has experience as a middle and elementary school English language arts teacher. She received her Ph.D. from New York University.

John T. Guthrie (Editor) is a professor of human development at the University of Maryland, College Park. From 1992 to 1997, he also served as co-director of the National Reading Research Center. In addition to administering the center, he conducted studies of motivational and strategic development in reading and the instructional contexts that increase long-term reading engagement, which have been published in the *Reading Research Quarterly*, the *Journal of Educational Psychology*, and the *Elementary School Journal*. Before coming to Maryland, he was Research Director for the International Reading Association. He began his career at Johns Hopkins University, where he founded a school for children with reading disabilities. He conducted studies of the cognitive, language, and neurological characteristics of these children. He received his Ph.D. in educational psychology from the University of Illinois. He is a recipient of the Oscar Causey Award for Outstanding Reading Research and is a member of the International Reading Association Hall of Fame. Currently, he is examining how classroom contexts facilitate the acquisition of reading as a multifaceted set of strategic, motivational, and conceptual processes.

James V. Hoffman is a professor of language and literacy studies at the University of Texas, Austin where he teaches graduate and undergraduate courses in reading. He is a past president of the National Reading Conference and former editor of the *Reading Research Quarterly*. Currently, he serves on the Board of Directors of the International Reading Association. His research interests are in the areas of reading acquisition, instruction, and teacher education at the elementary level.

Cynthia Hynd is a professor of reading in the Division of Academic Assistance at the University of Georgia. Her research interests include secondary and college students' learning with text in the disciplines of science and history. She is most interested in research dealing with texts in those disciplines that elicit conceptual changes in students.

Sarah J. McCarthey is an associate professor at the University of Texas, Austin, where she teaches undergraduate courses in language arts methods and graduate courses in sociolinguistics and reading research. She is a recipient of the American Educational Research Association Division K Young Researcher Award and earned a Spencer fellowship to study home-school literacy connections. Her work focuses on the home and school contexts that support students' literacy learning. Classroom interactions and the ways in which discourse supports or deters students' learning is her particular area of expertise. She has published numerous articles in such journals as the *American Educational Research Journal*, the *Reading Research Quarterly*, *Research in the Teaching of English*, and the *Journal of Literacy Research*. She has also written a book on school restructuring, co-authored with Penelope Peterson and Richard Elmore.

Peter B. Mosenthal is Associate Dean of the School of Education at Syracuse University and also serves as president of Proficiency by Design, Inc. His recent work has focused on the politics of literacy, the design of computer-adaptive programs for testing and teaching literacy, designing washback programs to optimize performance on high-stakes literacy and mathematics tests, and document/visual literacy. He received his Ph.D. from Ohio State University. For the past six years, he has served as Chair of the Reading and Language Arts Center at Syracuse University.

Louise Cherry Wilkinson is Dean of the Graduate School of Education and a professor of educational psychology at Rutgers University. Formerly, she served as a professor in and Chair of the Department of Educational Psychology at the University of Wisconsin–Madison, and as a professor in and Executive Officer of the Ph.D. program in educational psychology at the Graduate School–CUNY. Her extensive research on children's literacy and language learning has resulted in more than 100 articles, chapters, and books. She co-authored (with Elaine R. Silliman) *Communicating for Learning* (1991) and has another co-authored book in press, and has edited/co-edited *Communicating in the Classroom* (1982), (with Penelope L. Peterson and Maureen Hallinan) *The Social Context of Instruction* (1984), (with Cora B. Marrett) *Gender Influences in Classroom Interaction* (1985), and (with Leslie Mandel Marrow and Jeffrey K. Smith) *The Integrated Language Arts* (1994). Currently, she is a member of the editorial boards of two major journals in literacy, language development, and education. Her past achievements include fellowships from the American Psychological Association (1986), the American Psychological Society (1990), and the American Association for Applied and Preventative Psychology (1995), in addition to serving as an advisory board member of the National Reading Research Center. Her Ed.D. in human development is from Harvard University.

Index